demic and researcher, and has published widely on education
and the labour market, and on assessment, qualifications and
skills. She is currently Professor of Education at the University
of London's Institute of Education, where she directs the International Centre for Research on Assessment. Alison Wolf lives
in London and is married with three children.

WITHDRAWN

PENGUIN BOOKS

Does Education Matter?

Alison Wolf was educated at the universities of Oxford and Neuchâtel. She then lived in the United States, working largely for a federal agency and evaluating education policies for the US Congress, but also as a university teacher, journalist and researcher. Since returning to the UK, she has been an aca-

ALISON WOLF

Does Education Matter?

Myths about Education and Economic Growth

PENGUIN BOOKS

PENGUIN BOOKS

Published by the Penguin Group
Penguin Books Ltd, 80 Strand, London WC2R ORL, England
Penguin Putnam Inc., 375 Hudson Street, New York, New York 10014, USA
Penguin Books Australia Ltd, 250 Camberwell Road, Camberwell, Victoria 3124, Australia
Penguin Books Canada Ltd, 10 Alcorn Avenue, Toronto, Ontario, Canada M4V 3B2
Penguin Books India (P) Ltd, 11, Community Centre, Panchsheel Park, New Delhi – 110 017, India
Penguin Books (NZ) Ltd, Cnr Rosedale and Airborne Roads, Albany, Auckland, New Zealand
Penguin Books (South Africa) (Pty) Ltd, 24 Sturdee Avenue, Rosebank 2196, South Africa

Penguin Books Ltd, Registered Offices: 80 Strand, London WC2R ORL, England
www.penguin.com

First published 2002
6

Set in Monotype Sabon and TheSans
Typeset by Rowland Phototypesetting Ltd, Bury St Edmunds, Suffolk
Printed in England by Clays Ltd, St Ives plc

Contents

Acknowledgements

This book draws on many years' experience as a government analyst, a researcher, a consultant and an academic observer of education policy. During that time I have learned a great deal from colleagues inside and outside government and the universities, not least from arguments in which I sometimes changed my mind (and sometimes didn't) and sometimes convinced others (and often failed). I hope that, in reading this book, people will feel that I have dealt fairly with recent history, and excuse the fact that I have not been able to acknowledge each and every intellectual debt.

Special thanks are owed to people who provided direct research assistance when I was preparing the manuscript: Sutupa Choudhury, Nick Dean, Rhoda Mukasa, Wendy Robins, Chris Tryhorn and Alex von Tunzelmann. Claire Callender, Ron Dore, Harvey Goldstein, Tina Isaacs, Peter Robinson, Paul Ryan, Anna Vignoles, Jonathan Wolf and Martin Wolf all read some or all of the manuscript and provided me with detailed and very helpful comments (not least on sections with which some of them disagreed strongly). Responsibility for the final version is, of course, entirely mine. I am also very grateful to a number of people who, usually at ridiculously short notice, helped me by finding unpublished statistics, lost publications and stray facts. They include (in no particular order) Janet Sturgis, Stephen Pickles, Steve Kee, David Collins, Giliberto Capano, Annie Bouder, Samantha Parsons, Barbara Kehm, Jochen Reuling, Mike Coles, a number of anonymous Oxford college administrators, Peter Senker and Hilary Steedman; and I would also like to acknowledge the general excellence of the Institute of Education library.

This book would certainly never have been written without Susan Pollock, its original editor: my thanks to her, and also to *Prospect* magazine, where a 1998 article by me gave her the original idea. Martin Toseland, my editor at Penguin, has been admirably calm about continued delays and an excellent critical reader. My family has been remarkably patient and supportive, though I owe a particular debt to my mother, without whose constant enquiries ('Is it finished yet?') there might never have been a completed manuscript. Most of all, however, I would like to acknowledge the contribution of my administrative assistant, Magdalen Meade, who has typed up corrections, created complex figures, hunted down information and references, corrected my punctuation and my prose, and dealt with copy-editing queries, and to whom I owe an enormous debt of gratitude for all her help.

London, 2001

Introduction

Our number one priority for investment is education.

Tony Blair, 1999

Education remains [our] top priority.[1]

Labour Party manifesto, 2001

At the start of the twenty-first century, we inhabit a globe in the grip of consensus. The world's voters think their governments can and should deliver economic prosperity. Their elites agree with them – and even agree with each other on how to do it. Increasingly they sign up to the same package: free trade, market economics, the virtues of entrepreneurship – and education, education, education.

For decades now the British government – like governments in general – has become more and more fixated on education. It spends more and more money: on pre-school education, on Literacy Strategies, and on Technical and Vocational Education Initiatives; on new universities and new associate degrees in further education colleges; on city technology colleges, 'Youth Opportunity Programmes', national training organizations, and Modern Apprenticeship. In 2001, education spending by the public sector will have topped £50 billion: £850 for every man, woman and child in the United Kingdom – more than £1,800 for every payer of income tax. This is level pegging with the National Health Service, but considerably more than on defence and law and order combined.

Nor is it just a matter of spending. Prime ministers – from Callaghan to Blair – have made education the subject of their most high-profile speeches.[2] From their Whitehall fastnesses, education ministers have involved themselves ever more in the minutiae of educational practice, unwilling to trust so precious a charge either to the professionals or to local politicians. In the last quarter of the twentieth century British central governments busied themselves with creating a national curriculum, laying down the details of classroom practice, and bringing examination boards under centralized control. They nationalized apprenticeships and vocational qualifications, and established new bodies to monitor universities and create national standards for degrees. During the first three years of the Blair government, the Department for Education and Employment (DfEE) in London launched the equivalent of one new educational initiative or set of instructions for every single day of the year.

Have we become a nation of scholars? Hardly. Amid all this frenetic spending and organizing and reorganizing and spending, the idea of old-fashioned scholarship figures almost nowhere. Education is big because it is seen as the engine of economic growth, a sure-fire route to future prosperity and victory in a global competition. Politicians worldwide have signed up to this vision, and have the power (and taxpayers' money) to create ever larger, ever more expensive education sectors. But the belief in education for growth runs deep and wide beyond our political classes, replacing socialism as the great secular faith of our age.

One evening a year or so ago, I found myself at a 'working' dinner in a typical windowless conference room. My fellow diners were mildly eminent and seriously rich; the topic was how poor countries could follow Korea, Thailand, Taiwan and other 'tiger' economies into decades of rapid growth. The consensus was easy and total: the right policies were simple to identify (if hard to achieve). What was needed was the rule of law, market economies, access to overseas markets through free trade, and much, much more education spending. The sole educationist present, I demurred – just a little. More education spending might not, I suggested, be the top priority in most of the world's poorest nations. The reaction rather took me aback. As a social gaffe, mine went far beyond mistakes with the fish knife, or in passing the port. Questioning the automatic value of any rise in the education budget, it seems, places one somewhere between an animal-hater and an imbecile.

But actually it should not, for, as this book argues, an unquestioning faith in the economic benefits of education has brought with it huge amounts of wasteful government spending, attached to misguided and even pernicious policies. Just because something is valuable, it does not follow that yet more of it is by definition a good idea: that any addition, any increment, must be welcomed. Yet in practice this is what we seem to believe.

The 'knowledge economy'

Politicians' faith in education is fuelled by a set of clichés about the nature of the twenty-first-century world: globalized, competitive, experiencing ever faster rates of technical change. In this world, it seems, education is to be a precondition of economic success, and indeed survival, to an even greater degree than in the century before. Here, for example, is David Blunkett, the then Secretary of State for Education and Employment, in a speech given in February 2000:

> The powerhouses of the new global economy are innovation and ideas, creativity, skills and knowledge. These are now the tools for success and prosperity as much as natural resources and physical labour power were in the past century.[3]

Or listen to Charles Leadbetter, a policy adviser to Tony Blair and major author of the Department of Trade and Industry's 1998 policy White Paper on *Building the Knowledge Driven Economy*. Writing in a book whose jacket carries an endorsement by Blair, he argues that

> The generation, application and exploitation of knowledge is [*sic*] driving modern economic growth. Most of us make our money from thin air: we produce nothing that can be weighed, touched or easily measured. Our output is not stockpiled at harbours, stored in warehouses or shipped in railway cars . . . That should allow our

> economies, in principle at least, to ... be organized around people
> and the knowledge capital they produce. Our children will not have
> to toil in dark factories, descend into pits or suffocate in mills, to
> hew raw materials and turn them into manufactured products.
> They will make their livings through their creativity, ingenuity and
> imagination.[4]

Much of what Leadbetter says about the modern economy is (as we shall see in Chapter 2) untrue. But his general message is firmly and totally mainstream. One particularly influential analysis of the 1980s divided the world into 'high-skill' economies and poorly educated places caught in a 'low-skills equilibrium'.[5] No prizes for guessing which group we all want to belong to; and, sure enough, we have Tony Blair, in one of his major policy statements as Prime Minister, announcing that 'Our number one priority for investment is education ... Brainpower, skills and flexibility ... are the key to competitiveness. For the nation as a whole, it means shifting from a low skill average to a high skill average', and away from an economy 'built on mass manual labour, with little premium on higher skills'.[6]

From the premiss that a full-blown 'knowledge economy' is arriving now on our doorsteps, it is easy to slip into prescribing more and more of the raw material which apparently makes this possible: education. And of course it would be stupid to deny that education *is* central to any modern economy. Imagine the UK today – or the USA, or Greece, Japan, Brazil – being run by a population which is more than 90 per cent illiterate – the level of eleventh-century England.[7] Imagine Microsoft or British Aerospace research and development in the hands of people all of whom had left school after only a primary-school education, or a drug industry dependent on people whose academic training was the intermingled science and alchemy of Newton's day. Who could doubt that education matters?

But what doesn't follow is that vast amounts of public spending on education have been the key determinant of how rich we are today. Nor is it obvious that they will decide how much richer, or poorer, we will be tomorrow. The simple one-way relationship which so entrances our politicians and commentators – education spending in, economic growth out – simply doesn't exist. Moreover, the larger and more complex the education sector, the less obvious any links to productivity become. Developed countries have now moved well beyond providing basic education for all, and instead spend more and more on higher education, technical provision, vocational programmes, and adult training.

These are my main subject matter, for they are also the main recent targets of government policies inspired by ambitions for growth. Unfortunately, while an overwhelmingly strong case can be made for the state's responsibilities in basic education – and, indeed, for the latter's economic importance – not one of these newer enthusiasms deserves any such accolade.

Governments' expansion into ever larger areas of education and training has run parallel to their growing enthusiasm for detailed intervention. This is doubly unfortunate for, if the evidence in favour of indiscriminate education spending is weak, that in favour of government fine-tuning is even weaker. Most politicians, if asked directly, would probably deny believing that any and all education spending is a good thing regardless. What they do believe in, of course, is higher levels of spending 'properly' targeted to develop those high skills that the economy needs. Yet their record on just this point is largely dismal. The more overtly and the more directly politicians attempt to organize education for economic ends, the higher the likelihood of waste and disappointment. This book focuses largely on a quarter-century of British government activity, but British politicians are not unusual in believing that they can improve their country's economic performance through government-led education policies. What marks them off from their international counterparts is simply the speed with which, in our hugely centralized system, they can launch off one educational broadside after another.

In the process, we have almost forgotten that education ever had any purpose other than to promote growth. To read government documents of even fifty years ago, let alone commentaries and discussions of the nineteenth or early twentieth century, gives one a shock. Of course, their authors recognized that education had relevance to people's livelihoods and success, and to the nation's prosperity. But their concern was as much, or more, with values, citizenship, the nature of a good society, the intrinsic benefits of learning. When the hero of Thomas Hardy's *Jude the Obscure* tried desperately to enter the Oxford of a century ago, and when Greek was taught in the roadside 'hedge schools' of eighteenth-century Ireland because it was forbidden to the peasant schoolrooms, beating our national competitors was not top of teachers' or students' minds. The 'lad o'pairts', subsisting on a sack of oatmeal in his determination to take a degree, is central to Scots mythology and self-image. Of course, he hoped to be bettering himself materially in the long term, but the values this image reflects are primarily about enquiry, learning and scholarship.

In its tour around our modern articles of educational faith, this book concentrates on the post-compulsory years: on vocational, further and university education. This reflects a shift in education's own centre of gravity. Over the last century, the average length of education has increased inexorably throughout the industrialized world. In 1900 it was normal for children to leave school at twelve, thirteen or fourteen for full-time employment. Today it is sixteen at the earliest, and that ever more rarely; for more and more young people, education, with or without part-time work, stretches well into their early twenties. Chapter 1 sets the context by outlining the vast size of the contemporary education sector, and the ways in which it has been developing over the last half-century. Chapter 2 discusses in depth the argument about the relationship between education and growth, and identifies the two main areas in which this supposed link has generated major activity – vocational education and training, the subject matter of Chapters 3, 4 and 5, and university or 'higher' education, to which Chapters 6 and 7 are devoted. Together, as Chapter 8 concludes, these chapters demonstrate how misleading it can be simply to believe that 'education matters'. Instead, we are sorely in need of clearer thinking about *which* education matters, *how*, and *when*.

I   A truly world-beating industry: the growth of formal education

Bewilder'd in the Maze of Schools . . .
Alexander Pope, *An Essay on Criticism*, l. 26

To understand modern education, we need first to think size. For today's education sectors are huge. Education is a big player in the economy and labour market of any country you care to think of, and almost unimaginably enormous worldwide. Moreover, its sheer scale determines a great deal of how modern education operates, and how it affects people. It is also why education is inevitably a major concern to any politician, whose voters will necessarily use it, worry about it, work in it, and pay for it. As a prelude to understanding government policies, and what education can or should achieve, we therefore need a few raw numbers, and a sense of just what this vast sector comprehends. This chapter offers a brief, factual description of education's current profile and of recent changes.

Let us start at the global level. Table 1.1 summarizes the total number of students in the world, and the increase in numbers since 1970. We are starting a new century (and a new millennium) with no fewer than 1 in 5 of the globe's inhabitants inscribed as a student in formal education. This is a dramatic contrast with most of human history. It is not simply that for most of that time the vast bulk of the population was totally illiterate.[1] It is also that modern education involves armies of students and employees studying and working in large, bureaucratic, rule-driven organizations which are quite unlike the schools, as well as

Table 1.1   *Numbers of students in the world: 1997* [2]

Africa	138,714,000
America	191,468,000
Asia	679,366,000
Europe	137,645,000
Oceania	7,528,000
World total	1,154,721,000
Increase in world total since 1970	546,106,000
Percentage increase in student numbers since 1970	90%
Students as percentage of world population (1997)	19.7%

Source: UNESCO 1999

the workplaces, of previous eras. In the past, young people, in particular, lived and worked in small family groups; a formal apprenticeship typically meant living in your master's household, as did a first job as a young live-in servant, while the modal school was run by one or two individuals, whether it was a 'dame school' in a cottage parlour, a select seminary for young Victorian ladies, or the school of a successful Roman rhetorician, set up in the atrium of a noble's palace.

The very scale of today's student populations implies some far more industrial style of enterprise – as is indeed the case. The sheer numbers are difficult to comprehend: over a billion students in all; nearly half a billion students in secondary schools. UNESCO estimates that there are 88 million university students alone – a number far greater than the entire population of the United Kingdom. And almost all those students are to be found in huge, state-funded, public systems, created by governments, run by public-sector employees, and funded overwhelmingly from general tax revenues.

Equally striking is how recent all this is. In the West, universal (and compulsory) education has now been the rule for well over a century; elsewhere, large-scale primary education is a far more recent phenomenon. However, Figure 1.1 shows how much growth there has been, at all levels of education, in just the last quarter-century.

Figure 1.1 *Proportional increase in pupil/student numbers worldwide:*
1970–1997 (1970 = 100)

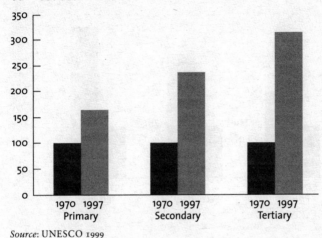

Source: UNESCO 1999

Primary enrolments have increased least in proportional terms simply because in many countries so much of the relevant age group is already in school that there is no one left to add. Such enrolments have nonetheless grown hugely in absolute terms, adding 257 million extra students to the 1970 tally. Meanwhile, at secondary level, UNESCO calculates that in the last quarter-century enrolment rates grew from 40 to 60 per cent of the entire eligible age group.[3] As for university education, there are now 60 million more university students than thirty years ago – a 300 per cent increase which, as we shall see later, shows no signs of tailing off.

Education on this scale has profound implications not just for students – who are predominantly young – but also for the adult workforce. The growth of organized education was an important factor underlying the huge twentieth-century increase in female labour-force participation, but it has also had a more direct effect on the structure of that same labour market. School systems must be managed and administered; buildings must be built, maintained and cleaned; and,

Figure 1.2 *Proportional increase in teacher numbers: 1970–1997 (1970 = 100)* [4]

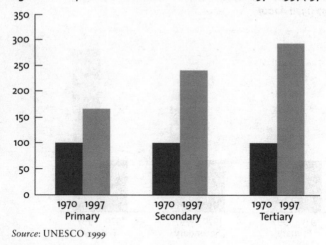

Source: UNESCO 1999

above all, students must be taught. The result is a teaching profession 54 million strong – double the size of thirty years ago. As Figure 1.2 demonstrates, this growth has again been most rapid in the upper reaches of countries' education systems. Not only has the secondary teaching force grown faster, but its absolute increase is higher than in primary schools; so there are over 13 *million* more secondary teachers than there were in the early 1970s (compared to 'only' 10 million more teachers in primary schools). Meanwhile, in the same few decades, the number of university teachers has almost tripled, adding 4 million or so more jobs to the total: the equivalent of every citizen of Birmingham, Glasgow and Greater Manchester joining the academic ranks in the space of less than thirty years.

If – as – the world grows richer, so too will this process continue. With wealth, countries expand first their primary, then their secondary, and then their tertiary education sectors. In Africa, primary teachers outnumber secondary ones pretty much 2 to 1. In Europe, the exact reverse is now true, because more and more European teenagers spend more and more years in full-time education. In Asia, dominated by the

Figure 1.3 *Students in state-funded primary, secondary and further education: England and Wales*

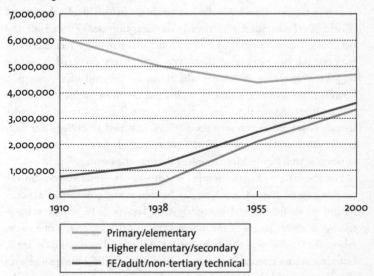

Notes: Independent schools were, for much of the twentieth century, included in official statistics only if they volunteered to be inspected; enrolments in independent secondary schools are therefore excluded. Free places held by former elementary-school pupils are included (1910, 1938). FE totals exclude art schools since they would today be listed as tertiary, but include day technical classes and day continuation schools, and (for 2000) A-level students in FE colleges.

Sources: Reports of the Board of Education; DES and DfEE *Statistics of Education*

still-poor giants of India and China, the gap between primary and secondary is closing rapidly as these same countries' incomes rise, and with them their citizens' access to education.

Look closer to home and the self-same pattern is immediately clear. Figure 1.3 summarizes twentieth-century enrolment patterns for England and Wales in primary and secondary schools, and also in further and adult education. This last is also huge, and predominantly part-time, based in myriad further education (FE) colleges, adult-education centres and community colleges up and down the land. Add in the 1.5 million full- and part-time students enrolled in different parts of the university sector and you have not 20 but a full 25 per cent of the population involved in formal education – and that is before you get to the people who work in it.

Figure 1.4 illustrates what this has meant for British life. By the Second World War, education was already the near-universal experience and occupation of anyone aged five to fourteen. For older teenagers this was not the case: many of them were completely divorced from any ongoing experience of formal education. By the end of the century, however, education's tentacles embraced far more of them, and for much longer. As we shall see in detail in later chapters, more and more teenagers stayed in school; more adults returned to college for later study; more and more universities were created. By the century's end, education well beyond fourteen had become the norm.

For the UK, as for the world, as enrolments grew, so too did the teaching force. Indeed, teaching can be seen as the quintessential occupation of industrial and post-industrial society. The village school-teacher is an archetype of the nineteenth century – especially in France, where the teacher was the embodiment of the secular, republican state, but also across Europe as a whole. In many families, movement into the growing middle classes began with a clever child thriving in the village elementary school; being invited to become a 'pupil teacher', serving an on-the-job apprenticeship teaching the younger pupils; then offered the prospect of a scholarship to 'normal school' or training college, and qualification as a fully fledged teacher.

Becoming a teacher continued to be the classic means of social mobility well into the twentieth century. This was even more true for women than for men (and is still the case in developing countries today). For decades, as girls' education spread, the one profession open to large numbers of women was teaching: as such, it attracted high proportions of the most able women. In their classic work, *Education and the Working Class*, Brian Jackson and Dennis Marsden traced the experiences of working-class children passing through the Huddersfield grammar schools in the wake of the 1944 Education Act. 'Over half of our sample entered' teaching, and 'only nine girls did *not* become teachers', they note.[5] The 30 per cent or so who did *not* become teachers but instead entered other middle-class professions were almost all from

Figure 1.4 *Enrolments in public-sector provision as percentages of the population aged five to fourteen and five to twenty-four: England and Wales*

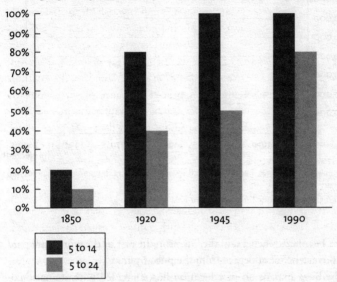

Sources: Carpentier 1999; DES and DfEE *Statistics of Education*

families which had in fact only just become working class: downwardly rather than upwardly mobile, or what the authors call the 'sunken middle class'. For the bright working-class child, teaching was, from the time that mass state education began, *the* route of occupational progress.

As twentieth-century education expanded, so too did the number of teaching positions and teachers. Figure 1.5 shows the growth in absolute numbers: from a quarter of a million in 1900 to a projected 1.2 million a few years from now. This is, by any measure, a huge workforce, and an enormous industry – one which marks our societies off from those of Rome, the pre-Columbus Americas or, indeed, eighteenth-century England quite as much as do our factories, television channels, motorways or telecommunications. Moreover, from a political standpoint, the huge teaching force is at least as pressing a concern as any of the

Figure 1.5 *Number of teachers: Great Britain**

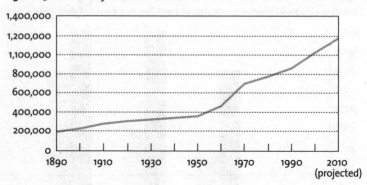

*All teachers – including, but not confined to, schoolteachers in maintained schools and university teachers

Sources: Census; Institute for Employment Research

latter. For these teachers, in the UK as in the rest of the world, are paid to an overwhelming degree from the public purse.

The huge expansion of education has coincided with its national-ization. Until the nineteenth century, the small-scale enterprises which provided the bulk of formal education were, typically, private concerns. The early universities were also independent; while in some societies there was an additional mixture of religious and charitable concerns. With the rise of the nation state, and the development of an industrial society, all this changed. Education came to be viewed as a core responsi-bility of the state, and came more and more under tight state control.

Although public provision of education became a normal activity for developed countries during the nineteenth century, the huge expansions of the twentieth century saw the cost soar. They did so, moreover, at a time of increasing government intervention and activism. The twentieth century was a period of apparently unstoppable expansion in govern-ment expenditure. Conventional wisdom has it that democratic govern-ments have reached the limits of what either voters or footloose global corporations will accept in terms of taxes (which are the flipside of government spending). But, as Table 1.2 shows, there are actually huge

Table 1.2 *Government expenditure as a percentage of GDP*

	c.1870	1913	1937	1960	1980	1990	1996
Australia	18.3	16.5	14.8	21.2	31.6	34.7	35.9
France	12.6	17.0	29.0	34.6	46.1	49.8	55.0
Germany	10.0	14.8	34.1	32.4	47.9	45.1	49.1
Italy	13.7	17.1	31.1	30.1	41.9	53.2	52.7
Japan	8.8	8.3	25.4	17.5	32.0	31.7	35.9
Spain*	n/a	11.0	13.2	18.8	32.2	42.0	43.7
Sweden†	5.7	10.4	16.5	31.0	60.1	59.1	64.2
Switzerland	16.5	14.0	24.1	17.2	32.8	33.5	39.4
UK	9.4	12.7	30.0	32.2	43.0	39.9	43.0
USA	7.3	7.5	19.7	27.0	31.8	33.3	32.4

Sources: Adapted from Tanzi & Schuknecht 2000: Table 1.1, plus IMF figures

* Central government for 1913 and 1937

† Central government only for 1870

variations in the share of GDP currently spent by governments, and the UK is nowhere near the biggest spender. What *is* consistent is the century-long trend – and the acceleration between 1960 and 1996. Even the Thatcher years in the UK, when rhetoric and intent both focused on reducing government-spending levels, achieved only a temporary reduction of a couple of percentage points in the public sector's take.

The steady upward trend in government expenditure reflects both an equally steady growth in demand for publicly provided services and an increasing tendency for government to involve itself actively in every area of social life. In the chapters that follow, we shall see both these tendencies manifested time and again in the context of UK education policy. Evident, too, will be the strains that come from the education sector constantly expanding while at the same time competing for resources with other state-funded activities. Table 1.3 underlines the huge growth that typically took place, during the twentieth century, in the percentage of national income devoted to publicly funded education – a fivefold increase in Britain, fourfold in France, a mere doubling in

Table 1.3 *Public expenditure on education as a percentage of GDP*

	1913	1937	1960	1980	1993	1997
Australia	–	0.7	1.4	5.5	6.0	5.6
France	1.5	1.3	2.4	5.0	5.8	6.1
Germany	2.7	–	2.9	4.7	4.8	5.0
Italy	0.6	1.6	3.6	4.4	5.2	4.8
Japan	1.6	2.1	4.1	5.8	4.7	–
Spain	0.4	1.6	1.3	2.6	4.7	4.8
Sweden	–	–	5.1	9.0	8.4	8.4
Switzerland	–	–	3.1	5.0	5.6	5.6
UK	1.1	4.0	4.3	5.6	5.4	5.1
USA	–	–	4.0	–	5.5	5.4

Sources: Tanzi & Schuknecht 2000: Table II.5; OECD 2000a

Germany, but more than a tenfold rise in Spain. However, it also indicates that at the end of the century this growth consistently levelled off or came to a total halt. Public education was still growing both in enrolments and in absolute spending levels, but in most cases it was no longer increasing its *share* of GDP.

The UK education system, which is the main focus of the following chapters, must thus be understood as huge in itself and as part of a vast, global industry. It developed as part of the Industrial Revolution which transformed our nations' economies and everyday lives, and it now structures all our childhoods and, increasingly, our young adulthood as well. Our societies are very rich, and they live by and through the ability of their citizens to use academic skills that were once the preserve of a minority. As such, they demand levels of reading, writing and mathematics which go far beyond the basic levels acquired by most of the 'literate' citizens of bygone centuries; people without such academic skills can offer very little to a modern economy, and their lives are accordingly blighted.

This explains why 'basic' education has grown in depth and length

Figure 1.6 *Labour-force fortunes: teachers and miners as a proportion of the economically active population*

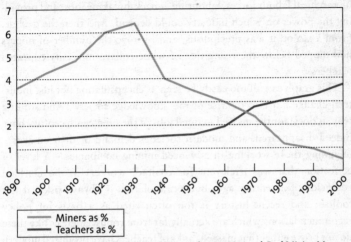

Sources: Census; Institute for Employment Research 2000; National Coal Mining Museum

– and rightly so. This book will be taking a very sceptical look at much recent education policy, but I do not want to deny or belittle in any way the importance of good in-depth, school-based education for all the world's citizens. The basic 'academic' skills with which primary and secondary education are concerned are also the main tools of survival in a developed economy, a precondition for running modern society, and, not least, a gateway to individual opportunity, enlightenment and knowledge which go way beyond the immediate concerns of work and occupation.

What I do query are the conclusions that so many people have drawn from the history of the last century about what education can and will achieve in the future. Figure 1.6. encapsulates a large and important part of that history, for what it shows are the relative shares in UK employment, over time, of miners and of teachers. Throughout the nineteenth century, and almost to the eve of the Second World War, miners were one of the greatest of occupational success stories, in the sense of recruiting huge numbers of adults to their ranks, year after year after year. They were the quintessential occupational group of the Industrial Revolution: manual workers, unionized, part of huge hierarchical labour forces, labouring at back-breaking jobs, and providing the power on which industry could depend. And then the decline. From 1940 on it was precipitous, and by 1970 the number of miners had dipped below the rising tide of white-collar, university-educated teachers.

This graph can all too easily be seen as encapsulating not just industrial change but also the rise of the 'knowledge society'. And so, in a way, it does: for the massed manual jobs of the nineteenth century have indeed disappeared, and modern societies demand of their citizens – including those working in advanced mining companies – a level of education that was irrelevant for coalface workers in the Durham coalfields of a century ago. But extrapolation is always risky, if not foolish; and recent history is too often cited as a basis for policy recommendations which are actually far from robust. Figures like these do not prove either that massed ranks of teachers have produced modern prosperity or that more education and more teachers are the best recipe for twenty-first-century happiness. As the following chapters show, the conventional wisdom is that we need more and more of the same. This is not at all obviously true – and in believing it we risk undermining the very quality of the education we supposedly value.

2 Elixir or snake oil? Can education really deliver growth?

> If we are to face the challenge of creating a high-tech, high-added-value and high-wage economy, we can only do so by skilling our people.
>
> Labour Party, *The Skills Revolution*, 1996

> Tony Blair says his priorities are education, education, education. Well, so are mine (but in a different order).
>
> Prime Minister John Major, in the run-up to the 1997 general election[1]

For twenty years, British politicians have been obsessed with education – convinced that it is in a uniquely parlous state, and that this matters as never before. As we saw in the Introduction, this passion for education rests on the belief that the world's whole economy has changed. It is now so 'knowledge-driven' that only those nations committed to 'lifelong learning' in a 'learning society' can hope to thrive. Lip-service may still be paid to learning for personal enrichment and development, but in politicians' speeches the emphasis is unremittingly on what education can do for the economy of the UK.[2]

There is nothing *parti pris* about these beliefs. In a 1991 White Paper signalling major education reforms, John Major's Conservative government defined its overarching purpose as being to provide 'young people going into work' with the 'skills and qualifications they will need for their future careers'. Education was to respond to 'the rising demand from employers for more and higher level skills to meet the growing challenge from overseas competitors in world markets'.[3] Seven years later, Labour's David Blunkett presented Parliament with *The Learning Age: A Renaissance for a New Britain*. 'Learning is the key to prosperity,' the document begins. 'Investment in human capital will be the foundation of success in the knowledge-based global economy of the twenty-first century.'[4] Three years in office did nothing to change Blunkett's view. 'Knowledge and skills are now the key drivers of innovation and change,' he announced in summer 2000. 'Economic performance depends increasingly on talent and creativity. And in this new economy, it is education and skills which shape . . . opportunities and rewards.'[5]

But is it true? Is education the elixir of economic growth? Does it deserve ever greater government expenditure and attention because it can deliver ever increasing prosperity? This chapter summarizes the figures which so impress all our politicians, and which indeed suggest a close relationship between education and wealth. But it then asks if they are quite what they seem.

The more educated do indeed tend to earn more, but there are good reasons to question how far this is because education made them skilled. We cannot conclude that if everyone had the same education as the top earners, they would have the same incomes; and the more we expand and lengthen further and higher education, the less reason we have to claim this. It is true that rich and developed countries tend to have high levels of education; but, again, the link between national wealth and education spending is a lot less straightforward than it appears. You can't conclude that more education, at any level, automatically spills over into benefits for society at large. Even the idea that education and success will be more closely linked than ever in the globalized twenty-first century is less obvious the harder you look. Politicians may think it is clear that everyone's work will soon be dependent on 'creativity', 'ingenuity' and 'knowledge capital' in a way that is quite different from in the past:[6] but it is no such thing. It is just as likely that we already have an over-educated workforce as that we need more graduates for a high-skills economic future.

Overall, as this chapter will argue, the links between education and growth are far less direct than our politicians suppose. Unfortunately, beliefs about these links dominate current policy. They have produced patterns of government spending, and detailed centralized controls over education, many of which are fundamentally misconceived. These are discussed in depth in Chapters 3 to 8.

It's the income, stupid

Whether or not education is financially good for their country, the past half-century teaches that it is certainly good for the educated. The more education you acquire, the higher your income is likely to be, and the less likely you are to experience long- or even short-term unemployment.

Figures 2.1 and 2.2 illustrate just how dramatic those effects can seem. They classify people by their highest qualification – whether academic (degrees, A and O levels, GCSE, CSE)[7] or vocational (ranging from Higher National Diplomas (HNDs) taken in higher education through the various BTEC, RSA and City & Guilds vocational certificates) – and then compare average earnings with those of the unqualified. Among British men born in the 1950s, a first or higher degree meant that, after twenty years in the labour force, you would be earning on average almost twice as much as someone who had left school with no formal qualifications. Even a single A level or five O levels left you half as well off again. For women the picture was the same – or if anything even more so. Not only did women seem to benefit hugely from A levels or degrees: as Figure 2.2 shows, higher vocational qualifications (typically nursing or higher-level administrative/secretarial diplomas such as RSA Higher) gave them a greater advantage vis-à-vis unqualified women than was the case for the male workforce.

The stepped shape of these figures tells a simple tale. Qualifications pay: but not equally. While men with vocational qualifications, such as a City & Guilds craft certificate, earn only a little more than men with no qualifications at all, a clutch of O levels or GCSEs at grade C or above[8] is associated with an income advantage of over a third. For women, a degree apparently more or less doubles income compared to the unqualified, while men and women with A levels alone are still

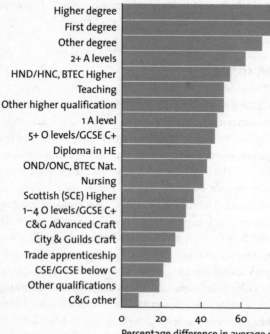

Figure 2.1 Male earnings by highest qualification held 1993–5: full-time employees evaluated after twenty years

Source: Robinson 1997b

pulling in incomes more than 50 per cent above the 'unqualified' average.

This looks like a pretty good advertisement for education – and nor is there anything particularly British about it: the same pattern holds for developed countries in Europe, North America and the Pacific Rim. Figure 2.3 shows this for a variety of countries – Denmark, with a strongly egalitarian Social Democrat tradition; three of our largest European neighbours, France, Germany and Spain; plus Australia and the United States. It takes completion of upper-secondary education as a benchmark (for example A levels, Highers, BTEC Diplomas,

Figure 2.2 Female earnings by highest qualification held 1993–5: full-time employees evaluated after twenty years

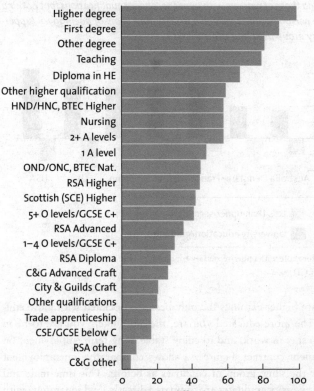

Percentage difference in average earnings compared to those with no formal qualifications

Source: Robinson 1997b[9]

baccalauréats) and compares it with higher and lower education levels. While the size of the gap between the less and the more educated varies from country to country, the basic pattern is exactly the same. Those who leave school without such an upper-secondary qualification earn on average about a quarter less than the benchmark group, and those with some university education earn an average of almost two-thirds more.

Figure 2.3 *Percentage difference between the average earnings of individuals with (a) less than upper-secondary education and (b) some university education, and those of workers with upper-secondary qualifications (but nothing beyond): persons aged twenty-five to sixty-four years of age, 1997/8 (upper-secondary group used as a benchmark)*

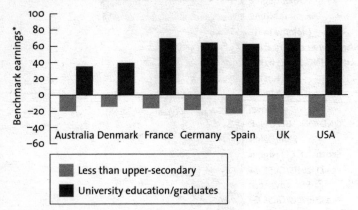

*Average for those with upper-secondary education
Source: OECD 2000

Nor are higher earnings the only benefit associated with more education. The more educated you are, the more likely you are to be in work, to stay in work, and to enjoy stable, long-term employment on a permanent contract. Figure 2.4 shows comparative unemployment rates for the same group of countries as before. This time male and female university graduates are compared directly (and separately) with men and women who left school before completing upper-secondary education – many of them with no formal academic qualifications at all. The unemployment rate for this latter group is calculated as a percentage of the rate for the university-educated: so, for example, we find that for German men the figure is over 300 per cent – meaning that the unqualified are more than three times as likely to be out of work as are the university educated. And in the USA the difference is more than fivefold.

The results here vary far more between countries, and indeed over

Figure 2.4 *Relative unemployment rates: unemployment rates for those with less than upper-secondary education as a percentage of rates for the university-educated: labour force twenty-five to sixty-four years of age, 1996*

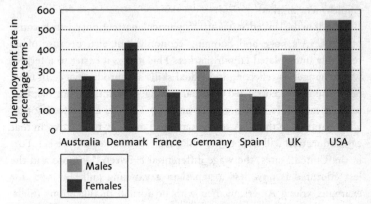

Source: OECD 1998

time, than do earnings (and remember that these are *relative* chances of being unemployed. Actual unemployment rates for both groups were far higher at this period in, say, Spain, than in the USA.) Nonetheless, the favoured position of the educated is confirmed again and again. Compared to graduates, the least qualified have two, three or even four times as high a chance of being jobless. Not all graduates may find the job of their dreams within a month of leaving university, and not all will be equally in demand. But, compared to their contemporaries, not only are their bank balances larger: their work lives are also more pleasant and secure.

Moreover, there are signs that the personal benefits of formal education are getting more marked, not less. The UK (in common, particularly, with the United States) saw big increases in wage inequalities in the last two decades.[10] Many of these occurred 'within groups'. That means that, if you took all the workers of the same age, education and gender in 1980 and compared them with the parallel group in 2000, you would find that the later, younger, group had much more varied earnings, with a larger gap between the top and the bottom. (This seems to reflect a number of factors: the jury remains out on the exact reasons.) But there are also widening differences *between* groups defined by their different educational backgrounds, suggesting that educational qualifications may be increasingly important to people's chances in the employment market.

Trends in the United States attract particular attention, partly because of the USA's huge and booming economy, but also because of its relatively unregulated labour market. This makes it easier to interpret wage changes as reflecting individual skills and productivity. (In most other countries, centralized wage bargaining, government controls, and/or political values have a greater impact.) There is also a feeling that what happens in the USA today may head our way tomorrow. In that case, education will start to look like even more of a sure-fire bet. For, in the United States, the wage differential between the more and the less educated is now less a gap than a yawning gulf. In 1970, for example, young American men with no formal qualifications (high-school dropouts) earned two-thirds as much, on average, as college graduates. By 1993 this had fallen to well under half. Put another way, by 1993 the gap between dropouts and those with just a high-school certificate was as large as the one between dropouts and graduates had been twenty years before.[11]

In the UK, meanwhile, the equivalent gap has also increased of late – albeit less dramatically. Figure 2.5 illustrates this for graduates, using average weekly wages. In the late 1970s, graduate men averaged 1.7 times as much per week as did the unqualified; over the next ten to fifteen years this rose to almost twice as much, while for women there was an even more marked difference. Meanwhile the benefits associated with other qualifications increased too, especially in the case of those, like HNDs, which are associated with higher or advanced further education.

Of course, these figures are averages.[12] Not all graduates, for example, earn more than people who left school at seventeen – or even expect to. (Vicars are an obvious example.) It matters for your future earnings what A levels and what sort of degree you did, what class of degree you got, and what university you went to.[13] People who went to independent schools tend to earn more, later in life, than those who went to state

Figure 2.5 *Ratios of weekly wages for degree-holders compared to those without formal qualifications.*

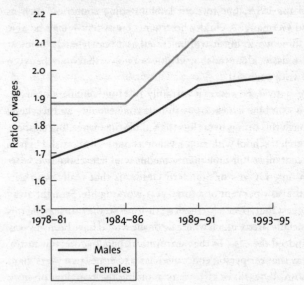

Source: Harkness & Machin 1999

ones.[14] And of course there are individual differences in skill and ability which matter irrespective of education. Nonetheless, the existence of Richard Branson, the Spice Girls or the odd homeless graduate selling *The Big Issue* in the streets does not change the general picture. Pick a highly educated and a poorly educated person at random, and by virtue of their education alone you can almost guarantee that the first will be earning more than the second.

So far, the news about education all seems to be good. At least for individuals, 'Get educated, get richer' seems like sound advice. This isn't quite the whole story though, because education isn't all free. Fees are the most obvious up-front cost; and while in the UK they affect only university and independent-school pupils, in many poorer countries they cut in well before university level. Less obvious, but no less real, is the income forgone by studying rather than working.

In developed countries like the UK this is rarely an issue until one's mid-teens (though it was in the past, and is for many countries today). Until then, school is compulsory: to sixteen in Britain and in most of Europe and the USA, but to even later in some countries, such as Belgium and Germany. A child who truants consistently may be able to pick up some work, but it will be casual and poorly paid; for most fifteen-year-olds, let alone those aged nine or twelve, the choice between school and work isn't real.

From age sixteen, however, it certainly is. Huge numbers of sixth-formers now combine education with part-time evening and weekend work, although this brings in far less than a full-time wage. But suppose someone who left school with an A level or a couple of Scottish Highers earns 5 per cent more full-time than someone who left school two years earlier with only GCSEs or Standard Grade. Is that really worth it? Two years is also 5 per cent of a forty-year working life. Straight away this may suggest that, over a lifetime, sixth-form studies are leaving this person financially pretty much where he or she would have been anyway – which is indeed the case. In the meantime, depending on your tastes, you could say that the person concerned has had either two years' hard slog with no ready cash, or two years avoiding the boredom of work and enjoying long school holidays.[15]

These costs of staying in education explain why it isn't enough simply to compare the average earnings of people with different education levels. We need also to see what people get from more education after allowing for both direct expenses and income forgone. This is what economists mean by the *net returns* to education. It involves thinking of your education spending (including what you don't earn) as an investment. What percentage return do you get, and how does it compare with other things: for example, saving that amount of money and putting it in a building society?

A lot of effort and ink has been expended on calculating such returns, with no great change in the general conclusion. Education, for those who can get it, still comes out looking like a pretty good deal in income terms – especially higher education. The UK's Dearing Committee of Inquiry into Higher Education reported in 1997, and its work will crop up frequently in the following pages. Student and university financing were a major topic examined, and the committee estimated the rate of return on students' (or their families') own investments at between 11 and 14 per cent, in real terms, allowing for inflation.[16]

Returns to school qualifications also look pretty good. The 'raw' wage difference between those with O levels/high-grade GCSEs and those with no formal qualifications at all implies a return of about 18 per cent – which is something close to pure gain, since you have to stay in school until you are sixteen anyway.[17] People born in the late 1950s who collected *three* A levels (rather than just one) look to have done even better. An average gain of over 20 per cent (or over 10 per cent for each year in the sixth form) is a very good bet indeed: well before you hit middle age your cumulative earnings should have pulled well ahead of someone who left school early with no qualifications. Different ways of analysing national data make little difference to the findings:[18] every year you stay in education beyond the school-leaving age appears to boost your income significantly, and by rates a great deal higher than the 4 or 5 per cent which, at the time of writing, is the most you could expect from your building society.

So, on this basis, individual enthusiasm for education looks pretty rational. But how about governments? Should they take the higher incomes of the more educated as a signal that education breeds wealth (and so growth)? Suppose – looking back again at Figures 2.1 and 2.2 – that most of the people whose GCSEs lurk around grade D instead got five GCSEs at C or above, which is pretty much the government's target. Can we assume that, even if they don't stay on for A levels, their incomes will duly rise by about 15 per cent? If they *do* stay on into the sixth form, as almost all with five or more good GCSEs now do, can we predict that, twenty years from now, their incomes will be more than half as high again as they would otherwise have been? Since only half the age cohort currently gets across this 'five A–C grades' boundary, this would suggest a very substantial increase in the country's overall wealth.

Most policy-makers appear to believe precisely that. 'Skills acquisition is "route one" to economic success,' announced one of the year 2000's public-sector reports.[19] But in fact you can't use the link between education and earnings to predict anything about future growth. The higher incomes of the more educated don't, in themselves, tell you anything, except that the educated are doing better than if national income were shared out equally. Before concluding that they 'deserve' it because of the wealth they themselves generate, or that the whole country benefits, and is richer, because of their skills, we need a good deal more evidence. Does such evidence exist?

Private incomes or national wealth? The search for social rates of return

People who look at the returns to education are at pains to distinguish between private returns – the benefits to individuals who receive the education – and social returns, which take into account costs and benefits to members of the society as a whole, not just the educated individual. Social returns are calculated in the same basic way whether academics or policy-makers are involved. That is, people work out how much income, further down the line, is received by the educated as a result of their education, and what sort of return this offers on the *total* amount spent, rather than just on the amount spent by the educated themselves.

These calculations of the social returns to education spending have, up to now, almost invariably given a positive result. Even though government is spending the vast sums described in Chapter 1, the calculations yield large, positive rates of return, suggesting that the country gets back substantially more than it puts in. This is one reason why the growth–education link is so deep-rooted a part of received wisdom. Unfortunately, when we look at how these calculations are made, it becomes clear that we can't make a leap from the pay of the educated to precise forecasts of economic success. Or, if we do, that it is in fact a leap of faith, and not based on hard evidence.

The problem is that the only real measure we have of whether people are productive and economically valuable is their wages. Government economists therefore assume that wages do indeed reflect the average contribution that people make in their workplace. In other words, the higher wages of the educated are interpreted as being a reward for their greater productivity. So, for example, if an average graduate is paid twice as much as an average school leaver with only a clutch of GCSEs, this is taken to mean that one graduate can in effect do as much for the economy, and take the place of, two sixteen-year-old school leavers.[20] The graduate is taken to possess a far higher level of *human capital* in the form of knowledge, skills or values which, like other forms of capital, 'yield income and other useful outputs over long periods of time'.[21]

What social-rate-of-return calculations do is adjust for costs differently from the individual calculations discussed above, and so provide a different take on the 'yield' to someone's education or human capital. Taxes cover the full costs of primary and secondary education for all students not in independent schools, and also most of the costs of university education; so there is an obvious difference between the net benefits of education to an individual and those which his or her education may bring to society. As an individual, you take into account whatever *you* pay, and whatever you might have earned if you hadn't been in school (which is not a lot when you are fourteen, let alone five years old). The state, by comparison, takes into account all the costs of education. By 2001 these amounted, in the UK, to £50 billion from public funds (equivalent to what is spent on the NHS). State spending swamps individuals' expenditure at school *and* university level.[22] Even in countries like the USA, where university students have traditionally paid fees, less than a third of university income comes from fees and so enters a 'private' rate-of-return calculation.

Working out the social rate of return on education – i.e. what education spending actually does for economic growth – still relies on people's wages as a measure of their productivity, but involves calculating the return that individuals' wages represent on the total educational spending or 'investment' that preceded them. Rate-of-return calculations sometimes also take account of the likelihood that those with the greatest natural ability in certain areas will also tend to be highly educated. This means that some of their wages may reflect natural ability rather than education, and so cannot be seen as a result of education or as a return to educational spending. Economists who try to adjust for this make a guess at how much of the returns are due to natural ability, and deflate the overall estimates accordingly. But basically the social returns to education will appear high if the highly educated are getting paid a lot more than their less educated fellow citizens, and not if they aren't.

Using this approach, we typically end up with figures which are considerably lower than for individuals, but still pretty high. For example, the Dearing Committee of Inquiry into Higher Education concluded that, since the late 1960s, 'the long run social rate of return [to higher education] . . . has run at about seven to nine per cent . . . This is above the six per cent rate regarded by the Treasury as a minimum acceptable return on public investment.'[23] In other words, education comes out looking like an excellent way of generating economic growth. Unfortunately, while using wages may be the best we can do when estimating people's economic productivity, as a basis for major policy decisions this is far from satisfactory. To see why, take everyone's favourite profession – the law.

The rebels in Shakespeare's *Henry VI* had a simple political programme: 'The first thing we do let's kill all the lawyers,' they decided (2 Henry VI, IV.ii). Few of us would go that far. We need lawyers – and not just when we are in trouble with the police. One really well-documented condition for economic prosperity is a proper legal system with enforceable contracts, for example. But it is very hard to see lawyers' salaries, and their share of GDP, as somehow reflecting closely lawyers' marginal productivity and contribution to economic growth. They have far more to do with the nature and volume of law and regulation in a society – most obviously in the USA, which has at least six times as many lawyers per head as Japan.[24] Opportunities for litigation, especially class-action suits, have hugely increased both Americans' direct expenditures on legal fees and the largely deadweight expense of spiralling insurance premiums for business, health and education, and for the law itself. Meanwhile, the money to be made in the law siphons off increasing numbers of the most able young Americans.

A detailed rate-of-return analysis in the US context would suggest that the fastest way to boost growth would be to send everyone to law school. This is clearly ridiculous, but it is an exact parallel with what happens when we use calculations of social rates of return to advocate particular education policies – such as the value of more higher education.

In reality, earnings reflect a great deal more than individual productivity. The amount paid to different groups and different individuals also depends heavily on the way in which a society is organized overall: how it runs services such as health and education; how much its public and civic cultures value equality; how professionals' fees are regulated. Look again at Figure 2.3, and in particular at Denmark and the USA. The USA has enjoyed a huge economic boom in recent years – but so too has Denmark. This tiny country has the highest proportion of its working-age population employed and the highest income per head in the EU, as well as a thoroughly high-tech industrial structure.[25] Yet returns to education are, apparently, markedly lower than in the USA.

Does this prove that education matters less and contributes less to the Danish economy than it does to the American? We would be most unwise to think so. Plenty of other developed-country 'pairs' offer comparable differences in relative rates of return, while fluctuations over time mean that they also change places in terms of which is apparently getting more for its education investment.

Or take a bus driver – a job found the world over, and involving highly uniform skills. Yet, in terms of purchasing-power, a bus driver in Germany is paid *thirteen* times as much as one in Kenya, and five times as much as one who faces the traffic chaos of India's commercial capital of Bombay. Clothing and textiles is one of the most global of industries, and 'unskilled' female textile workers form a large part of its huge workforce. In Indonesia, such a worker will be happy to earn a couple of pounds a day, $1,000 a year – if, that is, there is any work to be had.[26] Yet suppose that she – or the Kenyan bus driver – manages, by whatever means, to make it to the United States, the UK or Germany. Immediately either one can command far more for one hour's work than they previously earned in a whole day, because that is how much more we in the West pay our workers. Did something magical occur as they stepped across the border, endowing them with a whole new set of skills?

Rate-of-return analyses are hugely seductive because of their apparent precision: 'Society gets x per cent from upper-secondary education, Minister, but a hefty y per cent from more graduates.' Such comparisons can and do influence policy, but their apparent precision is spurious.

Earnings are a highly imperfect measure of an individual's 'productivity':[27] the statistics used in calculations of returns are often far from accurate; and social returns are, to quote a colleague, merely 'private returns tweaked a bit'.[28] In consequence, we cannot use rates of return to prove that more educational spending must be a good idea. On the contrary: it is no more self-evident that, since some education makes some of us rich, more would make more of us richer than it is that 'two aspirin good' means 'five aspirin better'.

To reach some firmer conclusions about education and growth, we need to go beyond the bare income statistics and look at what the underlying processes might be. We know that modern societies could not be run by illiterates, or without lots of scientists and engineers. But can we tell whether educated people are paid more because of specific skills which they learned at school and others did not? Or whether education spills over into economic development across the whole of society, with the educated doing us all a favour in the course of bettering themselves? Finally, can we tell, from current trends in our own and in the world economy, whether more education now is really the priority that our politicians proclaim?

Sorting by skill or just sorting? Why do the educated earn more?

The higher wages of the more educated *may* reflect education's contributions to growth and productivity. This is certainly the argument made when 'rates of return' are used to justify yet more government spending. But, as I pointed out above, our incomes depend on a lot more than our individual, school-learned skills. One additional factor is the overall level of industrial development in the society around us – which is why unskilled workers from the Third World can be so much more 'productive' (and better paid) if they make it to Europe or the USA. Another important influence may be aspects of our personality or basic ability which have nothing directly to do with education.

Employers are certainly using education when they hire. (Look at any job advertisement.) But might they be using it as something more than a measure of skills? Education is certainly signalling something. But is this skills, or just ability? Might education not be serving, essentially, as a simple way of ranking, screening and selecting people in a mass society?

The simple answer to this last question is 'Yes'. Education today is a socially acceptable way of ranking people which most employers would find it hard to do without. Indeed, its role in sorting and separating people and the impact this has on schools, universities and training schemes are a consistent theme of this book. But if selecting by education is so widespread, it must also be delivering more or less what the selectors need. So why are they paying more to the educated? Is it because this guarantees them employees with particular skills; or because the more educated tend to be naturally smarter and to work harder; or is it just that hiring-by-credentials is convenient, legal and unlikely to lead to trouble?

This is, quite literally, the billion-dollar question for education policy. It is obvious that education is a good bet for individuals: we saw this earlier. However, the vast amount of public money poured into it rests on the belief that high wages are a recognition of greater productivity, itself based on learned skills. Unfortunately, the question also turns out to be almost impossible to answer with any accuracy, because a lot of things are going on at once.[29]

Other things being equal, employers are generally on the lookout for the most able and intelligent people they can find. How long you stay in education is itself very closely related to how well you do in school; so years of education are a good proxy for the sort of general intelligence that school and university reward. Academic achievement fairly early on in school also determines what sort of courses and qualifications you take – how many and which GCSEs you take, and whether you do A levels or a vocational training course.[30] So the differences in earnings associated with different qualifications may say less about which skills these courses teach than about the different people who take them.

On top of that, years in education are also a reasonably good indicator of motivation, perseverance, organization – all top of employers' wish lists.[31] Of course, these aren't all that employers want, or jobs demand. Nonetheless, if one single indicator of educational success, like a degree or an American high-school diploma, wraps up a whole bundle of cognitive and personality measures then, from an employer's point of view, it is a pretty good bargain. What is more, the evidence suggests that employers are right to see cognitive skills (along with motivation and self-discipline) as good predictors of productivity. Measures of general cognitive ability are quite strongly correlated, for example, with how quickly people learn new skills, and with their performance on the job – at least in situations where we can get some reasonably objective measures.[32]

For many employers, education's usefulness as a signal of ability may be the salient consideration. However, this does not mean that concrete skills (learned through education) are totally irrelevant. Somebody who has very high cognitive abilities but is totally illiterate is not, in a modern developed economy, much use to most employers, and certainly couldn't substitute for many of the graduates currently parlaying their education into high take-home pay.

Suppose, though, that everyone left school for good at fifteen, or even twelve, instead of the modern habit of staying on longer and longer. Suppose too that, before leaving, everyone took some exams which provided a clear ranking of the population. How much less productive would the economy, and most of these people, then be? Conversely, is all the money poured into education and training beyond that point really having a substantial effect on the sorts of skills that people have, and their usefulness to employers?

Economists have devised a number of ways to provide some precise quantitative estimates of whether returns are to 'ability' or to 'skills'. However, all of them are open to serious criticism[33] – which is a major problem, given how much rates of return differ when calculated using a variety of perfectly plausible assumptions (and guesses) about how much screening for ability is involved.[34] We are left with the conclusion that returns to education partly reflect its use to sort people, and serve as a proxy for ability, and partly are a recognition of concrete skills. This is sensible enough – but not much help in planning an education system (let alone pinning down the best sort of education-for-growth). Can we instead say anything more about what *sorts* of skills seem to matter to employers, and how far they are the product of formal education?

Which skills matter?

So far, this discussion has been treating education as though all that matters is how much of it you get. So ten years is better than nine, and some college education is better than just going to high school. But, if the skills people acquire are important for growth, then this way of treating education looks rather odd. Do employers and the job market really reward you equally whichever GCSEs you take? Whichever A levels? Whichever vocational course? Whichever degree?

Perhaps they may if they are *only* using these qualifications as a general screen for ability.[35] Conversely, if they don't, this may provide some clues about which of the skills learned in school, college and university are more closely linked to the requirements of the economy than others.

Figures 2.1 and 2.2 showed very marked differences in the salaries associated with different qualifications. However, it is impossible to use these data as a source of skill needs, because (as Chapter 3 discusses) different qualifications have different status. If a degree 'pays' better than a City & Guilds diploma, this may be largely, or entirely, a result of that same screening for ability that we have just discussed: employers just assume that graduates are brighter and keep the better-paid jobs for them. So we need to look *inside* a group with equivalent education: for example, those same graduates for whom so many occupations are now reserved.

In every country for which we have data, it turns out that the market does indeed distinguish between different sorts of university education, and that there are major differences in the average earnings of graduates with different degree subjects. This is no doubt partly because some people and some degrees are not oriented towards high-earning opportunities: few of us conclude that being a religious leader must be a worthless, low-status occupation because it is badly paid. Again, some degrees (in education, nursing and medicine, for example) lead to occupations where the financial reward is state- rather than market-controlled: here, what people are paid says as much about national politics as it does about their productivity.

However, in other cases one is looking at what people get paid relative to each other in a fairly open market, and here it seems that the subject of a degree matters a great deal. Media-studies and English graduates are simply not paid as much, on average, as those with degrees in accountancy, economics, engineering or mathematics. This can partly be explained by differences in graduates' previous academic records – in the UK, with competitive and restricted entry into degree courses, courses on some subjects are harder to get into than others. That is only a part of the answer, though. Even when you control for A-level scores (and for the university that students attended), there are major differences in later earnings according to the type of degree. This strongly suggests that there is a demand for particular and specific skills learned after the age of eleven or fifteen, and that employers are not *solely* occupied with putting people in rank order. What this information does not do is translate into some sort of infallible policy of education-for-growth.

Table 2.1 summarizes private rates of return for different sorts of degree, but also looks at the social rate of return. This is calculated in the conventional way: by simply adding in the costs which are borne by government. Science degrees and engineering degrees are expensive, because they need a lot of equipment and more individual attention from staff. So, while they pay better than arts degrees from the individuals' point of view, once you add in the full cost of the degree (borne by the state) the social rate of return looks rather different. Engineers may have higher private rates of return (and average salaries), but the social rates of return look much lower for them than for graduates in the social sciences.

But does that mean that a government going for growth should ignore the salary evidence, look at the social rates, mothball the science laboratories, and channel everyone into social-science faculties? Packing thousands of students into halls to hear economics or business professors lecture (in the flesh or on a video screen) is certainly a very cheap way to generate credentials and increase graduate numbers. But a sure-fire way to growth? It hardly seems likely.

The returns to different degree subjects underline how limited a guide to policy these seductive numbers can be, and how dangerous it is to

Table 2.1 *Returns to different types of degree* [36]

	Wage premium for graduates (men: 1984–6 and 1989–91)*	Social rates of return (young men: 1986–9)†
Social sciences	20–25%	11–11.5%
Engineering	} 18–24%	5–6.5%
Science		4.5–5.5%
Arts	4–2%	–

Sources: * Harkness & Machin 1999. Wage differentials are relative/additional to A levels.
† Steel & Sausman 1997. This assumes that 60–80 per cent of graduates' pay premium is attributable to higher education rather than ability.

use them to peddle educational spending in a dash for growth. On the other hand, treated carefully, they *can* provide some indications of which concrete skills are important in the modern economy, and of whether governments' assumptions and spending priorities make any real sense.

For finding out which skills matter, the best data in the UK (and some of the best in the world) come from the National Child Development Study (NCDS). This remarkable study tracks all the children in the UK born in a particular week of March 1958; findings from it and its sister study (involving a cohort born in 1970) are a major resource for understanding how education really affects people in twenty-first-century Britain. Full information is collected at regular intervals on participants' education, jobs, family experiences, and health. In addition, as adults, participants have been asked to complete independent literacy and numeracy tests – that is, tests quite separate from anything required for GCSE or for their employers. The results are not known to anyone but the researchers, so again they provide a measure which can be used to see the effect of *skills* rather than formal education credentials.

The history of the study participants' lives underscores the enormous importance, in modern societies, of basic academic skills. Poor literacy and poor numeracy – especially the latter – have a devastating effect on people's chances of well-paid and stable employment. Moreover, this is not just because people with poor skills tend to have few GCSEs or other formal qualifications. Even after controlling for these, the effects of low skill levels are major and evident.

Figures 2.6 and 2.7 summarize the different employment prospects of those with good or poor basic skills. In order to compare like with like, they focus only on those who left school at sixteen, and who therefore could in principle have been employed for equal lengths of time. These people can be classified by their performance on a set of literacy and numeracy tasks which they were given at the age of thirty-seven, and, as the figures show, there were major differences between high- and low-scoring groups in their employment history. The groups were also very different in terms of the likelihood that they would be unemployed at age thirty-seven, and in the types of employment that they held. Moreover, there were still large and significant differences *after* researchers had controlled for any formal qualifications obtained before leaving school at sixteen. This suggests that people's work success was related to their actual skills, not just to screening by qualifications held. Further support for this idea comes from people's relative chances of being employed not just at age thirty-seven but also at twenty-one, twenty-four or thirty. For 'very low' scorers, and especially very low *numeracy* scorers, the gap widens dramatically over time: as young people, their relative chances of employment compared to the more skilled are nothing like as bad as they become later.[37]

At the other end of basic academic schooling, the NCDS data also allow us to see whether particular sixth-form subjects are more or less important in the labour market. Comparing one A level with another, the answer generally seems to be 'No': while having A levels will make you better off, this is because of the general skills that any A-level programme imparts, or because continuing to A level is so closely related to skills displayed at O level/GCSE, or because A levels are being used largely for screening.[38] There is, however, one major and

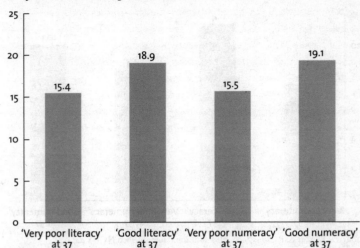

Figure 2.6 *Average years in full-time employment between ages sixteen and thirty-seven: men leaving school at sixteen*

Sources: Bynner & Parsons 2000, plus additional unpublished NCDS data

striking exception. Even after allowing for every other factor imaginable, people who took A-level mathematics earn substantially more – around 10 per cent more – than those who did not.[39]

To see what this means, imagine taking pairs of solicitors, pairs of store managers, or pairs of city bankers, in each case with the same numbers of A levels at the same grades, the same degrees and the same degree class, but where only one of each pair took maths. The ones with a maths A level would earn on average about 10 per cent more a year than the others. The reason why this finding is so interesting is that it applies across all occupations, however their wages are fixed or determined. Of course, we can't be sure that people are actually more productive because of their maths skills. But, given that we are looking at the effects of a qualification which most employers and colleagues won't even know that the individual possesses, it does seem very likely that this is the case. In which case, for once, we have found strong evidence for an economically valuable skill that is being rewarded as such.

Figure 2.7 *Average years in full-time employment between ages sixteen and thirty-seven: women leaving school at sixteen*

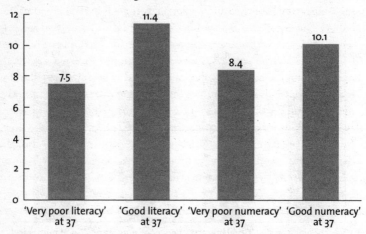

Sources: Bynner & Parsons 2000, plus additional unpublished NCDS data

Evidence from the USA also suggests that what are important – and increasingly so – are the traditional core parts of the school curriculum. The evidence again comes from large longitudinal studies – this time of young Americans who were in their final year of high school in 1972 or in 1980. These young people were given language and maths tests by the researchers, but the results were not known by their employers, or by any colleges they then attended. This makes it possible to look at whether skills, as measured on these tests, affect future earnings over and above the effects of any formal qualifications or of test scores which are public knowledge.[40] It seems that they do.[41] Moreover, the effects are higher for the 1980 than for the 1972 group, and higher six years into employment than two years in (which means that their effect is greater at the point when someone's substantive skills, rather than just bits of paper, will be more evident to employers). Moreover, it again seems to be mathematical skills which matter most.[42] The test results are, of course, likely to be highly correlated with (and proxies for) more general ability. However, their *increasing* importance between the 1972 and the 1980 cohort cannot easily be explained away on this basis.

So where does this leave us? First, none of this strengthens the case for using rates of return to different qualifications as a guide to education policy. The arguments that politicians advance for the importance of more and more education at higher levels – for more degrees, more higher education in colleges, more qualifications of every sort – rest ultimately on the apparent value of advanced education compared to schooling that ends at sixteen. Yet, in the context of a modern economy, this focus on returns to different qualifications risks devaluing core academic skills. Almost everyone who masters the latter properly now goes on to higher levels of education. So the 'returns' *look* as though they are not pay-offs to primary or even lower-secondary education at all, but only to later education levels and formal awards. However, because we have such high staying-on rates, we cannot conclude from this that the skills that employers are actually using and looking for are indeed the ones gained late in the day. The most valuable could have been acquired much earlier – by age fourteen, sixteen or eighteen – and we have seen strong suggestions that this may indeed be the case.

Second, the importance of 'old-fashioned' academic skills provides support for recent governments' emphasis on literacy and numeracy, but precious little for their parallel enthusiasm for vocational education and training. The evidence on skills suggests that employers in the brave new 'knowledge economy' are after just those traditional academic skills that schools have always tried to promote. The ability to read and comprehend, write fluently and correctly, and do mathematics appears more important than ever. It isn't obvious why this means pouring extra resources into more years of education, rather than maintaining quality in the places that already teach these skills.

Nonetheless, given that the data on screening and skills are so inconclusive, perhaps we will do better to look at a wider picture. Advocates of greater educational spending tend to argue not just that it increases the productivity of individuals, but that there are 'spillover' effects which raise the whole country to higher levels of wealth. This seems plausible enough. The unskilled worker whose wages quadruple as she crosses a border illustrates how much our welfare depends on where we have the luck to be born. Can we, though, come to any clear conclusions about how far *education* might play a key role in kick-starting or accelerating a country's growth, as opposed to other candidates – good governance, open markets, tax incentives, investment, and the like? Can we, in particular, find support for particular government policies to promote education?

Economic miracles and Asian tigers: was education the key?

If links between education and earnings within a country are less informative than most of us think, perhaps we will do better by comparing countries with each other. It is, after all, international comparisons that have really fuelled the UK's education panic. In the 1970s and 1980s Britain was increasingly preoccupied with its relative economic decline compared to other European countries and the Asian 'tiger' economies. Education and training became favourite culprits. Finegold and Soskice, for example, were the first to put forward an argument which, as noted in the Introduction, has captivated successive generations of politicians, including Tony Blair. The idea is that Britain was caught in a 'low-skills equilibrium' because its *relative* failure to educate and train its workforce had left it ill-equipped 'to adapt to the longer-term shifts in international competition'.[43]

The enthusiasm that politicians in developed countries now show for education (and not just in the UK) echoes that of many developing countries in their first years of independence. It is certainly self-evident that prosperous nations are also highly educated ones: any compendium of statistics shows that to be the case. But can we conclude that the education caused the prosperity, and that spending on schools and universities spills over into general well-being?

The short answer is 'No'. The experience of the developing world actually makes it all too clear that education cannot guarantee growth. It is certainly not enough on its own. The more interesting question is whether it is even very relevant.

A comparison of developing countries in the decades since the Second

World War suggests a rather weak link between educational and economic growth. In 1980, Egypt was the forty-seventh poorest country in the world (in terms of per-capita income), with GNP per capita of $580. Fifteen years later it was forty-eighth poorest, averaging growth rates of less than 2 per cent a year in the meantime. Yet, between 1970 and the mid-1990s, primary participation had risen to well over 90 per cent and secondary-school participation from 32 to 75 per cent of the cohort; while between 1970 and 1980 the rate of university participation more or less doubled, from 9 to 17 per cent of young people. Compare this with South Korea and almost the only common feature to be found is educational expansion. South Korea had a growth rate in per-capita income of over 7 per cent a year from the 1960s through to the 1998 crash (from which it is now recovering). In that period it also took primary education from near-universal to universal, and secondary participation from a quarter to the whole of the cohort; and, while in 1979 it had a smaller proportion of its young people in university than Egypt, by 1993 this proportion was much higher. So you grow economically and also expand your education system enormously; or, like Egypt, you fail dismally to achieve economic success, alongside huge educational expansion.

A number of recent World Bank analyses suggest that, across the world's developing economies, there exists a negative relationship between education levels and growth. In other words, *the countries which have done most to increase the education levels of their population have, on average, grown less fast than those which have devoted fewer resources to education*. What can be going on here?

The finding seems profoundly anti-intuitive.[44] However, when we look more closely at some of these economies, it becomes clear that, while spending on education isn't really *reducing* economic growth, educating people also doesn't, in itself, offer them many chances to bolster economic success. The belief that it does led many developing countries, notably in Africa, South-East Asia and South America, to spend a very great deal of money without creating successful economies in the process.

Egypt is a country whose government made a commitment to give graduates first call on jobs in the public sector. It very quickly found itself with a vast and underemployed army of civil servants, and a huge queue of students aiming at comparable sinecures for themselves. Sri Lanka and much of sub-Saharan Africa exhibit similar characteristics. In Sri Lanka, for example, the post-colonial governments inherited and continued a system in which school exams were used to ration access to a limited number of government jobs. Mounting pressure on these jobs, from educated teenagers in an economically stagnant society, was the trigger for two major youth insurrections and loss of life, in 1971 and again in 1988–9.[45]

In situations like these, rate-of-return analysis simply reflects back social inequalities. Compare the salaries of those who actually make it into government and other top jobs with the wages of the population at large and the figures will suggest that what is 'needed' economically is yet more university or academic upper-secondary graduates.[46] You could easily find yourself concluding that education in Egypt was contributing splendidly to growth, since the huge graduate-filled bureaucracy is paid a lot more than the vast majority of less-educated Egyptians.[47]

Countries which embraced central planning of the economy, of manpower and of public services were also particularly likely to believe in the importance of rapid educational expansion; to generate large numbers of expensively educated bureaucrats who had gone through both upper-secondary and university education; and to have low economic growth. In post-Thatcher New Labour Britain, a belief in central planning of the economy now seems like ancient history, but in the early 1970s an organization like UNESCO was behaving in a completely mainstream and uncontroversial manner when it identified its priority as establishing 'a close relationship between educational planning . . . and national overall plans for economic and social development'.[48] This may help to explain why, in comparisons of developing countries, education spending and growth can actually end up looking as though they are *negatively* related.

The obvious riposte is that neither developing countries nor the command economies of the period following the Second World War have much relevance to education's role in the most successful industrial countries. As a Whitehall mandarin might point out, no member of the OECD 'rich men's club', whether long-standing (like the UK) or new (like Korea), has practised manpower planning for many a decade. And what possible lessons can the heavily agricultural and low-productivity economies of Egypt or Sri Lanka have for the UK government's plans to foster economic growth?

But do comparisons of *developed* countries, older and newer, show anything different? More specifically, once you reach a certain point, does education spending change its effect, so that it really does become the engine of growth? Again, not obviously so. Reviews of the industrialized world do not produce anything quite so startling as an apparent fall in the growth rate being associated with high education spending, but they don't come up with evidence of any simple, positive effects either.[49]

Korea, as we saw above, now enjoys very high education levels and very high incomes. It is the favourite example both of development economists and of British commentators who want to make a case for educational spending and active government involvement in educational planning. They point out how Korea ran a massive national literacy campaign in the immediate post-war period; how it then expanded secondary schooling, with a strong emphasis on maintaining and equalizing school quality across the country; how it expanded vocational high schools and technical universities, even though this cut against the direction of student demand; and how there has been no problem with skill shortages throughout a fifty-year period of remarkable economic growth.

All true, and all very impressive; and it is hard to believe that this education policy did not help Korea's success. But did it *cause* it? Was it even a critical factor? If you want to argue that, you also have to find evidence that successful developed countries with poorer education policy, and lower spending levels, nonetheless experienced relatively and significantly lower growth rates than otherwise comparable states. However, among the most successful economies, there is in fact no clear link between growth and spending on education, let alone between growth and central-government involvement in education planning.[50] Surges in growth don't follow consistently from surges in educational achievement: nor is the reverse true. As Angus Maddison pointed out, 'the slackening in productivity growth' that marked the 1970s and 1980s cannot have been 'due to a slowing down in the pace of growth of educational capital. Indeed the evidence available shows more rapid growth in the educational stock in the 1970s than in the 1960s or 1950s.[51]

This is true even for the 'tiger' economies. Hong Kong had nothing like the central direction and planning of education evident in Singapore or Korea, but its growth rate has been comparable. In per-capita income terms, Switzerland was the richest developed country in the world in both 1980 and in 1993, and also, as we saw in Chapter 1, one with a history of relatively low public expenditure.[52] Its educational arrangements are a cantonal, not a national, affair; and the proportion of its young people in university or other higher education is way below the average for the developed world. Compared with the average for the 'rich men's club' of OECD countries, Swiss university enrolment rates have for much of the last quarter-century hovered at around a third of the *average* for the OECD, and some OECD countries registered rates five or six times higher.[53]

In the late 1990s there were headlines galore for England and Scotland's relatively poor showing in the Third International Maths and Science Study – or rather plenty for the maths results, and far fewer for science, where we were scoring near the top. This study, like a number of previous ones, involved giving the same tests (in translation) to large samples of primary- and secondary-age children at the same points in their school career.[54] A considerable number of developed countries participated. Singapore, Korea, Japan and Hong Kong were all at the top in the summary maths tables, while England and Scotland came just below the middle. But not only were the differences between most of the countries in the study not really very big: for the group as a whole, the correlation between maths scores and GNP per capita is so weak as to be insignificant by most normal statistical standards. Peter Robinson, who calculated the figures, also looked back at 1982, and the Second International Study.[55] Two of the countries which were to have the world's fastest-growing economies in the 1980s and 1990s took part in that study too. And at that point, on the eve of meteoric growth, the mathematics scores of the children who would deliver economic success were *not* higher than their English counterparts.

However, the country whose performance really deserves far more attention, in this context, than it usually receives is the United States, lurking consistently below England in these international league tables. Most European commentators register American education only to condemn it. In this they tend to echo Americans themselves, who have been sufficiently worried about their children's poor performance to publish official reports accusing themselves of 'unthinking, unilateral educational disarmament',[56] and who bemoan the 'dumbing down' of American culture and the low prestige attached to academic success by teenagers.

Critics have therefore tended to see American education as unproductive and inefficient. Indeed, Ashton and Green, in an analysis arguing for the importance of education *and* educational planning by governments, perceived it as being caught in something akin to a 'low-skills equilibrium': the state in which, as we saw earlier in this chapter, the UK stands accused of finding itself.[57] Such an equilibrium means that there is a self-reinforcing situation in which minimally skilled school leavers are being delivered into a labour market which must therefore concentrate on low-skill, low-value products. Ashton and Green's timing was unfortunate, for their analysis appeared in 1996, when the US boom of the 1990s was already under way. Suppose American education really is so poor, and education really so critical to growth. One may then well wonder why this same country not only enjoyed record-breaking growth in both output and employment, but was also the main source of innovation and product development throughout the last decades of the twentieth century, most of it the achievement of the US-born.[58] Do we conclude that American education was getting it right all along and should be copied? Or that the links are less obvious and far less direct than we once thought?

I would argue that there is no more guarantee in developed than in undeveloped countries that skills will necessarily be used 'productively', in the sense of fostering GNP growth. In discussing what set countries on the road to prosperity in the past, Douglass North provides a vivid example of how time and circumstance may steer 'human capital' into productive or unproductive channels. He points out that 'To be a successful pirate one needs to know a great deal about naval warfare; the trade routes of commercial shipping; the armament, rigging, and crew size of potential victims; and the market for booty.'[59] In other words, a successful pirate was (and is) a highly skilled human being. Moreover, in large parts of the world, through much of human history, piracy was one of the very few ways in which able young men from poor families could hope to make large sums of money. But pirates hardly generated economic growth, or enriched the whole society around them: indeed, the more skilled, the less so.

Modern developed countries give their trained and educated people strong incentives to go into more obviously productive, or socially worthwhile, careers than piracy. They may nonetheless vary enormously in how far their economies promote economic growth in other ways, and in how many people choose jobs which are 'deadweight' in terms of GNP growth. Lawyers and sheet-metal workers are both highly skilled (if somewhat less versatile than a top-rank pirate). But suppose the lawyers spend their time advising businesses on how to circumvent mutually inconsistent and badly drafted laws generated by a hyperactive legislature. Or that, as happened in the 1980s, sheet-metal workers are poured out into a saturated marketplace by government training workshops with targets to meet and a staff of highly experienced trainers whom industrial change had made redundant. What price growth then?

There is also another possibility. Maybe, at the levels of income and education that the developed world has reached, we are seeing things back to front. Could it be that growth causes education, rather than education causing growth? Hong Kong children, if this scenario is right, may be pouring into higher education, and outperforming the English at maths, *after* the meteoric growth rate of their economy, and indeed because of it. They are doing so in order to compete for jobs in an economy which, as the number of professional jobs grows, increasingly uses credentials for hiring. And their prosperous parents can now afford long schooling, and indeed encourage it, pushing them to compete academically and so get into the best classes, the best schools, the best universities.

American economists Mark Bils and Peter Klenow offer a test of this idea.[60] The basic argument of the 'education leads to growth' school is that education increases productivity and this is why the educated have higher wages. However, it is also the case that, as workers become more experienced, and build up time on the job, they tend to earn more. This is because of the skills they have gained while in employment: we can call it an 'experience premium'.

In most countries, over the last decades, the average duration of education for young workers in any given occupational area has increased markedly compared to their older workmates. If all this additional education has really increased their productivity – both immediately (since they have less to learn when they start work) and in the longer term (because they learn faster and more thoroughly) – then wage statistics should reflect this. Over time, we should find that the experience premium declines. Highly educated young workers should get paid more on entry than the previous generation did, but accumulate less of an 'experience premium' because they have less to learn. And those countries with the most rapidly narrowing premiums should be the fastest growing, as they benefit from educated young workers.

None of these patterns can be found; and the breadth or narrowness of the 'experience' bonus in workers' wages seems to bear no relationship to growth rates. If high-quality schooling is making any difference to the relative economic performance of countries, it is doing so in a very undramatic fashion, since its effects appear to be swamped or neutralized by other factors.

What Bils and Klenow's results do show, however, is that, while schooling may not have much obvious impact on growth, fast-growing economies *do* encourage further increases in schooling. Growth generates education, whether or not education generates growth. I have sketched out why this might happen above: namely that, if education is the recognized, legitimate and apparently sure-fire way to success, young people will increasingly crowd into education, with their parents' blessing – and with a hefty contribution of taxpayers' money. Later chapters return to this topic in detail; but the point is that, while this reflects *individual* self-interest clearly, it is not at all obvious that every extra bit of education is benefiting the economy, or is the best thing on which to spend public money.

The evidence I have just summarized pours further cold water on any simple equating of education spending with national economic success. Neither in the developed nor in the developing world can we conclude that education automatically delivers growth. Should we go even further, though? Should we argue that education is actually *ir-relevant* to growth?

The answer must be 'No', for all the 'obvious' reasons that fuelled our education panic in the first place. Modern economies *do* require educated people; and the latter command a premium in the marketplace in part, at least, because of their skills, not just because education serves as a sorting mechanism. And, while Switzerland may be educating fewer people for less time than France or Japan, it is still spending a lot, and supporting highly skilled research-and-development teams – many in private industry, but many others in universities. Equally, in a modern society, illiteracy brings misery to people, erecting barriers in front of them and their children.

So it would be bizarre to see our education systems as just a collection of huge white elephants. But then no one is seriously advocating closing down all publicly funded education, or even cutting 25 per cent off its budget. Plenty of people *are* advocating major increases in spending, and doing so not because people enjoy education, not because of its contribution to culture and learning, but because it leads to growth. Looking at the developed world over the last few decades – at Japan and Korea; at Switzerland and France; at the USA or the UK – one has to ask why. Just what evidence does the late twentieth century offer that suggests that education policy should take pride of place in a government's strategy for growth, or that further public spending on education is the way to deliver productivity gains? And answer comes there none.

Globalization and a new dawn?

To the sceptical arguments of the previous pages, there is one obvious riposte: everything is different now. All this looking back at the experiences of people born in the 1950s or 1960s and before is beside the point. We are now heading for a twenty-first-century economy in which, to quote Tony Blair, 'Brainpower, skills and flexibility – not cheap manual labour – are the key to competitiveness and productivity.' What is relevant is surely not evidence from the past, but the emergence of a new 'learning society', a new 'knowledge economy', in which only education can deliver growth.[61]

This view has been extremely influential and very widespread. The argument that a 'low-skills equilibrium' is disastrous in a world of integrated markets and new technologies has, as we have seen, found precise echoes in the speeches of Blair, Blunkett and others, as have the 'new economy' analyses both of small think tanks such as Demos and of whales such as the Confederation of British Industry (CBI). Senior business executives announce that 'Western economies [have] moved from manufacturing goods to manufacturing ideas.'[62] These ideas are why government enthusiasm for education has taken the particular forms it has – an enthusiasm for making everyone into a 'skilled' worker by means of vocational training, and for more and more higher-education graduates.

And yet, is current conventional wisdom really correct? It would be silly to deny the enormous importance of universities as generators of pure ideas, of applications and patents, and of practical industrial consultancy. But, although we may know that our economies need universities, does that mean they need more of them, or even as many as we have? We know that many jobs are highly skilled, and that well-educated, high-achieving employees tend to be more productive and quicker to learn in the workplace. Does that mean that the unskilled are in peril of losing their livelihoods in an emerging 'knowledge economy', and that we need to channel more and more of the young and of the adult workforce into vocational education and training?

There are two ways to help answer these questions. The first is simply to look at the way in which the labour force has altered over the last few decades. This gives us some broad idea of whether, as a nation, we are currently under- or over-educated, and whether we are heading for huge shortages of the skilled and educated and for mass unemployment for those with no qualifications. The second is to look for any clear evidence, not just at home but worldwide, of bonanzas for those societies for which 'high-tech'-related education is a public priority. Does pumping up the supply of graduates and of technicians deliver twenty-first-century-style growth, even if it couldn't guarantee earlier variants of economic development?

The occupational structure

On one point the new economy enthusiasts are absolutely right. If we compare the labour force in 1900 and in 2000, it is obvious that there has been a huge change in the sorts of jobs that people do. As we saw in Chapter 1, some of the huge workforces of 100 or fifty years ago have simply disappeared. In both 1900 and 1950, about 780,000 people were employed in the coal-mining industry. By the mid 1990s the number was 18,000.[63] At the same time, there has been a century-long growth in the proportion of jobs which count as 'professional', 'technical' or 'managerial', and a decline both in skilled manual jobs and in unskilled jobs generally. Moreover, these trends are expected to continue. Projections for the next decade are for a growth of 30 per cent (867,000) in openings for professionals, and for a continued, if less dramatic, growth of 8 per cent (290,000) in job openings for managers.[64]

This does not mean that we are all becoming computer programmers or biotechnology entrepreneurs. Tables 2.2 and 2.3 summarize recent changes, and make clear the decline in traditional manual jobs. As the sectoral figures show (Table 2.3), manufacturing jobs have declined particularly fast, as happened with agricultural ones before them. However, this is far from meaning that there are fewer and fewer jobs for the unskilled because the labour market is demanding only skilled labour. On the contrary, the percentage of jobs which fall into the 'skilled crafts' categories has fallen steadily throughout the 1980s and 1990s, and is projected to decline yet more.[65] Meanwhile, some occupations are thriving which require much less of a 'knowledge' base. The single fastest-growing job in the 1980s was 'postman'; that of the 1990s looks like being 'care assistant' in nursing homes and hospitals – i.e. an essential, low-grade, low-paid and pretty thankless service job. While professional and managerial jobs have certainly exploded in numbers, the greatest shrinkage has been among the skilled and semi-skilled manual jobs in the middle. Low-skilled openings still exist in their millions for people to do things like cleaning streets and offices, packing

Table 2.2 *Changes in the occupational structure of employment: percentage of total employment, UK* [66]

	1984	1990	1998
Managerial/professional/technical	29.1	31.8	36.6
Clerical/secretarial	16.1	17.0	15.0
Craft and related	17.7	16.0	12.2
Sales and personal services	14.3	15.0	18.8
Manual operatives	11.6	10.6	9.4
Other	11.2	9.6	8.0

Sources: Adapted from Robinson 1997a and Institute for Employment Research 2000

Table 2.3 *Changes in the occupational structure of employment: percentage of civil employment by sector: UK*

	1950	1971	1998
Agriculture	5.5	3.1	1.7
Industry	48.9	43.8	26.6
Services	45.6	53.1	71.7

Source: Feinstein 1999

and delivering boxes, staffing call centres, or operating supermarket checkouts.

There are all sorts of reasons why more education might benefit people who end up doing jobs like these – but they are not the hard-nosed education-for-growth ones so beloved of contemporary politicians. I find it difficult to construct a convincing argument that more sixth-form qualifications and more degrees are needed so that people will be educated enough to stack shelves, swipe credit cards, or operate a cappuccino machine effectively. And it is important to remember just how many jobs like this do exist, because to listen to a lot of the rhetoric you would think that every semi-skilled or unskilled job was going to vanish tomorrow, if not early this afternoon.

There are two particularly important (and interrelated) reasons why it is skilled manual jobs, and manufacturing jobs generally, that have declined. The first is the vast increases in productivity that have occurred in manufacturing industries over the last few decades, so that equal amounts of output can be produced with a small fraction of the old workforce. The second is that manufactured goods – unlike nannies or bus drivers – can be made abroad and imported in containers for sale. So countries with lower wages than ours can undercut our manufacturers, especially for products which need only semi-skilled workers.

This could mean, on the one hand, that manufacturers in developed countries have moved to high-productivity methods, involving more machines and even fewer (though more skilled) workers, even faster than they would have done in the absence of such overseas competition and, on the other hand, that companies which couldn't manage this simply closed. How far this has actually happened (and how far it is because of trade with lower-wage countries) is a subject of enormous debate among economists.[67] However, whatever the absolute impact of trade on manufacturing jobs, the general picture is the same throughout the developed world. In the foreseeable future, manufacturing is very unlikely to generate big increases in employment, and very likely to continue falling in size as a proportion of the workforce. The absolute numbers vary between countries: Germany, for example, has an economy which is much more manufacturing-based than that of the UK or of France, so the absolute importance of manufacturing has stayed higher there. But the trend is consistent, and there are no other major changes on the horizon which would generate big increases in demand for skilled manual jobs.

So what can we conclude about education policy from recent and projected labour-force trends? Governments' two most overtly growth-related priorities are, as we have seen, increases in vocational education and training and further university expansion. As Chapter 3 will describe, the public has been far less convinced of the merits of vocational education than have successive ministers and ministries, and the evidence above suggests it might be right. There have been large falls in the numbers of mid-level, skilled manual workers employed. So can a shortage of skilled workers and technicians really have been a major drag on recent British economic growth?

Governments seem on firmer ground with university expansion. Occupational changes certainly bear out the conventional wisdom that demand for highly educated people has grown: since 1961, the proportion of jobs classified as managerial, technical or professional has actually doubled. But even here it is not obvious that the current passion for yet more graduates makes any real sense. On the contrary, it is much easier to argue that we have an over-educated rather than an under-educated workforce.

The idea of 'over-education' is a slippery one on which a great deal of ink has been expended.[68] The usual, fairly common-sense, definition takes people to be over-educated if they have more education than is required to do their job. This begs the question of whether the 'over-educated' person is doing the job much better – or, alternatively, rather worse – than someone who has had less formal education. However, if some people have skills which they feel aren't being used by their jobs, or if others with the same skills and qualifications are employed elsewhere for much more pay, one can reasonably deduce that these people are not working up to their full productive capacity. In other words, the economy has more skills around than we apparently know how to use.

People who look at this issue in detail have almost unanimously concluded that, in these senses of the term, we definitely over-educate. A large number of UK economists – among them John Ashworth, Ewart Keep and Jim Murphy – have argued this forcibly in recent decades.[69] They point out that large numbers of jobs now 'demand' levels of education from their holders which were not required in the past. Spiralling numbers of people with formal qualifications mean that employers can now insist on employees having more education than in the past, and will also suspect that anyone without qualifications isn't worth having.[70] The result is that jobs which twenty years ago were done by people who had left school at sixteen or eighteen now go only to new entrants who have degrees.[71] Projected increases in graduate numbers seem bound to make this apparent mismatch even more marked.

At the time of the 1991 census, the proportion of people in professional, managerial and technical posts with degrees or other higher qualifications was still under half. This might suggest a considerable level of skill shortage, in spite of ever-rising entry requirements. But the phenomenon is highly age-related – older managers came to work straight from school, the young via university. Moreover, the category itself is more than a bit misleading, since, as Peter Robinson points out,[72] it includes huge numbers of owner/managers of small shops, hotels and businesses. It is hard to argue that a degree is a prerequisite for running a successful fish-and-chip shop, or a motor-repair business – though, on current trends, more and more proprietors are likely to have one.

The 'over-educated' may, of course, be more productive than their less-educated predecessors in a given job. However, this is another of those things that you can choose either to believe or not. There is certainly no firm evidence to suggest that 'over-education' does raise productivity; nor, conversely, that being better educated (or at least educated for longer) makes you less motivated or actually *worse* at your job. We can't use the 'over-education' figures to establish whether much current education is economically a waste of money. However, we equally can't get much support from occupational changes for the idea that we are currently seriously under-educating for our new century's economy.

Social spin-offs

There is one final possibility to be considered. Earlier in this chapter we looked at the historic link between education spending and growth on an international basis, and found it far from self-evident. Perhaps, though, the twenty-first century is going to be different, and we will find that those countries which are economic powerhouses are also those which have educated their way into a 'high-skills' equilibrium.

A simple comparison of occupational trends doesn't show anything obvious of this nature. The general direction is the same everywhere in the developed world – less manufacturing and more services, although countries differ in the absolute size of each sector and the speed of change. A more sophisticated analysis is associated with 'neoclassical endogenous growth theory'. This term enjoyed some short-term notoriety after a speech on the topic by the Chancellor, Gordon Brown, provided a field day for diarists and cartoonists. What it actually refers to is some highly technical literature which examines whether, in the new economy, highly educated people don't just produce more themselves but create an environment in which *everyone* is more productive. This would mean that their education spills over to everyone's general benefit: the whole is more than the sum of the parts.

If true, this would be very good news indeed for enthusiasts of education spending. Instead of muttering about students lolling around for three years at taxpayers' and parental expense, we could see them as future benefactors of the nation; and, rather than seeing 'over-education' as a mistake, we could confidently expect that the whole workplace was benefiting from those extra skills.

But, as with so many other ideas, there is very little hard evidence either way.[73] Of course, if you look at somewhere special like Silicon Valley, something on these lines is certainly happening: the energy, ideas and creativity generated by a critical mass of very clever and skilled people are greater than if you scattered that group evenly across the United States. But there is no clear or consistent empirical support for the idea that a higher 'volume' of education in a whole society creates spillover effects and, as a general rule, raises everyone's productivity. Nor is there anything to suggest that, in this respect, the new economy is vastly different from the old.[74]

Conclusion

Throughout the developed world, politicians take it for a fact that education and economic growth are directly linked. They translate this into an enthusiasm for yet more education spending – and yet the balance of evidence is clearly against them. One argument after another falls apart on closer examination: there is no clear indication at all that the UK, or any other developed country, is spending below some critical level, or that pumping more money into education will guarantee even half a per cent a year's extra growth.

At the same time, we do have some indication of what is particularly important. We know that employers use qualifications partly as a simple screening device, and that, in a modern economy, people are well aware of this on their own and their children's behalf: industrial economies create their own demand for education. At the same time, schooling and qualifications do signal certain substantive skills – and people's earnings are related not just to their paper qualifications but also to their relative academic ability and to (some) things that they have studied and learned. We know that basic literacy and numeracy matter a great deal, and that the labour market rewards mathematical skills. We also know that technical progress depends on the best scientific and technological research; but that there is no evidence that education spills over to raise productivity in a general, economy-wide way.

Of course the opposite applies as well. We can't happily recommend cutting educational expenditure in some sweeping fashion, and we don't have any idea of how much less education we could get away with from a purely economic point of view. But all this suggests that a government which is serious about economic growth needs to be quite careful and discriminating in its education spending. It needs to eschew sheer quantity and think about where there is a clearly demonstrated demand, about where and for what governments should be paying, and about the quality of what is provided. As later chapters on higher education will show, it is all too easy for developed as well as developing countries to sacrifice quality to quantity – a process more likely to reduce growth than to encourage it.

Are our governments up to this fine-tuned decision-making? Those of the UK certainly have believed they are, and that they can not so much tweak as remake education in the country's economic interests. As we have seen, their main preoccupations and the areas of greatest new public activity are vocational education and training and higher education – both seen as necessary to a new economy which demands ever higher skills. In both these domains governments have hugely increased central control over education during exactly the same period as they have seen it as an elixir of growth.

The result, unfortunately, has been some seriously bad policy, while the way in which policy-makers view education has been narrowed and distorted. The following chapters describe, in detail, the recent history of vocational education and training and contemporary changes in higher education. They show how inadequate and wasteful such a simplistic equating of education and growth turns out to be, and how problematic it is to try to fine-tune education from inside a government ministry. We start, in Chapter 3, with vocational-education policy, and government attempts to steer the young into staffing the government's conception of a 'high-skills' workplace.

3 A great idea for other people's children: the decline and fall of vocational education

Vocational qualifications will in future:

be of equal standing with academic qualifications.

Conservative ministers, 1991

be a positive choice with as much status and esteem as academic.

Labour ministers, 2001

I am doing A levels; I do not intend to do any training.

English sixth-former planning to enter nursing or physio-therapy, 1994

NVQs are No Value Qualifications.

English grammar-school student, 2001[1]

For over a quarter of a century, British governments have been making determined attempts to enlarge, redesign and promote vocational education. They have been convinced that this is necessary if the economy is to reach the apotheosis of a 'high-skills' equilibrium, as well as being in the best interests of the nation's young. The activist policies of one minister after another have reflected the parallel belief that the education system, left to itself, is incapable of recognizing economic imperatives. Nor can the young and their families be trusted to perceive where self-, as well as national, interest lies. Central government must intervene.

The main target of attention has been and remains the tally of vocational qualifications. The thrust is clear: numbers of students achieving vocational qualifications were too low, are too low, and need to keep increasing. Equally explicit is the commitment to raising the status of vocational education for young people. Minister after minister has pledged his or her government, Conservative or Labour, to achieving 'parity of esteem' for vocational and academic awards. Mr Blunkett, in 2000, did so in words that were almost identical to those of Tim Eggar in 1991, David Hunt in 1993 or James Paice in 1995.

Both policies, as this chapter shows, have met with comprehensive failure. There has been no major increase in the number of vocational qualifications awarded, and no change in the relative status of vocational education either. If anything, the opposite has occurred. The story of this failure helps us understand how today's labour market actually works. It shows why, for the foreseeable future, other efforts to promote vocational education are going to founder in their turn. And it demonstrates how little one can rely on governments' ability to fine-tune education effectively for short-term economic ends.

Too little too late? Vocational awards in the twentieth century

To understand why so much effort has been poured into developing and promoting vocational qualifications, we first need a little history. A century ago, the education systems of the developed world – essentially Europe and North America – were actually far *more* similar to each other than they are today. The vast mass of the population attended schools which concentrated on the three Rs, plus some handicrafts – woodwork for boys, needlework for girls – and which they left at about age thirteen or fourteen. Alongside this mass system there existed a very small, high-status academic sector which concentrated overwhelmingly on classics and mathematics, and from which a minority, even of these privileged students, went on to university.

As the century progressed, the industrialized countries gradually developed mass systems of upper-secondary schooling, which took on a variety of forms – quite different in, say, Germany from Sweden, or in the Netherlands from Scotland or Spain. They also developed very different approaches to vocational education.

We all have a fairly clear idea what 'vocational' schooling means – which, of course, speaks volumes in itself. It does not mean a medical or veterinary degree; or a postgraduate law-school course; or taking one's accountancy examinations while working for one of the big City accounting firms. It does not even mean nursing or teacher training. 'Vocational education' instead refers to courses for young people which are offered as a lower-prestige alternative to academic secondary schooling, and which lead to manual, craft and, more recently, secretarial jobs. 'Technical' education slots into the hierarchy above vocational and below academic, and leads, in theory, to the technician jobs which increased in number during the twentieth century.

In the educationally more uniform world of the nineteenth century, apprenticeships were the main source of formal vocational training – as indeed they had been for centuries before. As the twentieth century advanced, so apprenticeship patterns diverged. Some countries, such as France, developed a large range of school-based vocational qualifications, so that students mostly remained in full-time education in order to obtain vocational training. French apprenticeships, meanwhile, became a residual, rather low-status option, followed mostly by those entering the traditional artisan occupations – construction, catering, agricultural trades. Spain abolished apprenticeships altogether (then later reintroduced them); in the USA they withered away except in a few highly unionized manual craft areas; in Italy they now exist only as an informal system, with no official qualifications associated with them at all. In other countries, however, notably Germany, Austria, Switzerland and some of the Scandinavian countries, apprenticeship instead expanded, encompassing new occupations. For a majority of young people in these countries, it became the regular route from school to work.

British apprenticeships were distinctive in two ways: continuing lack of government involvement and the absence of compulsory examinations (or formal qualifications) at the end of an apprenticeship. While apprenticeship in most European countries was heavily regulated, in the UK it remained an industry- or even firm-specific concern; both content and apprentice pay were negotiated between employers and the relevant craft unions. There were no major reforms or expansion of apprenticeship, but for most of the twentieth century it remained important. In 1961, 34 per cent of fifteen-year-old boys (though only 7 per cent of girls) left school and went directly into apprenticeships; in 1974 the figure for boys was still only just below a third.[2] From there, as we shall see, decline was to be both precipitous and hastened by government policy. It was also largely invisible, since from a Whitehall (or a media) viewpoint it involved only other people's children.

During the twentieth century, countries' secondary-school systems also diverged. While everyone organized things differently from everybody else, a segmented secondary sector was (outside North America) the rule. Most countries had academic high schools plus quite separate vocational ones. In Germany the *Gymnasium* provided the academic route to university; but, from the end of elementary school on, most pupils were (and are) in the *Hauptschulen* or *Realschulen*, where the prescribed curriculum combined vocational and general elements. The French vocational secondary schools were set up quite separately from the academic *lycées*: today, after the comprehensive *collège* (for eleven-to-sixteen-year-olds), French children continue to feed into distinct 'vocational' and 'general' *lycées*. The Spanish system was similar. The Dutch – who divided their children from age eleven into the most complicated and segmented system in Europe – included in their provision a network of full-time vocational secondary schools which were the accepted route into respected artisan jobs.

The UK had 'grammar' and 'modern' schools at secondary level, but no comprehensive network of vocational schools. It did develop vocational qualifications, but largely independently of any government initiative. 'City & Guilds' (the City and Guilds of London Institute), which was to become the largest of the country's vocational examining bodies, was an initiative of the City of London's livery companies, and was established in 1878 to improve 'the technical knowledge of those engaged in the manufactures of this country'. The RSA (the Royal Society for the Encouragement of Arts, Manufactures and Commerce) had started to set examinations even earlier, and became especially important in the commercial field. From 1920 onward, various chartered

Figure 3.1 *The growth of City & Guilds vocational awards: 1900–1960*

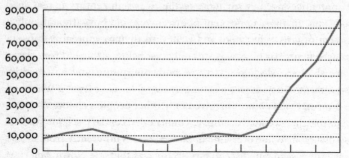

Source: City & Guilds 1993

occupations[3] started to set examinations – first for National Certificates (or 'Ordinary National Certificates' – ONCs), taken by part-timers, and then for Ordinary National Diplomas, taken by full-time students. From the mid 1920s onward, groups of local education authorities also started to form regional examining unions whose activities included technical subjects.

The rather motley collection of examining bodies which developed early in the century survived well into the century's third quarter, with different organizations dividing up the market between them more or less amicably – or at least avoiding too many public turf battles. New occupational groups set up their own specialized awards, while local authorities increasingly paid for evening and part-time day classes in technical colleges or evening institutes – the forerunners of today's multi-site, multi-purpose colleges of further education. Figure 3.1 shows the development of course provision by City & Guilds (as the largest of the vocational examining groups). In addition, many technical students, until quite recently, enrolled for classes but did not obtain formal qualifications.

By the 1930s, one employed person in fifteen was enrolled for some form of part-time education, and there were more than 1.25 million part-time students in technical colleges or institutes. After the war, as we saw in Chapter 1, further education numbers surged again, reaching 2.25 million students by the mid 1950s. There were five times as many full-time vocational students in technical colleges in 1955 as in 1931, and eleven times as many part-time *day* students (generally on day release from their employers). Evening enrolments were more heavily 'general' and 'recreational'; even so, the rise in enrolments over that same quarter-century saw numbers of evening vocational students rise from 300,000 to almost twice that number.[4]

None of this involved anything that could be seen as a European-style system of technical and vocational schools. Junior technical schools had enjoyed a steady but unspectacular growth in the inter-war period. The 1944 Education Act, which introduced universal secondary education, also provided for a tripartite German- or Dutch-style system with grammar, technical and modern schools. By 1946 there were 324 Senior Technical schools in the UK; but by 1953 numbers were down to 250, more than half of them housed within further education colleges. Technical schools were far more expensive than their general equivalents, and they had no powerful friends to argue their case in Whitehall. In 1953 their 79,000 pupils amounted to 4 per cent of secondary enrolments; in 1965, 3 per cent of senior pupils were in technical schools; by 1975 this was down to just half a per cent.[5] At the same period two-thirds of the equivalent German age group were in vocational high schools.

We need one more piece of history before we can understand the vocational alarms and excitements of the last few years, and why they were – and are – the equivalents of fingers in a dyke. In 1969 the indigestibly named Committee on Technician Courses and Examinations of the National Advisory Council on Education and Industry produced the 'Haslegrave Report' (named after its chairman). The report was designed to tidy up the complex structure of vocational awards that I outlined above, and recommended two new quasi-governmental bodies: a Technician Education Council and a Business Education Council (TEC and BEC).

Duly established, they were housed at first within City & Guilds, whose own technician awards were, in the process, merged into a new set of National Certificates and Diplomas. But the two broke away, with government approval, and formed BTEC (the Business and Technician

Education Council), developing and accrediting their own wide range of upper-secondary courses as well as the advanced Higher National Certificates and Diplomas. Though furious at the loss of its technician courses, City & Guilds replaced them, in volume terms, with customized certificates for individual companies and trades, and qualifications for lower-achieving sixth-form and FE students. BTEC also extended its range, adding lower-level First Diplomas to its main Diploma range.

The result was a steady if unspectacular growth in both the numbers and the proportions of young people and adults taking vocational qualifications. By the early 1980s, 15 per cent of British sixteen-year-olds were in full-time vocational programmes; over the next decade, this doubled. These were a major part of the teenage population, albeit still well below the 60 per cent of Swedish young people completing vocational upper-secondary programmes, or the 40 per cent of French young people obtaining vocational diplomas in the 1980s and 1990s. What the numbers do not and cannot show, however, is the underlying and seismic shift in the nature of 'vocational' awards, and especially those taken by young, full-time students.

For 100 years or so, a slowly expanding, non-governmental vocational-education system had, as its central clientele, apprentices and ambitious part-timers whose past, current and future jobs lay in particular industrial sectors. In 1938, part-timers in technical colleges outnumbered full-timers by 25 to 1. But, between 1938 and 1978, part-time student numbers grew only threefold, compared to a twelvefold increase for full-time students. The typical 'vocational' student of the late twentieth century was a very different creature from her pre-war or 1950s counterpart. She was also, unfortunately, outside the government's line of sight. As policy-makers geared up to expand vocational numbers, they combined rhetoric about the future with a surprisingly backward-looking vision.

Thwarted reformers: cries on deaf ears

Britain's lack of technical secondary schools is a well-established target for critics of the education system. It epitomizes, for them, the blinkered anti-growth or elitist attitudes of a ruling class presiding over economic decline.[6] Moreover, the consensus is entirely non-partisan. Andrew Neil, the passionately Thatcherite editor-in-chief for Press Holdings and former editor of the *Sunday Times*, could be found, in summer 1999, lambasting current and previous governments for their failure to raise 'the status of secondary moderns by turning them into high-quality technology and vocational schools'.[7] A year later, almost to the day, we find Nick Davies, a star writer of the left-wing *Guardian*, in similar vein. In a major series of articles on the need for school reform, he mourned the failure of the 1944 Education Act to deliver on its promise of 'parity of esteem' for different modes of education. 'Why have we accepted for so long that education is academic?' Davies asks. Other countries know better, apparently, and offer proper vocational pathways to their schoolchildren. In those vocational classes, 'disaffected . . . pupils are learning . . . Their attitude is better . . . They are enjoying school . . . And it is on an equal footing with academic learning.'[8]

The British state's neglect of technical education was not, however, for want of urging. On the contrary, calls to create, renew, reform and expand run like a thread through the past 130 years of English (and British) history. Decade after decade, one finds government commissions, reports, speeches and yet more commissions all emphasizing the need for more technical education, and the parlous fate that awaits industry and the economy in its absence. Even the unflattering comparisons remain constant: in 1868 commentators are bemoaning the UK's performance vis-à-vis Germany, and in 1988 their successors are doing exactly the same.

Take, for example, the following:

> The development of technical education is the greatest need of this country.
>
> We find that our most formidable assailants are the best educated peoples . . . For some time past, whilst we have advanced, they have advanced faster still; they have driven us from several of their domestic markets and they are sharply competing with us in the markets of other nations.
>
> [Other countries] are making an immense effort to train more scientific and technical manpower and . . . we are in danger of

being left behind ... Much depends on strengthening the base of
the pyramid of technical education.

... industry in this country has been short of skilled labour ...
There is no doubt that shortages of skilled manpower have been
an important factor in holding back the rate of economic expansion
... the rate of industrial training must be increased.

England is very much behind hand as regards the provision for the
commercial as well as the technical education of the proprietors
and principal managers of industrial works ... [Germans] are better
fitted to do the work required of the middle ranks of industry than
any that the world has ever seen.

The dates are 1924, 1884, 1945, 1962 and 1919; the writers a prime
minister (Ramsay MacDonald), an industrialist heading a government
commission (Bernhard Samuelson), a politician turned university
administrator (Eustace Percy, in the Percy Report on Higher Technological Education), an anonymous civil servant (in the 1962 White Paper
on Industrial Training), and the pre-eminent economist of his age
(Alfred Marshall). The sentiments remain the same – change the writing
style slightly and there is no way one could date them blind. There is
an equal consistency, over the better part of a century, in the plaintive
verdict on British employers. 'There is a disquieting indifference on the
part of employers' to training, complains the 1927 Balfour Committee
on Industry and Trade;[9] while in the 1930s the government's Chief
Inspector of Technical Education moans that among employers 'It is
not generally believed that technical education can play a most important part in the struggle to increase the national well being.'[10] In 1962,
the Ministry of Labour complained that 'Much [training] is barely
adequate and some definitely unsatisfactory. Many firms do not make
adequate use of facilities for technical education.'[11]

Commissions, committees and advisory councils followed thick on
each other's heels: Table 3.1 does no more than list the major government reports. And yet nothing very much really happened. Decade
after decade, industries trained – or didn't. Elementary schools were
reformed, and secondary education expanded – but no substantial
technical sector was added. Further education colleges grew rapidly but

Table 3.1 *Government reports relating to vocational and technical education*

1867–8	*Report from the Select Committee on Scientific Instruction*
1872	*Report from the Select Commission on Scientific Instruction* (Devonshire Report)
1884	*Report of the Royal Commission on Technical Instruction* (Samuelson Commission)
1895	*Report of the Royal Commission on Secondary Education*
1906	*Report of the Consultative Committee on Higher Elementary Education*
1915–16	*Report of Committee of Privy Council for Scientific and Industrial Research*
1918	*Final Report of the Departmental Committee on Juvenile Education in Relation to Employment after the War*
1919	*Labour Conditions and Adult Education*, Ministry of Reconstruction
1926	*Report of the Consultative Committee of the Board of Education on the Education of the Adolescent* (Hadow Report)
1927	*Report of the Committee on Industry and Trade* (Balfour Report)
1928	*Report of the Committee on Education and Industry* (Malcolm Report)
1937	*Co-operation in Technical Education*
1938	*Report of the Consultative Committee of the Board of Education on Secondary Education with Special Reference to Grammar Schools and Technical High Schools* (Spens Report)
1945	*Recruitment and Training of Juveniles for Industry*, Joint Consultative Committee of the National Joint Advisory Council (NJAC) to the Ministry of Labour
1945	*Report of a Special Committee on Higher Technological Education* (Percy Report)
1946	*Report of Committee on Scientific Manpower* (Barlow Committee Report)
1949	*Report of Special Committee on Education for Commerce* (Carr-Saunders Report)
1950	*The Future Development of Higher Technological Education*, National Advisory Council on Education for Industry and Commerce
1951	*Higher Technological Education*
1955	*Report on the Recruitment of Scientists and Engineers in the Engineering Industry*
1956	*Technical Education*, Ministry of Education White Paper
1958	*Training for Skill* (Carr Report): NJAC Subcommittee, reporting to the Ministry of Labour and National Service
1969	National Advisory Council on Education for Industry and Commerce: Haslegrave Report (*Report of the Committee on Technician Courses and Examinations*)

piecemeal, adding on a City & Guilds course here, two or three A levels there, adult-literacy courses in their satellite annexes. Apprenticeships were negotiated between management and unions, without government concern. Then, suddenly, in the 1980s all this changed. Vocational education was no longer simply the rallying cry of reformers in the wilderness: it was a central plank of activist government policies, backed by Prime Minister and Cabinet, by civil servants, by legislation, by an ever changing clutch of quangos – and by a very great deal of cash.

Too much too late? Economic decline and the 'intermediate certificate' solution

The vocational-educational crusade of the 1980s and 1990s began inauspiciously enough. In the early 1970s a series of government interventions in industry training policy included the creation of a new quango, the Manpower Services Commission (MSC). The MSC, at its height, employed 22,000 officials, 12,000 of them working directly on vocational education and training. But it was not an obvious maker of revolutions. On the contrary, it started off as a corporatist body, with Commission members representing employers, unions, local authorities and educational organizations. And in its early years its activities were largely reactive. The 1970s were a period of recession, spiralling inflation, and labour unrest. The late 1970s and early 1980s saw unemployment rates rising to their highest levels since the 1930s Depression. The MSC's job was to 'do something': in practice, to set up temporary make-work schemes, subsidize temporary jobs for adults, and run short emergency courses teaching painting and decorating, typing and the like. 'Youth Opportunity Programmes' and 'Training Opportunities Schemes' (YOPS and TOPS) reduced the unemployment rolls, but even the most enthusiastic spin doctor could hardly portray them as heralding a breakthrough in technical education or industrial skills levels.

Then, in 1981, the MSC issued a consultative paper, *A New Training Initiative*, endorsed by the new Conservative government and leading to legislation later that year. Much of its content was familiar stuff. 'Training is not given enough priority in Britain,' the NTI authors proclaim. 'We must exploit new growing markets . . . [where] there are more and stronger competitors now than there used to be . . . Firms need to change or upgrade . . . skills . . . [But] our methods and attitudes contrast markedly with those of . . . our major foreign competitors such as West Germany and France.'[12]

The specific objectives also seem innocuous and familiar enough: to open up opportunities for adults to update skills, to have all young people involved in some education or training up to the age of eighteen, and to open up and develop apprenticeship and skill training on the basis of 'agreed standards of skill'. References to these skill standards reoccur from time to time in the NTI document, along with references to the need for a 'new approach to identifying . . . achievements of anyone at any age' and for employers and unions to focus on what 'standards' of performance should embody.[13] Few people noticed these sentences, or saw them as in the least bit controversial. Fewer still could have guessed at the huge 'standards programme' that would ensue.

With unemployment still rising (to over 3 million registered unemployed in 1981, and topping 20 per cent for young males),[14] 'doing something' about youth unemployment remained a critical part of the MSC's function. But it was now determined to create a high-status vocational route for young people, emphasizing practical skills and 'work-based learning'. The architects of the Youth Training Scheme, formally launched in 1983, believed that they were transforming the nature of post-compulsory education and training for British young people. 'YTS is going to be a permanent feature of our training system,' ministers and officials insisted at every opportunity, and would mark a 'permanent change in the way we regard young people'.[15]

YTS started as a one-year programme and was quickly expanded to two years, designed to give sixteen- and seventeen-year-olds vocational training plus instruction in 'transferable skills' (sic), and to provide them with formal qualifications. YTS places were ideally with employers, with periods 'off the job' to receive formal instruction, though many were in fact in specially established organizations run by 'training providers'. The whole approach was avowedly inspired by German apprenticeships, but it was equally clearly not built around traditional British apprenticeships.[16] Apprenticeship numbers at this point were in rapid decline, but there was no enthusiasm for reviving the institution. Conservative ministers and left-leaning officials alike saw apprenticeships as a source of restrictive practices, artificially inflated wages, and/or barriers to entry and equal opportunity. YTS trainees were not to waste years in time-serving, with their training dragged out irrespective of what they had learned, thereby reducing the numbers qualifying and increasing the wages of those in the trade. Instead they would be trained from the start to achieve clear skill standards, or, as they were increasingly known, 'standards of competence'. Norman Tebbitt, the Employment Secretary, launching YTS with a £2 million advertising campaign, called it the 'most far reaching and ambitious proposal ever put before Parliament'. In their 1985 report, the MSC hierarchy expressed the aim of attracting no less than two-thirds of sixteen- and seventeen-year-olds on to their Youth Training Schemes.[17]

A new era required new qualifications: if YTS was to be more than a 'stop gap programme', it needed certificates with value.[18] The Review of Vocational Qualifications, set up in 1985 by the MSC and the Department of Education and Science, delivered conclusions that were largely established before it ever met. The current system of vocational qualifications was a 'jungle', and a new, clearer, structure was needed. Standards for vocational qualifications should be set by industry (roughly the German pattern, but with the role of unions downgraded), and the notion of 'competence' was to be the defining characteristic of vocational qualifications. Finally, the Review recommended yet another brand-new quango, the National Council for Vocational Qualifications (NCVQ), which would promote and revolutionize vocational qualifications in Britain. In 1986 NCVQ was duly born. Its deputy director, and the chief architect of its approach, was Gilbert Jessup, fresh from the MSC. He was convinced that this new approach could and would 'force a fundamental review of the objectives of education and training'.[19] The current system was one of 'discontinuities and overlaps [and] unnecessary entry restrictions', which 'discourage people from continuing with education and training'.[20] The new one, with its specification of standards, would provide 'the key to unlocking the . . . system', and creating a 'more highly skilled and more flexible workforce'.[21]

The Manpower Services Commission was a favoured child of government for a number of reasons. The catalyst for change was partly the record level of youth unemployment; but there had been plenty of economic downturns (and full-blown recessions) before. More important was the government's, and especially Mrs Thatcher's, determination to change British attitudes, which she saw as dismally antagonistic to business and to economic success. Individuals were also important, especially David – later Lord – Young, chairman of the MSC, later Secretary of State for Employment, and a huge favourite of Mrs Thatcher because he 'understood how to make things happen'.[22] Young shared with Sir Geoffrey Holland, MSC director and later the permanent secretary of the Department of Employment, an enthusiasm for training that was joined to an equally strong belief that government programmes could change the world.

Most important of all, however, were a group of intellectuals who never held government office. Their championing of vocational education and training echoed that of previous generations – but they were both tenacious and convincing, they spoke to an elite obsessed with the UK economy, and they found that this time the world (including the Minister for Employment) was listening. They castigated previous generations for their 'pseudo-aristocratic' frivolities in promoting education removed from any 'purposes related to life and work in the modern world', and for denying 'parity of provision and status' to technical schools.[23] They provided an explanation of decline at a time when the UK economy seemed doomed to fall further and further behind the rest of Europe for ever. Better still, they offered a solution. British productivity was dismal because the UK lacked a qualified and well-trained workforce. Increase training and qualification levels – and especially the numbers obtaining 'intermediate' vocational qualifications for skilled workers – and you would usher in a new dawn.

The analysis is encapsulated in *Competence and Competition*, a research report commissioned and published jointly in 1984 by the MSC and the National Economic Development Office, a corporatist body representing the 'social partners' of government, unions and employers, which was created well before the Thatcher era (and later abolished) but had real influence on policy-making. *Competence and*

Competition compared England's education-and-training system with those of Germany, Japan and the USA. All these, the authors concluded, were superior to the UK's, and in each case 'underpin their [nation's] economic competitiveness, and . . . support their effective response to changing markets and a rapidly changing economic environment'.[24]

An array of tables documented the failure of UK training, while the text emphasized the need for industrial and vocational routes to be developed 'in a way which will enable us to compete effectively with Germany, the US and Japan'. 'Effective performance at work . . . is not a traditional aim of Education and Training in the UK,' the report charged, and we therefore risked falling 'further behind in producing the key competences needed today'. It was time 'for individuals to . . . become more conscious of the types of competence in demand in internal and external labour markets'. *Competence and Competition* was especially concerned with what came to be known as 'intermediate' skills. New, work-related training routes were needed for young people, it recommended, so as to 'avoid future severe skill shortages amongst competent craft and "middle level" people', and employers 'should take the lead in proposing training outcomes and standards'.[25]

The authors of *Competence and Competition* were close to MSC policy-makers, and within the civil service the report was very important. However, in creating a consensus over vocational education and training, it was not the most influential. That accolade belongs to a series of small green-covered booklets and of articles in a staid academic journal, both emanating from the National Institute of Economic and Social Research (NIESR). They reported on studies of productivity in different industries, comparing the UK most often with Germany but also with the Netherlands and France. Highly detailed, and based around case studies of firms, their message was consistent and relentless: UK productivity was invariably lower, and the major culprit was the low quality of its workforce.

For example, in German hotels 'three-quarters of all housekeepers . . . had attained craft-level qualifications, following a standard three-year apprenticeship; in the British sample not a single housekeeper had attended any external courses in hotel work'.[26] In engineering companies, better training and higher skills led to the 'greater general ability of Continental firms to meet customers' specialized needs';[27] in woodworking, the result was higher quality in German fitted kitchens; in clothing, far lower numbers of supervisors. 'The more complex the work, the greater was the gap observed between Britain and the Continent in the proportions of the workforce with vocational qualifications,' concluded Sig Prais, leader of the research team, looking back over fifteen years' work.[28]

The NIESR studies were read across Whitehall, used by the CBI in its submissions to government, cited in House of Lords debates on education and training, and hugely influential among other academics.[29] Their authors had the ear of ministers, and their analysis became the conventional wisdom of the time. The NIESR gave a particular emphasis to Germany, and this reinforced a long-standing British obsession. *Competence and Competition* had looked at the USA and Japan as well, neither of which makes much use of formal vocational qualifications, but its concrete recommendations for future action all signalled an infatuation with German approaches. As we saw earlier, British policy-makers are preoccupied with German competition, German education and German training. This has been the case ever since the 1867 Paris International Exhibition, where British manufacturers won almost none of the prizes they had confidently expected. The basis for attraction is clear: Germany's top manufacturing companies not only are highly impressive, but also can be easily visited and admired (much more so than the financial-services or music businesses that top UK success lists). Germany's apprenticeship system not only wipes out youth unemployment but also occupies a hugely respected niche in the German national psyche. In addition, German education and training appeal to civil servants, rationalistic policy wonks and centralizing politicians because they are – or appear to the outsider – so tidy, controlled and encompassing.

The fixation on German training was nonetheless a great pity. Borrowing policies from other countries is always problematic. Trying to do so with a country whose industrial structure, main industries, political organization, school system and employer–union relations are all so hugely different from one's own pretty much guarantees disappointment. However, the German model it was. The UK set out to create a massive new work-based training route for young people. It also followed the academics in their preoccupation with numbers of certificates. However, while the researchers saw qualification numbers as simply a means of highlighting an absence of training, government policy upended this. The goal became to heap up intermediate vocational qualifications as a direct route to an industrial renaissance.

NVQs: aspiration and reality

In 1987 the Manpower Services Commission was spending well over £2 billion a year, including large amounts of money for school- and college-based programmes allocated to it by a government mistrustful of its own education ministry. Some 420,000 young people, and a quarter of sixteen-year-olds, were enrolling on YTS.[30] And NCVQ had just been established, with its own London headquarters,[31] ready to create a complete national system for vocational qualifications. Ten years later, MSC, YTS and NCVQ were gone and all but forgotten. What happened, and why?

NCVQ was born on a wave of optimism. Its remit was not merely to tidy up the 'jungle' into a clear, neat system organized by level and content, but to improve quality as well. The purveyors of existing qualifications would not be forced to meet the criteria needed for these to earn the badge of a 'National Vocational Qualification', but it was assumed that this would be a highly sought-after prize, and that qualifications would duly be brought into line. Those that failed to change or make the grade would be spurned in favour of fully fledged NVQs.

The existence of new, superior, awards was expected, in turn, to transform the choices of young people, and also to turn shop floors into centres of learning, creating a virtuous circle of training and productivity. NVQs were to be different from any previous award, because they would be competence-based – in the MSC's words, award-holders would have demonstrated the 'ability to perform activities in the jobs within an occupation, to the standards expected in employment'.[32] So any award-holder would offer a future employer the *guarantee* that he or she could perform at the level of a highly competent worker in the relevant field, whether a barman, a plumber, a manager or an accountant. Moreover, NVQs could be acquired without having to follow a boring, classroom-based course, or take irrelevant paper-based examinations: if you possessed the relevant competences (*sic*), you could present yourself for assessment directly, and gain the relevant credit.

Government officials confidently predicted that NVQs would be taken up quickly by employers and employees. Individuals would acquire them because of their high value in the marketplace. Employers would appreciate their value as the embodiment of standards and quality, hire those possessing them, and use them to develop highly efficient training programmes with an immediate pay-off. In Whitehall they expected A levels to remain as a choice for the academic young, but that other options, such as full-time college-based BTEC awards (and notably the National Diplomas), would simply wither away as young people plumped for NVQs acquired in the workplace. Further education colleges, one manager of a training scheme assured me in 1986, would pretty much vanish in the next few years.

The passionate reformers at the head of NCVQ saw NVQs as the vanguard of a whole new approach to education and training. I described earlier how the MSC's New Training Initiative had introduced the idea of skill standards, and these soon took shape as 'occupational standards', defined by the industrial sector concerned, as the touchstone for high-quality vocational training. Standards, in turn, became the focal point of NVQ development. To become an NVQ, a vocational award had to reflect industry-set standards absolutely and precisely. The standards, in turn, had to be expressed entirely in a particular form: as 'outcomes'. To gain an NVQ, you had to demonstrate every single outcome fully and comprehensively; and the award could not be tied to any formal training or course of study.

As the reforms gathered pace, the MSC (transformed in 1988 into first the Training Commission and then the Training Agency) turned its attention to accelerating 'standards development'. The imperative for ambitious civil servants and officials became the establishing of as many 'lead bodies', representing different industries, as possible. These, in turn, were encouraged to write the standards on which NVQs could be based. By 1996 there were 180 lead bodies, each provided with government funding in order to develop detailed 'standards of competence' defining the skills needed to perform different jobs.

At the height of activity, in the early 1990s, large numbers of civil servants were devoting their time to establishing lead bodies, chivvying them to develop standards, publicizing and marketing NVQs, and encouraging their use by industry. 'Standards' acquired a mystique and vocabulary all their own. A plethora of rules developed which had to be followed if standards were to pass muster with NCVQ as the basis for a new NVQ. Above all, it was decreed that every single part of an NVQ must be not only directly related to current workplace practice in the particular job concerned, but also assessed as far as possible by observing performance of real, practical activities. That was what would make NVQs attractive to employers, and ensure their contribution to the productivity of 'UK plc'.

The rhetoric proclaimed that industries themselves were to specify their requirements and concerns. In practice that was hardly the case. Large companies were, inevitably, hugely over-represented in the lead bodies, but even they were unwilling and unable actually to write the standards. Only a very small band of MSC-approved consultants were able to produce the relevant vocabulary, layout, analysis of underlying 'functions', and myriad detailed pages needed to get the standards approved by the overseeing bureaucracies. Figure 3.2 provides an example of the standards that actually resulted from this process and which ran, for even quite low-level awards, to literally hundreds of pages.

NCVQ's theory was that standards could be so clear and all-inclusive that anyone, in any factory, office or playgroup, would be able to use them to assess and measure performance accurately.[33] As reality stubbornly failed to fall in with NCVQ's vision of perfect clarity, the level of detail required by the Council and the complexity of standards layout increased. It became more and more desirable for industries to acquire, along with their brand new lead body, the services of an experienced all-purpose standards writer from the government's approved list. In any case, it was all being paid for by the government . . .

Accrediting qualifications as NVQs involved slow passage through

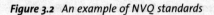

Figure 3.2 *An example of NVQ standards*

Performance criteria from an element of competence for a worker with young children (for example as a playgroup assistant)

'Identify the language and communication abilities of an individual child'

1. Observations of the child's interaction with other children and adults provide objective information about his/her spontaneous speech and communication skills

2. Activities and methods of communication are selected which encourage the child to communicate and are adapted to suit the child's interests and abilities

3. Information about the child's ability to communicate in the home setting obtained from discussion with parents is treated as confidential and used only as necessary to develop a picture of the child's language and communication skills

4. The child's hearing and understanding of stories, instructions and other communication is regularly checked by observing and interacting with the child

5. Identification of the child's language and communication abilities is based on relevant sources of information

---

Source: NVQ standards approved by NCVQ and the Department of Employment in 1992

the NCVQ bureaucracy, but by May 1995 the target for coverage was all but met: 95 per cent of occupations were covered by standards, and 794 different sorts of NVQ had been created and accredited. Well over a century before, Trollope had lampooned the academic cleric Mr Jobbles, who dreamed of a day when the whole world was divided into 'classes and sub-classes [and] . . . The greengrocer's boy should not carry out cabbages unless his fitness for cabbage-carrying had been ascertained.'[34] Mr Jobbles's day had, it seemed, finally arrived. But in the workplace itself the plot was going heavily awry.

As NCVQ's tenth birthday approached, it was clear that at least half of its brand-new NVQs were effectively unwanted and unused: 364

had never been awarded to a single candidate, while another 43 had each involved a single award to a single individual. For many others, the numbers awarded fell short of double figures.

Looking at the cumulative numbers awarded by 1996, it emerged that just 10 NVQs out of nearly 800 were accounting for 16 per cent of all certificates awarded to date, and just 42 awards for 83 per cent of the total. Moreover, most of these 'successful' NVQs were simply direct replacements and reworkings of long-established craft awards run by City & Guilds for decades (and were offered largely through the FE colleges so despised by enthusiasts for workplace-based, lecturer-free qualifications). The government never published figures for the cost of the standards programme and for NVQ development, but, using 1995 figures, I estimated development costs at from £100,000 to £300,000 for a new set of standards, and from £20,000 to £100,000 for each NVQ based upon them.[35] For high-uptake NVQs this gave development costs of a few pounds per qualification. For those with a few takers it meant that, for every NVQ awarded, £4,000–£5,000 had been spent just on developing the paperwork. And for those with no takers at all . . .

Worse, other qualifications were not disappearing: there was no sign at all that the whole vocational area was coalescing into a single unified framework. Even though NVQs were the favoured and increasingly the only qualifications offered on government-funded training schemes, in 1996 they only accounted for 25 per cent of the vocational awards made, and there was no sign that 'traditional' awards were fading away. Even in City & Guilds, which had obediently transformed most of its major craft qualifications into NVQs, 1995 registrations ran at only one NVQ for every three 'other' awards. The main effect of NVQs appeared to be some more thickets in the jungle.

Doubts about the underlying argument were nonetheless pushed aside (as were increasingly vocal criticisms of the quality of the awards themselves). The reform slid into something reminiscent of the cargo cults of Polynesia. Worshipping replicas of planes was thought, by cult adherents, to bring the showering of gifts from the sky, because the arrival of planes had heralded the arrival of gifts and largesse in the past. Similarly, it became an article of faith that awarding enough NVQs could and would somehow transform the nature of the UK economy, bringing productivity in their wake. If this was not happening, it was because of temporary difficulties in making assessment available, or because the 'awarding bodies' who actually assessed and awarded qualifications were dragging their feet, or simply because not enough had been done to publicize NVQs.

The few sceptics inside government who attempted to force any rethink of the policy got nowhere. They faced a solid phalanx made up of true believers plus senior officials who had told too many people for too long that everything was working to start admitting the opposite now. Big business in the form of the CBI sprang to NCVQ's defence. NCVQ spokesmen assured critics that NVQs were arousing great interest among other countries: when Oman (population 1.7 million) bought into the system, after heavy British selling, the event was publicized widely – a first swallow which signally failed to bring the spring, let alone the summer.

It is hard to know how much and for how long civil servants and ministers were victims of their own spin. They were certainly adept at it, a decade in advance of the Blairites. The New Training Initiative documents are full of praise for the despised Youth Opportunities Programme even as the MSC was privately condemning it and planning for the new Youth Training Scheme. In 1990, Lord Strathclyde, the government's education spokesman in the Lords, was happy to follow his civil servants' briefings, and announce that 'YTS has been a triumph',[36] at a time when enrolments on YTS were plummeting and less than half of all trainees were gaining any sort of qualification.

But did the enthusiasts really believe their own full-page advertisements in the national press? These showed a photogenic girl with a computer manual under her arm. The caption read, 'Look out Japan! Lindy's coming.' Lindy was meant to be a YT trainee gaining an NVQ. (She was actually an A-level student with a sideline as a photographic model.)[37] As Ron Dore has remarked, 'the charitable explanation of why the MSC spent those tax payers' thousands on the improbable story of Lindy' is that at least some of its staff actually believed it.[38] But teenagers didn't. They knew a low-prestige, low-return option when they saw it, and were in no mood to realize NCVQ's vision of a brave new world of competence-based vocational education and training.

Figure 3.3 *Percentage of sixteen-year-olds studying for A levels: England and Wales*

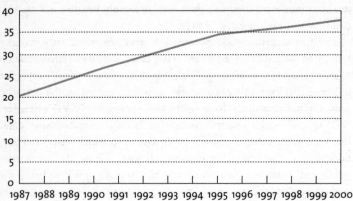

Source: DES/DfEE 1981–

From Figures 3.3 and 3.4 one might conclude that government enthusiasm for workplace learning was a kiss of death. With every year that money was lavished on industry lead bodies, NVQs and Youth Training Schemes, and with every ministerial speech proclaiming parity of esteem for vocational education, there was an increase in the proportion of young people plumping for full-time academic education instead. By 1995, 36 per cent were following A-level courses, designed originally for the 3 per cent entering the elite universities of the 1950s. Numbers following other full-time courses rose in unison. Meanwhile, numbers in Youth Training, the main route to NVQs, followed a steep decline. Young people had no questions in their minds about the relative worth of 'training' compared to school-based options. When Lorna Unwin interviewed a sample of teenagers in full- or part-time education, typical responses included, 'I doubt if I want a job with training', 'I am not going into a career that needs training', 'I am not going to the sort of employment where training is necessary.' This trio had career aspirations in teaching, nursing and physiotherapy,[39] and they spoke for their generation.

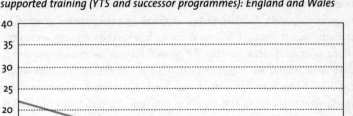

Figure 3.4 Percentage of sixteen-year-olds in work-related government-supported training (YTS and successor programmes): England and Wales

Source: DES/DfEE 1981–

Modern labour markets and the rational teenager

Why were young people so resistant to the highly specialized vocational-training qualifications which government saw as the answer to Britain's economic problems? Were they blind to the rewards which education and qualifications apparently bring in the labour market? Perhaps they were uninformed and unaware of the advent of the 'high-skills' economy, and believed there would always be an ample supply of unskilled and semi-skilled jobs for the taking. Or were they, perhaps, clearer about both their own self-interest *and* the nature of the modern labour market than were the creators of YTS and NVQs? The answer, I think, is very much the last of these, as we can see by looking more carefully at the nature of modern employment and the cumulative pressures it places on young people.

In many countries, as this chapter noted earlier, a large proportion of teenagers take a 'vocational' upper-secondary programme. In some (as Chapter 5 will discuss in more detail), apprenticeship remains important and/or large-scale. The hostility of British young people to 'training' partly reflects particular characteristics of what they were being offered. Government schemes had a hybrid origin as an emergency response to youth unemployment as much as a determined attempt at labour-force reform. 'YT' was more or less forced on many teenagers when unemployment benefits for school leavers were ended in 1987; correspondingly, its image was that of a last-resort destination for the least able, least motivated and least advantaged. A period on a government scheme of this type was not something to boast of, even if vocational qualifications themselves might have some value: indeed, at least one academic study suggested that the major effect of months on YT was to *depress* your future earnings.[40]

The peculiar characteristics of NVQs also played a role. In the hands of visionary reformers, these had become quite unlike any other vocational qualification the world had ever seen – and, in the process, hugely complex and difficult to administer. The numbers who started and then managed actually to complete an NVQ were correspondingly low. NVQs also attracted increasingly vocal and hostile criticisms for being not merely unmanageable and expensive, but also *less* reliable than the old-style qualifications their advocates despised, and for being preoccupied with trivial skills at the expense of knowledge and theory. In cases where older qualifications survived alongside new NVQs – whether certificates in vehicle servicing and repair from City & Guilds or awards in personnel practice from the Institute of Personnel & Development – it was the older, traditional, awards that pulled the punters in.

However, the behaviour of young people in the late 1980s and 1990s went far beyond antipathy to particular government programmes or qualifications. In only a few years, the UK moved from being a country in which the 'normal' pathway after compulsory schooling was to enter the labour market as fast as possible to one in which the vast majority remained in full-time education at sixteen and on into their upper teens. Youth Training numbers did not fall because the economy revived (although it did). They fell, as did the numbers of teenagers actually in the labour force, because the vast majority of young people opted for full-time education.

Figure 3.5 *Percentage of sixteen-year-olds remaining in full-time education: England and Wales*

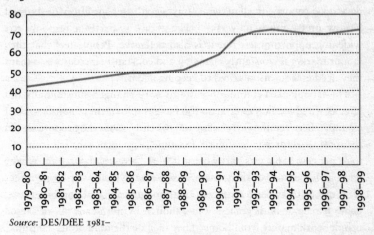

Source: DES/DfEE 1981–

Figure 3.5 shows *total* participation rates for sixteen-year-olds – not just for A levels, but for *all* types of full-time education. As government geared up for its vocational crusade, and as larger and larger numbers moved into A-level classes, so, too, increasing numbers of other sixteen-year-olds opted for other full-time courses.

The most important alternatives to A levels were BTEC National Diplomas, one-year 'prevocational' courses, and full-time GCSE resit programmes. The government's game plan was for all these to fade away. The number of different qualifications, in the government's view, confused students and employers. It meant that people didn't know what a qualification was worth, and this in turn reduced the incentive to acquire vocational skills. In the sunlit uplands of successful reform, there would be just A levels and NVQs, and the simplest and clearest of frameworks. Indeed, considerable pressure was put on BTEC to turn its awards into NVQs. Aware of its market, it resisted. Sure enough, far from fading away, enrolments by young people for non-A-level, non-NVQ, classroom-based full-time courses persisted and grew.

This rapid shift reflected the way in which young people and their families saw the labour market changing. More and more they felt it necessary to gain formal qualifications of a general academic kind. In this, they shared the views of their contemporaries in every single other developed country. In all of these, 'staying on' after age fifteen or sixteen is now pretty much universal.[41] The choice is partly a response to widening opportunities, but it is also defensive. People feel that the labour market is constantly changing and constantly insecure, and that they need an education suited to keeping afloat.

The labour market and job patterns *have* changed substantially of late, as we saw in Chapter 2. So too have employment conditions. For example, between the early 1980s and the early 1990s the proportion of the total workforce in 'standard' full-time permanent jobs fell from 70 to 62 per cent. This was partly because of the growth of part-time work and partly because of the growth of self-employment – up from 7 per cent in 1965 to 13 per cent in 1991, with roughly a quarter of this group being female at both points. Some, though by no means all, of these people work mainly from home. They include the ubiquitous 'consultant' – highly paid and/or recently redundant – but also the more traditional, large and overwhelmingly male group of skilled workers such as plumbers who work from a home base rather than *at* home.[42] There is also a general perception that employment has become significantly less secure in the industrialized countries. Whether this is actually the case is the topic of much academic debate. The average length of time for which people hold jobs has actually hardly changed since 1975, so the general perception of much greater insecurity may just mean that the professional classes have become more exposed to levels of insecurity that the rest of the world has always taken for granted.[43] What is certain is that very few people indeed can expect to do anything approaching the same job in the same company over a lifetime of employment.

The labour market also – as it always has – looks very different for men and for women. The proportion and numbers of women at work have increased hugely in the last fifty years, but, in the process, the nature of women's working life has changed. Since 1940 there has been a move from a pattern where women worked continuously until marriage (or, in the case of unmarried women, until retirement) and then stopped altogether, to one where women typically move in and out of the labour force a number of times. Women also make up a large proportion of those working part-time. Part-time work is relatively rare among men – in 1995, 8 per cent of British male workers were part-time, compared to 44 per cent of women – and male part-timers are usually students or close to retirement. For women, part-time work is common, and for many it is a positive choice. It may be politically incorrect to talk of men and women as being different, but in their working lives they *are*.[44]

A typical pattern of employment has also developed for young people. It consists – for an increasing proportion of them – of

- part-time Saturday and/or evening employment while in full-time upper-secondary school;

- a combination of work and study while in college/university;

- frequent changes of job and of occupation during one's early and mid-twenties, even after becoming entirely, or mostly, an employee rather than a student.

Student jobs are now the norm, among both secondary-school and university pupils. This is not, on the whole, because of poverty. On the contrary, teenage life follows the general rule: unto those who have it shall be given. More teenagers from well-off families are able to find jobs than those from families with unemployed parents. Affluent areas offer jobs for affluent teenagers. Clearly some students work because they have to; but most do so to supplement their incomes and as an antidote to the prolonged dependence inflicted on them by ever lengthening education. Working while in college is associated with greater success later – having a job helps you find another, looks good on your CV, develops social skills.[45]

Nor is this solely a UK pattern. Throughout the developed world, more and more young people move into the labour market gradually, via a period of extended more or less part-time study and part-time more or less casual work. In their twenties, people not only change jobs extremely often, they often change the occupational area they work in as well. The most rapid job changes are among the very young –

teenagers in part-time jobs. But job turnover remains very frequent up to the age of thirty: over half of all job changes involve workers under the age of thirty, and an individual of twenty-four is almost five times as likely to change his or her job in a year as is someone of sixty. Moreover, both the rate of job change and the difference between the young and the old in this respect have been increasing.[46]

As people move into their thirties, they tend to settle not only into a given occupation, but also into a given company or job. This does not, however, necessarily mean the cocoon of a huge company or chain – NatWest, Unilever, BT. In the early 1990s only 50 per cent of UK jobs were in firms employing more than 100 people (and many of those were part-time jobs in large shop chains.) The rest were split between small (11–99 employees) and very small companies. Looked at the other way round, only 5 to 6 per cent of the country's businesses employ more than 100 people. This leaves us with a minority of male, and a small minority of female, workers for whom either stable employment by a large company or a lifetime's occupation in the same trade is a likely pattern. Moreover, within companies, even if employment is steady, frequent restructuring and sideways movement are the rule.

The changing nature of modern economies has hardly gone unnoticed. On the contrary, accelerating technical change, the need for flexible skills, and 'portfolio careers' are the very stuff of political discourse. Indeed, the whole vocational-education revolution – the whole argument for NVQs – takes off from this very same point. Which makes it all the more remarkable that what actually emerged from a stupendous central-government effort was so ill-suited to its apparent purpose. Back in the early 1990s I conducted a study of why so few of the people who started NVQs inside companies were finishing them.[47] By far the most common reason was that they had changed what they were doing within six months of starting the award. As a result, many of the competences on which they were meant to be assessed and accredited were no longer part of their remit. The NVQ which they had started no longer matched their job, because their company, very reasonably, was in a state of constant updating and change.

The idealized vision of many education planners is of a smooth progression from 'appropriate' education and training to a well-matched permanent 'job for life'. This may have been the experience of yesterday's miners, as well as its bank managers, but it bears little resemblance to today. Young people, with their own lives and interests at stake, know this. They may not have a detailed grasp of labour-market trends, but they are aware of general ones – and so are their parents. Would you advise your own seventeen-year-old to abandon general education in favour of a highly specific vocational training which leads directly into a highly specific trade – and only into it – especially when that trade itself may disappear tomorrow? No – and nor did the civil servants and ministers who somehow persuaded themselves that everyone else should do so.

As a preparation for the labour markets of the late-twentieth and the twenty-first century, it is hard to think of anything less suitable than a suite of qualifications based narrowly on the specific large-company practices of a given year. This is not a novel observation. Fifty years ago Robert Hutchins, the chancellor of the University of Chicago, was pointing out that 'In a fluid, industrial, scientific democracy, the more specific an education is, the less likely it is to achieve the only purpose that it has – to prepare the student for a particular kind of economic activity.'[48]

Yet qualifications based on highly specific, atomized and current tasks are precisely what the huge NVQ effort set out to, and did, deliver. Faced with this offering, the rational choice of any sixteen-year-old, male or female, was to reject NVQs. Indeed, all those with good enough GCSEs opted for a more general education. A levels, diplomas and degrees were the way to keep your options open, and to present yourself as a desirable, flexible individual with general skills and abilities. And general skills were what success in the modern labour market demanded.

Getting ahead on a moving staircase

At the same time, a second – even simpler – set of forces was at play. Young people chose education rather than vocational training not just because narrow vocational awards were unsuited to the labour market, but because everyone else was doing the same. Nor was this just peer pressure: following the pack was exactly the sensible thing to do.

Increases in participation, over time, generate yet more increases. The point comes when, for the large majority of young people, it is no longer a question of whether it makes sense to stay on longer, but of whether they can possibly *not* stay on without putting themselves at a serious disadvantage. That is pretty much the situation which we reached in the UK in the early 1990s, so that, all over the country, parents were quite rightly telling their children that while they themselves might have done OK without formal qualifications, or A levels, that was not possible for a sixteen-year-old today.

As we saw in Chapter 1, the twentieth century was the century of mass education. At the start of the century, less than 20 per cent of European young people attended secondary school: in Britain secondary education became universal only in 1945. In 1900 only 0.9 per cent of the age cohort attended university, and even in 1950 only 3 per cent did so.

Today, in the UK, over 90 per cent of a cohort have GCSE awards; 50 per cent have five or more 'good' GCSE grades; 35 per cent have A levels; and 40 per cent are on track to gain degrees. Looking across to two of our European neighbours who are ahead of us on this road, in France 80 per cent have followed an academic upper-secondary programme, while in Sweden 90 per cent now complete a three-year upper-secondary programme which meets the prerequisites for university entry.

If only a tiny proportion of young people acquire advanced qualifications, then most of an employer's prospective workforce falls outside this group, and he is almost bound to recruit from the vast mass of the less qualified. But suppose you move to the situation where two-thirds of the population have advanced qualifications? The assumption that employers will and do make – in their behaviour, whatever they may say – is that the educated majority are pretty much the same as the 'top two-thirds' of the ability distribution. What's more, as we saw in Chapter 2, the 'academic' curriculum – including maths, analytic writing, and comprehension of complex prose – is not only very general in its likely relevance but suited to just that expanding category of professional and technical jobs that we want for ourselves and our children. So employers opt for the academically educated; and the educated land the good jobs.

What, in this situation, does a rational young person do? Exactly what the English teenagers of the last twenty years have done. They have torpedoed governments' attempts to generate vast numbers of vocational diplomas: such awards are of dubious value as ways to acquire skills for a changing economy, and of zero worth in positioning oneself well in the competitive struggle for employment. If teenagers don't have good enough GCSE results for A levels, they have plumped for full-time semi-vocational courses of the BTEC type, which offer general education as much as specific vocational content, and offer an alternative route into higher education. And they have availed themselves of the same governments' almost open-ended commitment of public money to the expansion of higher education.

We return in Chapters 6 and 7 to the effect of explosive growth on the universities themselves. What needs emphasizing here is just how enormous and just how spontaneous this growth has been. During precisely the period when the government machine was devoting its efforts to promoting and praising vocational education, enlisting minister after minister in its cause, the university sector was growing exponentially, without any need for spin-doctoring or expensive advertising campaigns to bring in the punters.[49] In fact the growth was so unplanned that one suspects that even the Treasury had fallen victim to the government's own rhetoric. While the university expansion of the 1960s was the result of major deliberations and national debate, that of the 1980s and 1990s began with a funding formula which offered institutions an almost open-ended financial incentive to expand their numbers. It would appear that neither the Treasury nor the Cabinet had any conception of the results. Did they believe that most of the young would be trooping off to complete their NVQs?

In step with the world

YTS and the NVQ reforms were inspired by the German apprenticeship system and by more than a century of British preoccupation with German education and its apparent contribution to economic prosperity. The UK, however, came nowhere close to creating a German-style system. A decade into the reforms, as we have seen, 'training' was a dirty word to British teenagers. Enrolments were soaring – but for general education, not vocational. YTS had become a last resort for those with minimal, or no, GCSEs, and no job either. Meanwhile, old-style apprenticeships were ignored, bypassed or even undermined.

Other European countries, meanwhile, continued to operate vocational and technical schools and programmes as a major part of upper-secondary education. It is a considerable exercise in wishful thinking to believe, as many British people apparently do, that vocational schools and apprenticeships enjoy the same prestige in Germany, or the Netherlands, as do academic ones. They don't, and they never have.[50] Nonetheless, during most of the twentieth century they were the standard route into artisan and skilled-worker jobs all over Europe. Their graduates provided much of the workforce during the post-war period of rapid European growth, when incomes per head in Germany, France, Scandinavia and the Netherlands grew so much faster than in the UK. Moreover, European countries' statistics suggest that many of their young people are continuing to show enthusiasm for vocational options: Eurostat figures, for example, show 'vocational' programmes enrolling over half the upper-secondary-level students in eleven out of fifteen EU member states.[51] Do our European partners have a different, better, view of what skills the twenty-first century requires? Does this bode well for mainland European economies, and ill for the UK's?

On the contrary. A closer look shows how deceptive these statistics are, and that the grass is equally green (or brown) on either side of the fence. In a recent study of all the EU member states, two colleagues and I established that, in every case, the content of a country's 'vocational' tracks was being substantially changed to make it more and more general and academic. This was happening without any comparable changes in the academic tracks, to bring them closer to the vocational. The changes came about because of pressure from the young (and from their parents), all of whom want to be in the high-prestige academic classes. Only the promise that they can still progress to higher education from a vocational programme keeps any equilibrium in the system.[52]

Austria, for example, appears in all the charts as having high vocational enrolments in upper-secondary programmes; it is also a country which during the twentieth century developed a huge apprenticeship system involving the majority of young people. One of its senior education officials notes that, today, 'the vocational credentials of these programmes seem to become outweighted by the simultaneously-provided entitlement to transfer to university':[53] in other words, what matters to young Austrians on these courses is not the vocational skills at all, but that the courses offer an alternative route on and up. Who can blame these young people?

Earlier in this chapter, I mentioned the Netherlands and its vocational schools. These were the traditional training ground for skilled craftsmen and artisans, many of whom went on to become highly successful small businessmen. These schools have been an inspiration for advocates of more vocational education and training – including, as we saw earlier, journalists such as the *Guardian*'s Nick Davies, but also the NIESR researchers who were so influential in British policy-making. Yet, pre-occupied with the UK's problems, these commentators missed what was happening in the society around these schools. In the 1980s, as Professor Jaap Dronkers of Amsterdam shows, junior vocational schooling 'became a rubbish-bin' for children who had consistently failed academically, and especially for the children of the immigrants (largely from old Dutch colonies) who form the new Dutch lower class.[54] In France, parents fight for their children to be allowed to repeat years at school rather than leave the track which leads to an academic rather than a vocational *baccalauréat*. Even in Germany, where the apprenticeship programme plays a central role in selecting and training skilled workers and lower management, the same pattern is apparent. The proportion of the cohort entering apprenticeship is falling, while that entering higher education rises; and in many sectors German employers are having to build in opportunities for apprentices to continue into higher education – otherwise they cannot attract the quality of recruits to which historically they are accustomed.[55]

An A level by any other name?

The last act in the short history of NCVQ also encapsulates the forces that really drive vocational education. Earlier in this chapter I described the wishful expectation that NVQs would become the major, and increasingly desirable, alternative to A levels – and the stubborn refusal of the country's young to behave accordingly. By the early 1990s it was obvious, at least to the senior officials in the departments of Employment and Education, that full-time educational alternatives to A level were not simply going to fade away, and that a major attraction of these, and especially of BTEC Nationals, was that they offered an alternative, and by then well-trodden, pathway to advanced training (such as in nursing) and higher education.

In 1991, therefore, the poacher turned gamekeeper. Instead of trying to turn the full-time semi-educational, semi-vocational courses into 'real' NVQs, the government (still Conservative) decided to recognize a third pathway between A levels and NVQs. However, it was still determined to create a tight national system of qualifications, and also to promote the intermediate vocational skills that industry 'needed'. There would, it announced, be a completely new set of 'General' NVQs, which, unlike the BTEC diplomas, could be awarded in schools as well as in colleges. These would not be a BTEC monopoly, but would be awarded by all three major vocational awarding bodies (BTEC, City & Guilds, and RSA), following a centralized curriculum and rules developed by NCVQ.

GNVQs were designed to look as much like NVQs as possible in their curriculum and assessment approach. The new awards were, it was officially announced, to 'offer a broad preparation for employment' and be 'clearly related to the occupationally specific NVQs'. They were also, finally, to nail that elusive beast 'parity of esteem'. GNVQs were, the government stated, to 'be of equal standing with academic qualifications at the same level'.[56] The titles included 'Business', 'Health and Social Care', 'Leisure and Tourism' and 'Manufacturing'. This last was never taken by more than a handful of students, and owed its existence entirely to central government's conviction that vocational education must have some connection to traditional notions of industry, with its heavy shop-floor machines.

Within a year of their general release into schools and colleges, it was clear that GNVQs had found a clear niche – and that it had precious little to do with either vocational preparation or parity of esteem. What GNVQs provided was a full-time alternative for young people whose

GCSE grades were not good enough for entry on to an A-level programme. The Advanced GNVQ attracted those whose grades fell just
short of the usual A-level threshold of five A–C grades in subjects
including maths and English. So, whereas the average number of GCSE
points for A-level students was around 45 in the early to mid 1990s, for
Advanced GNVQ students it was 35, and only about a third of these
students had a C in their maths GCSE. The one-year Intermediate
GNVQ attracted students with lower grades still: typically 25 GCSE
points, which placed almost all of them below the national mean, and
largely in the thirtieth to fortieth percentiles of the student population.[57]

The GNVQ structure offered a clear set of sixth-form alternatives
for the less academically successful. What it didn't do was steal many
students from A levels. On the contrary, GNVQs basically just dis-
placed students from the National Diploma route, in particular by
allowing schools to retain students who would otherwise have trans-
ferred to FE colleges.[58] In the latter, National Diplomas nonetheless
lived, and live, healthily on.

The qualifications hierarchy formed itself immediately, and with
complete clarity as far as those on the ground were concerned: a
GCSE-based ranking that went A levels, Advanced GNVQ, Intermediate GNVQ – and, below that, off to Youth Training. At central level,
denial set in. To report on this hierarchy was, for some listeners,
apparently to have created the situation out of malice. But when I
conducted a major evaluation of the new qualification, from 1993 to
1997,[59] I found GNVQ teachers to be, on the whole, both hugely
committed to the course and also quite realistic about its recruitment.
'You have to remember these are GNVQ students,' they would say,
discussing their teaching approaches; or 'Well, they wouldn't be on
GNVQ if they had those grades.'

GNVQs were also, from the start, clearly and predominantly educational in their focus, rather than vocational. The students themselves
were very clear about this. Far and away the most important thing they
hoped for from their courses was progress into higher education. The
large majority of Advanced GNVQ students saw themselves completing
a two-year full-time course, then moving on to degrees, or nursing, or
other higher-education courses. Intermediate students, with very poor

GCSE grades behind them, expected a longer slog – first Intermediate GNVQ, then progression on to Advanced, and then on to higher education.

Nor were their aspirations stupid ones. Those who finish their Advanced courses have gained places on degree and higher-diploma courses, though high failure and dropout rates make them a minority of those who start out on this road. And no less than half the students on Advanced courses were graduates of Intermediate GNVQs who had made it back on to the post-GCSE academic ladder. What students didn't do, and were not going to start doing, was treat their GNVQs as a way of preparing for a specific career. (In the study I conducted, only a tiny minority went from a GNVQ to a job in any way directly related to it.) They would have been foolish, in fact, to regard GNVQs as a sensible way to do this. GNVQs were taught in classrooms by teachers: if you *are* wedded to a highly specific career, it is far better to go for that NVQ.

GNVQs had the potential for success – though not for reasons that had anything to do with vocational training, or industrial skill shortages. Unfortunately, they were also burdened with an extremely complex 'competence-based' assessment and grading scheme, designed by NCVQ. Teachers with GNVQ classes averaging from eight to fifteen pupils found themselves spending thirteen hours a week simply meeting assessment requirements.[60] GNVQs experienced high dropout rates and consistent criticism from staff, college administrators, inspectors and researchers. At their launch, ministers had confidently predicted that 25 per cent of young people would be taking GNVQs by 1996. The 20 per cent who started one (and the 10 per cent of the cohort who actually completed and passed their GNVQ) were not enough to save NCVQ, which in 1997 vanished into a super-quango, the Qualifications and Curriculum Authority, dominated by the once-despised school establishment.

As the new century began, YTS – that 'permanent feature of our training system' – vanished altogether, replaced by an attempt to resuscitate and rebrand apprenticeships. Vanished, too, are GNVQs. After two total redesigns, a multi-million-pound in-service programme for teachers, three new experimental curriculum and assessment regimes, and a near-mutiny by the examining authorities, a Labour minister delivered the *coup de grâce*. Mr Blunkett clearly agreed with the general public about which qualifications it really made sense to obtain: namely those with an established, high-status, academic name. Advanced GNVQs were relabelled 'vocational A levels' and Intermediate GNVQs were also smothered, to be reborn as 'vocational GCSEs'.

The new GCSEs were launched by Blunkett in a major speech delivered in January 2001 (and published in pamphlet form). They are, of course, to be of 'the highest standards', 'a positive choice' for young people, 'an important modernisation of comprehensive secondary education'. As for their predecessors, they are simply airbrushed from history. Not once in the whole 11,000-word speech did the term 'GNVQ' even appear.[61]

Conclusion

Governments' activist policies in the 1980s and 1990s were in large part about extending central-government power. Vocational qualifications had, until then, been effectively unnationalized and unregulated, the product of examining bodies' and occupational groups' perceptions of market demand. The reformers of the Department of Employment, the MSC and NCVQ believed that they could do better, and increase demand, quality *and* economic relevance by developing tight, clear, national frameworks. They also thought that, in the process, they could definitively alter teenagers', parents' and employers' views of the relative value and desirability of different sorts of education.

In all of this they failed. Their rationalized, bureaucratized, centrally planned qualification structure proved less successful than the messy and complex one they had inherited – to which employers and students remained stubbornly attached. Nor could they buck the worldwide trends in both the labour market and the education world which make vocational courses a low-status and undesirable choice. As millions of teenagers demonstrated, education in late-twentieth-century Britain mattered to them – but not in the way that governments and intellectuals wanted.

Do these vocational-education failures matter? And has the government learned anything from the experience? The answer to the former is 'Yes, but not for the reasons you might think.' To the latter, unfortunately, it is 'Not obviously.'

The ultimate rationale for all that happened was economic growth. Vocational education was, supposedly, failing to deliver enough qualifications of the right sort to ensure efficiency, productivity, and success vis-à-vis our competitors. In the 1980s, when the reforms were launched, Britain was slowly emerging from a period of economic crisis and high unemployment. It was easy, and plausible, to compare our situation with Germany's and conclude that every difference between the two countries must be important *and* growth-related. Since then, however, and with exactly the same apparently under-trained and non-vocationally educated workplace as before, the British economy has been transformed. It does not have the *same* successful industries as Germany (and why should it?); but it has car and chemical plants with world-class productivity levels, as well as large successful service industries, and some of the highest growth and lowest unemployment rates in Europe. In this context it becomes rather hard to argue that reforming our messy, unsuccessful vocational education system is an economic priority.

There is, however, an important caveat. For many jobs (and most office ones) the best vocational education is an academic one; but this is not universally true. The old crafts, in particular, have not vanished from the occupational scene. Plumbers, hairdressers, electricians, thatchers, upholsterers and bricklayers remain as important as ever. Moreover, while openings for skilled manual workers in industry have fallen dramatically, this is not the same as vanishing. An occupational grouping which has been shrinking by 10 per cent a decade may not be the one you advise your children to aim for; but from the point of view of key sectors (toolmaking and engineering, energy supply, steel) there are still well over a million jobs to be filled, and close to 50,000 new recruits needed every year.[62]

In all these areas, apprenticeships had developed as the natural training route. Moreover, as Chapter 5 discusses further, they survived the 1980s and early 1990s out of industrial necessity, while the government at worst undermined and at best ignored them, building and dismantling different ambitious national schemes meanwhile. However, engineering companies now find it increasingly difficult to attract high-calibre apprentices – young people with the academic grounding that a skilled trade demands. Recruitment to construction, meanwhile, has been in crisis for decades, with constant, well-attested shortfalls to which anyone in search of a plumber can readily attest.

The incentives that young people now face can only make things worse. Teenagers are entirely rational in their quest for academic qualifications: as we saw in Chapter 2, these seem to pay much better on average than vocational ones, as well as currently opening up far more alternatives in a mobile, changing economy. Ninety per cent of those with 'good' GCSEs[63] now stay in full-time education at seventeen; yet these include exactly the people who used to enter engineering or electrical apprenticeships. Successive governments have reached for universal revolutions, for comprehensive 'qualification frameworks', and for regulatory arrangements that encompass all occupations in exactly the same way. In doing so, they have not only, and quite inevitably, failed to generate a vocational-education fuelled economic take-off. They have also failed to register the particular problems of particular sectors, and the way that general educational pressures are actually *harming* their growth.

The January 2001 speech in which David Blunkett launched his plans for vocational GCSEs marked, definitively, the end of the love affair with 'VQs' and the old MSC reforms. It seems a good place to discover what central government has learned from the last twenty years. What one actually finds is very much analysis-as-before.

'In the past,' the Secretary of State informs us, 'we have failed in this country to develop high standards and esteem for vocational and technical education . . . The divide between education and employment was pervasive and debilitating.' Fortunately, however, his government is poised

> to bridge the historic divide between academic and vocational education, and to match learning to employment needs at national, regional, sectoral and local level . . . Our primary purpose is radically

> to improve the education and training available to our young
> people and adults – and, particularly, to secure an excellent system
> of vocational and technical education fit for the new century. This
> is vital if we are to meet critical skills shortages that employers
> currently face ... I want to build ... a new vocational ladder for
> many more young people. In the future, vocational and technical
> education will be a positive choice, not a second-class fallback, with
> as much status and esteem as academic education.[64]

The rationale, as always, is economic – our labour market may be
fine, but 'the enhancement of productivity growth in the UK is a
challenge we must meet'. The comparison group is also the usual one:
British mistakes 'were not made in countries like Germany'. But in
future our awards will be 'as good as the best in Continental Europe,
against which they will be benchmarked'. And the government's role is
still seen as critical. It is to 'invest on the supply side of the economy',
in order to 'promote demand and growth' and equip people with
the 'skills and the creative, inquiring minds that will drive ... [the]
Knowledge Economy'.[65]

And how is this to be achieved? Essentially through those vocational
GCSEs which, moreover, are *avowedly* aimed at low-achieving young
people. Parity of esteem for vocational education is to be promoted by
encouraging those young people who are failing academically to drop
most of their ordinary GCSEs in favour of vocational courses from the
age of fourteen onwards. This group is then expected to progress on to
the higher-level apprenticeships or vocational A levels.

'Plumbing to be taught in schools,' proclaimed *The Times* approvingly.[66] 'Engineering' is to be a GCSE, says the Secretary of State. But
to be a good plumber is intellectually demanding, and the skills required
to be a good craft (let alone a graduate or postgraduate chartered)
engineer are not something you pick up in a school workshop in a few
hours a week. It is extraordinary to believe that targeting vocational
education on the lowest-achieving fourteen-year-olds will solve our
specific, but real, skill shortages, let alone transform the relative attrac-
tions of vocational and academic awards. Do our policy-makers really
believe that anyone (even other people's children) will be more attracted

to vocational courses as a result? Do they truly expect that these new GCSEs will spawn a productivity revolution? If so, I would be willing to bet a large sum that they are wrong. Fine-tuning or kick-starting the economy via state-run vocational education is a misconceived endeavour, and it is time that governments recognized their inability to do anything of the sort.

4 Does business know best?

> **Our training system must be founded on standards ...
> identified by employers.**
> Conservative White Paper, 1988
>
> **[We will] encourage better links between education and
> business.**
> Labour White Paper, 2001[1]

Governments, as we have seen, have had huge aspirations towards
remoulding education in the service of the economy and of industrial
skill needs. Between aspiration and actuality, however, the gap is huge.
Government bureaucracies are totally ill-suited to this sort of activity.
But could business itself do any better? The 1980s and 1990s were a
good time to find out, for they were a period when business – and
especially big business – exerted unprecedented influence not just on
workplace training policies but on education as a whole. Especially in
England and Wales, business opinions and advice were taken very
much at face value by policy-makers and fed directly into major policy
decisions. In this policy climate it was assumed that education mattered
a great deal to business. Who better, then, to advise on it than business
itself?

In fact, as this chapter shows, there is very little to suggest that
business knows best about what the education system should provide:

certainly not if, by 'business', we mean its official representatives. Individual employers may well know a lot about their immediate hiring priorities, and the qualities that make individual employees succeed or fail. Business bureaucracies, on the other hand, proved no better than central-government ones at getting detailed education policy right. In its entanglement with NVQs, its creation of national targets, and its commitment to 'core' skills, 'business' helped to create and maintain a new set of centrally managed policies with effects that ranged from neutral to expensively harmful. It also, as this chapter describes, promoted its own interests in some very effective ways.

Welcoming business in

The fact that business influence over British education reached its highest point to date in the 1980s and 1990s is, at first sight, something of a paradox. British governments' enthusiasm for education as an engine of growth has been particularly strong because of their equally marked dissatisfaction, not to say panic, over the UK's economic performance. But who were the most visible players in that same economic scene? Obviously, the big companies – and particularly the manufacturers: the engineering sector, the car manufacturers, the chemical and pharmaceutical companies, the steelworks, the producers of china, textiles, electronics. It is in considerable part because these companies' own performance was less than stellar during the period from 1950 to 1980 that politicians found themselves so occupied with Britain's economic growth. To take an example, in 1960 there were still five major British-owned car manufacturers. Now there are none;[2] while between 1960 and 1995 the UK's share in world machinery exports more than halved.

Business might therefore seem to be the problem, not part of the solution. Nonetheless, under the Tory governments of the 1980s and 1990s, business opinions consistently carried more weight than those of the educational establishment. And Labour is not obviously any different. One of its first acts was to set up a National Skills Task Force, to look at skills gaps and their implications for productivity. Its 'wide-ranging remit', which the Secretary of State emphasized as a sign of government's seriousness about 'long-standing problems of skill deficiency', encompassed recommendations for the whole of post-sixteen education. Just three of its members were from mainstream education, compared to ten from the private business sector.

The road to Whitehall: industrial training policy

To understand how business representatives have used their influence, we again need a little history. Britain has never been a very corporatist country – at least not by European standards. Membership of the EU has introduced the term 'social partners' into academic and policy talk, but it is not one which trips readily off anyone else's tongue. Trade unions and employer organizations do not find it natural to sit comfortably alongside each other, determining joint policy – not even in the New Labour new millennium. Our politics also tend to be confrontational rather than consensual: governments are just as inclined to see both unions and employers as vested interests as they are to seek partnerships.

Nonetheless, post-war governments did establish a number of 'social partnership' organizations in the area of economic policy-making – especially concerning policies relating to industrial training and skill development. In the economic area, the largest number of the great and the good were attached to NEDO, the National Economic Development Office. In the 1980s, as we saw in the last chapter, NEDO's joint publications with the Manpower Services Commission, notably *Competence and Competition*, were important in helping to establish a national consensus on the importance of vocational training. Much older was the National Advisory Council for Education in Industry and Commerce (NACEIC), set up after one of our periodic panics about technical education and international competition (in this case the one that produced the 1945 Percy Report). The Council was an early attempt to bring systematic business advice into the planning of mainstream education, and was set up to 'advise the Minister of Education on national policy for the full development of education in relation to industry and commerce'. But there was no serious appetite in Britain either for manpower planning or, at that period, for central control of education. Consequently, NACEIC creaked along for twenty years largely ignored.

The twenty-year wave of panic over Britain's industrial performance which began in the early 1960s was easy enough to justify. Table 4.1 gives some comparative and summary statistics relating to economic growth; by the mid 1960s the effects of differential growth rates on living standards were obvious to even a casual observer.

Policy-makers looked admiringly at countries, such as France or Japan, with corporatist institutions and national planning staffs and grew impatient with British industrial management. Interventionist policies of various kinds gained in popularity, and among these – from a Conservative government nominally committed to leaving industry alone – was the Industrial Training Act of 1964.

The act involved a major increase in direct governmental intervention, not least because it affected so many companies, and 15 million workers, all at once. It rested on the long-standing conviction (to which we return in Chapter 5)[3] that firms were spending much less on training than the national interest required, and on a belief in rational planning systems – in this case to be devised by twenty-seven industrial training boards (ITBs). Each of these encompassed a different sector and had

Table 4.1 *Comparative economic success: 1960–87*

	Annual average percentage increase in output per hour worked: manufacturing industry			Annual average percentage changes in per-capita GDP	
	1960–73	1973–79		1960–68	1960–87
Britain	4.1	1.0	Britain	2.4	2.1
France	6.6	4.4	Japan	9.3	5.5
Germany	5.7	4.2	Italy	5.0	3.1

Sources: Adapted from Owen 1999 and Meen 1988

the power to exact a financial levy from firms in this sector. This was commonly 1 per cent of payroll, but could go much higher. Indeed, in the engineering industry it rose as high as 2.5 per cent – a figure to attract the attention of even the most dozy board of directors.

The principle behind the ITB levy was that firms that trained would be compensated, and could actually get more money back as a grant than they paid out as a levy; while those who 'poached' skilled labour, without providing their fair share of training, would now have to contribute to the cost. Of course, en route from firms to ITBs and back again, a good deal of the levy was likely to trickle off to support training-board staff and activities – the more so the more activist the board and the more it set itself to change the actual nature of training, rather than just its recorded volume.

The creators of this new interventionist policy had little faith in businesses' ability to make decisions about the content and quality, let alone the desirable volume, of training. With hindsight, opinions differ on whether the ITBs achieved anything of value. At the very least, they were helpful in encouraging the growth of group training associations, with dedicated training centres catering for groups of small employers, and especially for the initial training of apprentices. (Most of these have now disappeared again.) However, they also gave firms an incentive to 'at least get the levy back', irrespective of whether the training involved was worth having in the first place.

By the late 1960s, vehement complaints from industry were being echoed by academics and politicians, especially over the volume – and cost – of the form-filling and ITB bureaucracy. Their views found a spokesman in Enoch Powell, a Conservative MP, but also an impassioned advocate of the market economy in what was then a deeply statist Tory party. The Industrial Training Act, he argued, had

> ignited a prairie fire of bureaucracy and profligate spending . . . Freed from its anchorage in profit and loss, it was predictable that training would rise like a balloon and float up into the stratosphere. So it has done, so it is doing, and so it will continue to do until the premise of the 1964 Act itself is revoked . . . [B]ack to square one? I hope so, but it is the hardest square ever to regain. Great political

and material vested interests lie, like an army in order of battle, across the path. I will say nothing of the chief training administrators, the regional officers, the training officers, the research officers, the public-relations officers, the secretaries, and all the other job-holders in this new and growing industry of raising levies, paying grants, claiming grants, analysing syllabi, producing manuals, organizing courses, making reports, reading reports, sending out forms, collecting forms. Of these I will say nothing except that if they could do something better at as good a rate they would not be doing what they are doing . . . No wonder the phrase 'the Great Training Robbery' is going the rounds.[4]

The ITBs nonetheless survived into the 1980s, when the Thatcher government's determination to cut government expenditure made common cause with critics of any government-sponsored 'compulsion' involving businesses' training programmes.[5] Free-market think tanks, such as the Centre for Policy Studies, argued that in a statist environment the whole rationale for a professional training officer's existence became simply gaining grants or justifying levy exemption. 'The bias must be towards waste and inefficiency', and the training undertaken would be decided not by its value but by whether 'it is possible to identify exact costs . . . [and so] fit neatly with bureaucratic methods'.[6]

In such a climate the ITBs' prospects were poor. In 1982 all but seven were duly scrapped; within a few years only two remained. They left behind, however, a business world with a strong aversion to 'compulsion' and a determination not to let levies return.

An invitation to the driving seat

The end of ITBs was not the end of government training policy. On the contrary. It coincided with the high summer of Manpower Services Commission influence – the New Training Initiative and the creation of YTS, and the increasing emphasis on vocational qualifications. Increasingly, business opinion became a touchstone, not only in training but also in education policy more generally. 'Local employer networks' were created in 1986 to ensure a substantial input from employers into technical and vocational education and training. Then came the 'industry lead bodies', set up – all 180 of them – to develop the skills standards, or 'occupational standards', on which NVQs were in turn to be based. These organizations might choose to include representatives of unions (as they sometimes did) or of education (as they very occasionally did); but what they *had* to include was employers.

As I described in the last chapter, the New Training Initiative, launched by the Manpower Services Commission in 1981, embraced a huge increase in vocational training and heralded the whole NVQ experiment. While strongly in favour of more government involvement and spending (and, by extension, a greater role for the MSC), in other ways the NTI was highly Thatcherite. Many unions had, over the previous decades, negotiated increasingly high wages for apprentices; this was seen as a major reason for recent declines in apprentice numbers, and an obvious market distortion. Under a standards-based system, the training radicals argued, there would be open access to qualifications and no more 'time-serving' – that is, dragging out the length of training irrespective of whether the apprentice had reached the required level of skill.[7] Instead, anyone who met the standards would get a certificate.

But where were these new standards to come from? It was hard to see civil servants as the oracles of marketplace requirements, or as repositories of knowledge about the practical, the innovative or, indeed, the efficient. Teachers and educators, including those in vocational programmes, were alternatively depicted as out-of-touch, opposed to the market, or perpetrators of 'producer capture' – that is, of using their employment for their own ends rather than their clients'. The unions, already a general target of the government, were ruled out as being interested primarily in limiting access to qualifications. Only the employers remained. Their economic competence or incompetence became irrelevant: they were the ones who must set the standards, based on analysis of their companies' needs and practices. Standards could be legitimate only to the degree that they were employer-created; and if they *were* employer-created – that is lead-body-created – their validity was assumed.

Twenty years before, Whitehall had lobbed training boards and levies into companies' plants and offices, affecting budgets and operations alike. Now Whitehall was inviting the employers in. For 'employers', however, read 'large employers' – and especially the CBI.

Most British employers belong to one of two very different national organizations: the Confederation of British Industry (CBI) or the Institute of Directors (IoD). Locally, they may also belong to a Chamber of Commerce; but, though Chambers of Commerce have a national umbrella organization (the British Chambers of Commerce), they do not have the same high profile or distinctive voice. For those not familiar with them, the CBI and the IoD are easy to characterize. The CBI represents the big employers; so when journalists write about what 'captains of industry' are telling the government they are almost invariably reporting on a CBI position. IoD members, by contrast, hold individual rather than corporate membership and are generally directors of smaller and newer companies. The IoD is far more adversarial, more distrustful of any government; and, except on a few fairly obvious issues (such as the level of business taxes), one can safely predict that, if the CBI takes one position, the IoD will opt for a polar opposite. The CBI is comfortable in government committees, in the corridors of Whitehall and Brussels – an instinctively emollient, well-connected insider. It was the CBI which provided all the business members of the Manpower Services Commission, as of other quangos before and since. And in the new educational climate of enthusiasm for business, it was the CBI that made the running.

In the industry lead bodies, large companies were inevitably and hugely over-represented. Who else could provide personnel and training officers willing and able to spend days on end in workshops involving the 'functional analysis' (*sic*) of an occupation? Who else had time for discussions with the government-funded consultants drawing up the standards, or to comment on the drafts, or to respond to criticisms and demands for amendment before NCVQ would accredit the results?

But involvement went far beyond this. Under the activist leadership of the headquarters staff at Centre Point – the concrete skyscraper which dominates London's West End skyline – the CBI set out to influence and make education policy in an unprecedented way. It shared the dominant belief that education's primary function was to contribute to economic growth – the implication being that business is education's primary customer. It also believed that it, the CBI, could speak for business needs; and, in the late 1980s and 1990s, governments were suddenly very ready to listen.

A businessman's vision? The CBI's policies for education

In 1988 – shortly after NCVQ's creation – the CBI set up a task force on vocational education and training. Staffed by permanent CBI employees from the Education and Training Directorate, it was chaired by Sir Bryan Nicholson, chief executive of the Post Office, but also a past chairman of the Manpower Services Commission and a future one of NCVQ.[8]

The CBI task force reported in 1989 with a widely publicized document entitled *Towards a Skills Revolution*. Echoing and endorsing the general Zeitgeist, it called for 'a quantum leap in the education and training of young people to meet the needs of the British economy'.[9] At the time, rather few of the people actually working in the education or training sector took much notice of its detailed suggestions. Nor did most of them ever see, let alone read, the other glossy CBI monographs which followed at regular intervals over the next decade. It is unlikely that many chief executives or finance directors in CBI companies paid close attention either, other than to assume that 'their' staff were probably talking more sense than the trendy progressives commonly supposed to be ruining UK education. But the credibility and influence of the CBI with government meant that, over the next decade, CBI recommendations had a major impact on policy.

The CBI's 1989 task force combined the usual call for expanded vocational training (and government funds to support it) with a number of quite specific and less predictable policies. First and foremost, it called for *targets*: 'The Task Force believes that it is necessary to set world class targets ... the ... targets will have to be reviewed and raised until the United Kingdom is on a par with its main competitors.'[10] Targets are usually associated more with the defunct central-planning regimes of Eastern Europe than with an association representing capitalist employers, but, nonetheless, targets followed. In 1991 the 'National Education and Training Targets' were adopted and developed by government. Enshrined on hundreds of thousands of plastic wallet-sized cards, these were distributed up and down the land by more or less believing civil servants. The National Advisory Council for Education and Training Targets (and a separate Scottish equivalent), with the CBI and TUC as official partners, was established in 1993 to 'monitor progress', 'advise Government', and 'provide business leadership' of the national effort to achieve these National Targets.[11]

In a pamphlet on *World Class Targets*, published to mark the Advisory Council's inauguration, the CBI announced that

> All those who support this report believe that the UK must know where it is going on skills and that world class targets will help each organisation set and pursue relevant objectives within their area of responsibility ... [T]he targets provide the required challenge for the nation ... Without qualifications targets, there is a danger that the year 2000 will find policy makers still debating the challenge rather than evaluating the progress made ... [T]he primary source of competitive advantage lies in investing in people. *The UK cannot afford to debate this issue, it must believe it.*[12]

Unlike the league tables which list pupils' scores on national assessments and GCSEs school by school, the National Targets have passed most people (and most parents) by.[13] Not so in government departments. Here, they were – and are – highly visible: the potential embarrassment if no progress is made looms large. And the CBI was very proud of them. In a 1993 report to its members, it announced that 'The National Education and Training Targets were initiated by the CBI. They set the efforts of employers, schools, colleges and training providers into a national context and are the glue which holds together the different initiatives in this field.'[14]

Although targets were first introduced by a Conservative government, the incoming Labour ministers of the late 1990s embraced them with enthusiasm (and duly multiplied their numbers). The 1997 Labour consultation document on *Targets for our Future* noted that the

National Targets 'were originally launched by the CBI ... They drew attention to the serious skills gap that existed between the UK and a number of its foreign competitors.' For David Blunkett, the Secretary of State, 'National Targets ... are critical because ... they can mobilise and focus everyone's effort on clear goals.'[15] Progress 'towards achieving the Targets ... will show visibly how well the country is doing'.[16]

They certainly created a focus for civil servants. With targets in their sights, government agencies set themselves to piling the qualifications high. In a centrally funded and increasingly regulated sector, incentives and payments were organized around successful delivery of the qualification targets summarized in Table 4.2.

As Table 4.2 shows, NVQs were central to the first formulation of the targets – as indeed they were in the CBI's original proposals. So 'NVQ level 2 or equivalent' encompasses GCSEs, Scottish Standard Grade and the like; and 'NVQ level 3 or equivalent' sweeps up A levels, National Diplomas and Scottish Highers. In the early years of target-shooting, NVQs were also the major focus of government action. The easiest institutions to manipulate were the eighty-two Training and Enterprise Councils, or TECs, which funnelled government funds for youth and adult training to a host of private 'providers', as well as to FE colleges. They duly became the front-line troops in the effort to meet the Targets.[17]

TECs were established in 1990 with the idea that local organizations, with boards made up of business people, would get business genuinely involved in directing training funds to meet local training needs, and encourage enterprise and business efficiency. The reality was very different (which is why no one mourned their demise and replacement, in 2001, by yet another set of quangos). TECs were not about economic regeneration or the enterprise culture. They were about administering government-funded low-status training programmes for the young and unemployed – and about growing NVQs.

Budgets for these programmes came from central government on an annual basis. Very quickly the National Targets became the key measure of TECs' progress, and the most important indicator by which they were evaluated by their paymasters. TECs' contracts with central

Table 4.2 *The National Education and Training Targets: successive formulations*

1991	1995	1998
By 1997, 80 per cent of all young people to reach NVQ level 2 or equivalent	By 2000, 85 per cent of all young people to achieve five GCSEs at grade C or above, an Intermediate GNVQ or an NVQ level 2	By 2002, 50 per cent of sixteen-year-olds achieving five or more GCSEs at grades A*–C and 95 per cent achieving one or more GCSEs at grades A*–G
By 2000, 50 per cent of young people to reach NVQ level 3 or equivalent	By 2000, 75 per cent of young people to achieve level-2 competence in communication, numeracy and IT by age nineteen, and 35 per cent to achieve level-3 competence by age twenty-one By 2000, 60 per cent of young people to achieve two GCE A levels, an Advanced GNVQ or an NVQ level 3 by age twenty-one	By 2002, 85 per cent of nineteen-year-olds with a 'level-2' qualification By 2002, 60 per cent of twenty-one-year-olds with a 'level-3' qualification
By 1996, all employees should take part in training or development activities	*No employee target*	*No employee target*
By 1996, 50 per cent of the workforce aiming for NVQs or units towards them By 2000, 50 per cent of the workforce qualified to at least NVQ level 3 or equivalent	By 2000, 60 per cent of the workforce qualified to NVQ level 3, Advanced GNVQ or two GCE A-level standard By 2000, 30 per cent of the workforce to have a qualification at NVQ level 4 or above	*No workforce target*
No adult learning target	*No adult learning target*	By 2002, 50 per cent of adults to have a 'level-3' qualification By 2002, 28 per cent of adults to have a 'level-4' qualification

Sources: DfEE & DENI 1997; NACETT 1999; DfEE 2001

government were drawn up annually to cover the funding of a set number of training places, and a set amount of assistance to local businesses, and committed TECs to so many NVQs being awarded in consequence.[18]

A targets-oriented funding mechanism which accompanied these arrangements generated wonders in the very short term and disaster in the slightly longer term. 'Outcome-related funding' was a new label for payment by results. Among TEC-funded programmes, a sizeable amount of the funding per trainee was paid to the 'training provider' only at the end of training, and then *only if an NVQ was actually achieved*. The proportion paid over in this way varied by TEC, but typically in Youth Training about 60 per cent was paid for providing the course and the remaining 40 per cent when, if, and only if the trainee got his or her NVQ. In other programmes the proportion of funding tied to actually obtaining the NVQ was often higher.

The logic was obvious. Too few trainees were qualifying, so introducing outcome-related funding would spur providers to greater efficiency (measured in NVQs) in exactly the same way that payment on delivery spurs performance in supermarkets and hairdressers, or among home-builders and manufacturers. It also made trainers as NVQ-obsessed as the TEC staff who paid them.[19] The effects on NVQs' quality and reputation could have been predicted by anyone half-acquainted with the old Eastern Bloc economies. Corner-cutting and inflated qualification counts followed, as night does day. Government departments might perhaps have overlooked this logic. But a large business organization, devoted, in theory, to the principles of the market? Yet the CBI seems never to have anticipated or recognized what targets actually do.

One reason for this was its passionate determination to promote the NVQ. The CBI had not invented NVQs in the way that it had invented the targets, but it came to cherish them as though it had. The first set of targets shown in Table 4.2 were the ones most influenced by the CBI, and far and away the most NVQ-oriented. To the CBI, NVQs were businesses' own qualifications, and it would fight their corner with government, with education, with academic critics, and even with its own indifferent members.

'A fundamental change for the better': the CBI to the rescue

As Chapter 3 described, NVQs were intended to reflect the realities of workplace competence: a holder of an NVQ was presumed to have shown that he or she could carry out every single component part of the competence at the level of someone actually doing that job, and to have done so in a realistic context – either the workplace itself or somewhere which faithfully reflected workplace conditions. NVQs were to be 'owned' by business, not by educators and trainers: businessmen would set the occupational standards which defined the content of an NVQ. Businesses would know, as a result, that anyone with an NVQ relevant to a company really could operate as a fully productive worker from the word go.

The promise was seductive, and many businesses and trade organizations were eager to help. When, in the early days, Employment Department civil servants rushed to create a mass of industry lead bodies, they found companies very willing to release staff for meetings, to circulate and respond to documentation, and even to contribute directly, with cash and not merely time, to the costs of the exercise.

In book publishing, for example, senior figures from large publishing houses were enthused by the vision of lonely freelancers collecting their valuable NVQs. They gave not only their own time but also substantial resources from publishing charities to match and build on the usual government grant. Offices were rented and staffed; a suite of qualifications was developed, consulted on, redrafted and approved. A major national launch was held in London; by 1993 no fewer than 140 NVQ assessors had been trained and a chief examiner had been hired. Only the candidates failed to materialize. As Table 4.3 reveals, by 1997 a grand total of fifteen certificates had been awarded for the whole industry with its suite of eleven awards. Over the next two years, just two more certificates were gained.[20] A similar story in many other sectors produced the national total of 364 NVQs never taken by anyone, to which we referred in Chapter 3, and the hundreds of others with only a tiny number of candidates.

Table 4.3 *Total (cumulative) number of book-publishing NVQs ever awarded*

	Total number of certificates awarded up to September 1997	Total number of certificates awarded up to September 1999
Book Commissioning	1	1
Book Contracts	2	2
Book Design	1	1
Book Editing level 3	7	7
Book Editing level 4	0	0
Book Editing (Editorial Management)	0	0
Book Production	4	5
Book Promotion and Publicity	0	0
Book Publishing, Publicity and Promotion	0	0
Book Publishing Rights	0	1
Book Rights	0	0
Total	15	17

Sources: NCVQ, *Data News: Annual NVQ Statistics Supplements*, and QCA, *Data News: Annual NVQ Statistics Supplements*

In some companies, NVQs were designed to fit specific jobs and training programmes. For these companies NVQs were a useful and usable way of delivering training and certifying achievement. But in many companies the bureaucratic complexities of actually running an NVQ, and the lack of grass-roots enthusiasm, percolated even to chief executives. Nonetheless, as the attacks on NVQs grew, the CBI became their staunchest defender.

The most vocal critics of government policy were, inevitably, from education and the policy world. (Business people, after all, have businesses to run.) Prominent among them were the academics of the NIESR, who had so championed the cause of better vocational education for young people[21] and who saw NVQs as a travesty of their original ideas. NVQs' critics attacked them as too narrow for young people. They also questioned their quality. The absence of external assessment or tests was a particular issue. NCVQ saw written tests as a typical product of despised old-style education – largely irrelevant to true vocational competence, and a barrier to the less advantaged, whose practical experience and abilities they obscured. Consequently, NVQs were assessed task by task (or 'performance criterion' by 'performance criterion'), generally by a trainer who ticked off the fact that a particular practical task had been achieved.[22] The CBI was determined that educators should not get hold of NVQs and change this basic approach. NVQs must remain under employer control, based on authentic demonstrations of real workplace skills, or they would not be attractive to industry. The chairmen of large companies were encouraged to cheerlead for NVQs by the CBI as much as by government.

From 1991 onward the CBI's central staff produced a series of glossy monographs, each of which reiterated support for NVQs and for the increasingly beleaguered National Council. In *World Class Targets* (1991), the CBI pronounced that 'The targets call for extensive use of the NVQ framework by employees with support from employers . . . A much higher proportion of training should contribute to NVQ certification with half the workforce making some use of the framework.'[23] In 1993 (*Training: The Business Case*) it was prodding its members to remember that 'It is important for the future competitiveness of British industry that NVQs are accepted in the workplace . . . In the past employers have been hampered in their training efforts by a lack of appropriate qualifications . . . The new National Vocational Qualifications (NVQs) are designed to redress this situation.'[24]

The 1994 publication *Quality Assessed* mounted an extensive defence of NVQs as a 'fundamental change for the better' and 'part of a sustained revolution to raise . . . skills'. The report pushed for the abolition of any vocational awards (such as BTEC Diplomas or City & Guilds certificates) that were not full-blown NVQs. It reiterated that

> **The CBI has given consistent support to the principle of the NVQ framework since its inception. The criticisms of the previous vocational qualifications system . . . echo the frustrations and waste**

> experienced by employers who have used them ... Significant
> business benefits have been reported by employers using NVQs ...
> All Awarding Body [*i.e. all formal vocational*] qualifications should
> either be NVQs or constructed to be compatible with and allow
> progression to NVQs.[25]

A year later, *Realising the Vision: A Skills Passport* announced
that 'NVQs and SVQs[26] are strongly supported by employers. The
competence-based national vocational qualification – incorporating
employer-determined standards – is acknowledged as the world leader
by many countries interested in adopting it.'[27]

The support for the qualifications extended also to NCVQ, which by
the mid-1990s needed all the friends it could get. (The 'many countries
interested in adopting' NVQs had by this time crystallized into just
Oman.) Forced to acknowledge that 'the take-up of NVQs to date has
been relatively slow' and that 'CBI members have also been identifying,
in addition to the benefits, obstacles to the take-up of NVQs',[28] the
CBI nonetheless saw the remedy as more powers and more public
resources for NCVQ. 'Marketing is best in the hands of those committed to the product ... [E]mployers prefer NCVQ to be given prime
responsibility for NVQ marketing ... If given an expanded marketing
role, as this Report recommends, then it is essential that NCVQ has
the resources and staff expertise necessary to fulfil that role.'[29] Better
still, the CBI argued, let a body with a business orientation expand to
regulate the whole of upper-level education and training, including A
levels. 'One qualifications framework should result in one assessment
body at 16 plus,' it urged. 'SCAA [the Schools Curriculum and Assessment Authority] should be responsible only for curriculum and assessment from five to 16. The 16 plus part of [its] remit should instead be
merged with NCVQ.'[30]

This recommendation may have planted the idea of a future super-
quango, but in the short term it was dead in the water. CBI support
notwithstanding, by 1995 the complaints about NVQs had reached
such a level that the government felt obliged to mount an inquiry into
the system.

The source of trouble was not the academic critiques, let alone any in-depth research and evaluation. It was, instead, the payment-by-results funding regime which I described earlier, and which had seemed such a clever touch, guaranteed to deliver large numbers of NVQs and do so within a penumbra of market rhetoric about efficiency, prices and customers.

Unfortunately, training schemes financed entirely by quangos are about as far from a market as one can easily get. In this case, a single paymaster (government) was paying its totally dependent subsidiaries (the TECs) on the basis of how many training places and NVQs they could register. They in turn paid training providers – many of them again completely dependent on one customer – on the basis of how many trainees completed an NVQ. Since NVQs were assessed by the trainers themselves, it was not long before some trainers were, in the prevalent phrase, 'shelling them out like peas'; and not long, either, before a few scams – such as non-existent trainees receiving NVQs – made the national press. That many people had predicted that this funding method would do for the quality and reputation of NVQs precisely what Soviet planners had done for Russian tractors was no consolation. Tabloid scandals were bad news, and civil servants were charged with sorting things out.

Given the central place accorded to NVQs in training policy, and the cheerleading for them written into ministers' speeches, this was not an exercise to which civil servants applied themselves with any vast enthusiasm. What they set up was 'a review of 100 of the most-used NVQs and SVQs' rather than of NVQs in general, thus neatly side-stepping the fact that most NVQs were not used by anyone at all. The review was also based in and staffed by NCVQ itself. Business and employers were to be the key audience. Elevated as the ultimate authority on vocational-training matters, so they must equally be the arbiter of whether the NVQ system was an appropriate use of public funds and governmental powers. The chair of the review was correspondingly chosen from business – more specifically, from among the CBI's own long-standing committee members.

The review duly reported in 1996 with a document written entirely in terms of what employers (supposedly) desire (while remaining remarkably data-free).[31] Overall, it concluded, everything about NVQs was just fine. For the sake of 'UK plc' (*sic*), everyone just needed to keep criticisms in perspective and be a bit more 'customer focused'. Everyone concerned needed to use powers 'sensitively but firmly', to establish procedures with 'clear boundaries, but ... framed to guide and enable' – and to increase employer influence yet more. On this one point the 'Beaumont Report' was very clear indeed. NVQs were for employers, and employers needed more say, not less. In fact the one concrete change the report proposed was that employers (through the lead bodies) should be given additional powers, acquiring the job not only of writing the standards which comprised the NVQ curriculum, but also of deciding exactly how NVQs should be assessed – the task normally carried out by professional examining bodies such as City & Guilds.

The Beaumont Report, along with continuing CBI support, probably ensured that no very dramatic changes were made to NVQs – then or since. However, neither this nor the commitment to NVQs of a few major companies could offset the wholesale and near total neglect of most NVQs. Developed 'for' and supposedly by business, they were consistently neglected by vast numbers of employers, both before and after Beaumont. Senior managers were happy to assure government researchers and surveys that they not only had heard of NVQs, they were also making them available to their workforce. But the facts spoke otherwise: by the mid 1990s only 2 per cent of that workforce actually reported themselves to be working towards any sort of NVQ, employer-supported or not.[32]

NCVQ itself did not long outlast the Beaumont inquiry. A year and a half later, in 1997, a consultative document paved the way for its merger with SCAA, the schools curriculum and examinations quango, creating the Qualifications and Curriculum Authority. However, while the CBI two years before had advocated a merger which gave NCVQ overall control of the whole post-sixteen sector, the QCA's first group of top executives numbered four from SCAA and just one – since departed – from NCVQ. The despised education establishment was making a comeback.

'What industry wants': basic skills, core skills, key skills, and then some?

The CBI's three great educational enthusiasms were for targets, for NVQs, and for core skills. Targets, as we have seen, established themselves firmly in the hearts of both main political parties. NVQs have had a rockier ride. How about core (or 'key') skills?

The history of core skills encapsulates the growing, and unusual, influence on UK education that business enjoyed during the 1980s and 1990s. Asking industry about vocational training is an obvious enough thing to do, although government bureaucracies (whether central or local) generally keep firmer control over events than in the British case. Far more novel was the idea of taking business advice about the mainstream school curriculum.

For the most part, businessmen's views about the public education system were – and are – quite simply expressed. They are that schools turn out pupils who simply do not have the relevant skills or personal qualities. They can't add up; they can't write a business letter; they don't know how to work in teams, or talk to customers, or understand the need to turn up to work on time . . . In fact the schools are doing a dreadful job for a lot of money and need to improve, fast. To quote the Institute of Directors this time, 'Without high calibre school leavers and graduates, the capacity of business to compete is seriously jeopardised . . . we must make good the shortcomings in education and training for the world of work . . . The IoD's [1991] survey . . . reveals directors' concerns about falling educational standards and an education system which is a poor preparation for employment.'[33]

This negative view has chimed with that of both politicians and media commentators. Ever since James Callaghan, the Labour Prime Minister of the mid 1970s, expressed 'the unease felt by parents and others about the new informal methods of teaching',[34] the view of most politicians and business leaders, and almost all the press, has been that English education is run by a progressive educational establishment with no interest in standards.

This view, along with the belief that education 'matters', has helped propel education to the forefront of recent election campaigns. It has also destroyed the trust which underlies any professional relationship: in this case most clearly between teachers and the state.[35] Another effect, following directly from this view, has been to legitimize alternative sources of advice on the curriculum and the conduct of education. The education establishment's loss was business's gain – the more so because of the growing political preoccupation with education and growth.

Core skills figured large in the concerns of civil servants for years before the wider public had any inkling of their supposed existence. This was because they were presumed to reflect what business 'really' wanted from education. And in late-twentieth- and early-twenty-first-century Britain what business wanted was what it behoved government to provide. After all, if the main purpose of education was to develop the skills required in the workplace, who better to identify them than business itself?

Core skills first saw the light of day with a speech by Kenneth Baker, the minister who was also responsible for introducing the National Curriculum and national tests for seven-, eleven- and fourteen-year-olds. He is also generally perceived, in school circles, as a supporter of 'standards' – a back-to-basics Conservative, leading the offensive against the supposedly laid-back, anything-goes educational consensus. And when Baker launched core skills on the world, in a 1989 speech to the annual general meeting of the Association of Colleges of Further & Higher Education (ACFHE), he was supporting 'an initiative to promote further education' that was relevant to a changing economy and to business needs.

In his speech, Baker announced that

> As I see it, there are a number of skills . . . which young people and adults in future will all need. They could be expressed as a list of core skills . . . say, the following:
> - communication – written and oral. How to explain a complicated working procedure, or deal with a tricky customer.
> - numeracy. Not simply adding a column of figures, but understanding orders of magnitude.
> - personal relations – team working and leadership.

- familiarity with technology . . .
- familiarity with systems . . .
- familiarity with changing and social contexts . . . especially foreign language knowledge.

The speech (and the list) appeared just a few months before the launch of *Towards a Skills Revolution*, the CBI task-force report which, as we have just seen, launched the National Targets. The close relationship between government and business thinking is clear from the similarity of ideas, and indeed language. The CBI too wanted 'core elements', present in all young people's education and training programmes as 'a basis for working life', and its list (shown in Figure 4.1 and at this point labelled 'Common Learning Outcomes') covered extremely similar ground to Baker's.

Figure 4.1 *The CBI's list of 'Common Learning Outcomes'*

> Values and Integrity
> Effective Communication
> Applications of Numeracy
> Applications of Technology
> Understanding of Work and the World
> Personal and Interpersonal Skills
> Problem Solving
> Positive Attitudes to Change

Source: CBI 1989: 21

Baker himself seems to have forgotten about core skills almost as soon as he launched them. They figure nowhere in his autobiography; indeed, his only related comment is that, as Education Minister, he soon became 'suspicious of certain phrases widely used in education which had a meretricious ring about them. One was "problem solving" . . .'[36] Problem-solving has, for all that, enjoyed a ten-year curricular career, starting when Baker launched it with his own unremembered speech. So too have core skills in general, which for the moment are a central plank in the sixth-form curriculum and in government-funded training schemes and apprenticeships, and a supposed priority for higher education.[37]

For if Baker soon forgot core skills (and moved on from Education to the Conservative Party chairmanship), his old department did not. Later that year, letters from the Secretary of State for Education – by now John MacGregor – asked both the National Curriculum Council, the quango responsible at that time for the school-level curriculum, and NCVQ to advance the incorporation of 'core skills' into post-sixteen course provision. NCC evinced a marked lack of enthusiasm, and on the academic side they were shelved for the better part of a decade. NCVQ, on the other hand, greeted the idea with enthusiasm, reflecting both its own educational ideas and its closeness to the CBI. It eventually settled on a list of six core skills:

- application of number,
- information technology,
- communication,
- problem-solving,
- working with others,
- improving one's own learning and performance.

NCVQ officials argued that, using 'performance criteria', it was possible to define exactly what each of these meant at a variety of different 'levels', and then use these definitions to assess and accredit performance. Draft upon draft of performance criteria were accordingly produced, on the basis of which one might purportedly assess 'Problem-Solving Level 3', or 'Communication Level 1'. Figure 4.2 provides some examples of the achievements (and the detailed 'performance criteria') on the basis of which people would receive their awards. So, for example, you could be well on your way to getting level-1 Problem-Solving if you followed standard solutions to any common problem in any workplace – provided that you also, for example, did so 'in an appropriate timescale' and followed 'laid down procedures' (see Figure 4.2: performance criteria for level 1.) For level-2 Communication, one

Figure 4.2 *Sample core-skill elements and performance criteria*

Communication *(1993: accredited version)*	**Problem-Solving** *(1992)*
Level 1 1.1 Take part in discussions with known individuals on routine matters.	*Level 1* 1.1 Select standard solutions to fully-described problems.
Level 2 2.1 Take part in discussions with a range of people on routine matters. 1. Own contributions are clear and appropriate to the subject matter. 2. Own contributions are made in a tone and manner suited to the audience. 3. Contributions from others are listened to attentively. 4. Own understanding of points made by others is actively checked and confirmed.	1. All information about the critical features of the problem is used in order to identify the solution. 2. Solution is the appropriate response to the problem. 3. Solution is identified in an appropriate timescale. 4. Laid down procedures for identifying the solution are followed accurately. *Level 2* 2.2 Select standard solutions to routine problems.
Level 3 3.1 Take part in discussions with a range of people on a range of matters.	*Level 3* 3.1 Select procedures to clarify problems with a range of possible solutions. 3.2 Identify alternative solutions and select solutions to problems.

Source: NCVQ 1992 and 1993

of the 'elements' to be completed was 'taking part in discussions'. Again (see Figure 4.2), discussing any routine matters would do fine when it came to being judged 'competent' at this level, but to get your award you did have to be ticked as having listened to others and having used a 'tone and manner suited to the audience'.

The essence of the core skills was that they should be embedded in vocational activity. Workplace supervisors or vocational trainers were expected to observe and catch them on the wing, recording them as they passed by. So, for example, in some situations, the trainer might conclude that a seventeen-year-old on YTS (or, indeed, an adult on the shop floor or in the office) had selected 'standard solutions to fully described problems' and so should receive credit towards Problem-Solving Level 1. Another day, he or she might 'identify alternative solutions' and clock up credit towards not just level 1 but level 3 (see Figure 4.2). NVQs had no formal academic content, and a settled aversion to written tests, but NCVQ believed that core-skill certificates would become a valuable credential in the labour market, and trainers were encouraged to accredit trainees with core-skill 'units' at different levels. Core skills also became an official part of GNVQs, although the government would allow only some of the units to be mandatory.

In all of this, NCVQ enjoyed strong and consistent support from the CBI. It was quickly forgotten that the 'core-skills' label was not originally the CBI's: by 1992 a new Secretary of State for Education was referring in official statements to 'what the CBI describes as "core skills" ... I think industry can reasonably expect people to leave education at all levels with these skills.'[38] In 1995 the CBI can be found urging the government that 'All learning should develop core skills. They should be integrated into all qualifications to the appropriate level and separately assessed. A Core Skills Task Force should be set up to agree and implement a strategy for core skills in all learning.'[39]

Evidence from school and college inspectorates, as well as from academic researchers, was consistently critical of attempts to deliver core skills meaningfully, let alone assess them to some clear standard. However, the CBI was unfazed. In arguing the case for core skills, it could point to employers' consistent preoccupation with qualities such as time-keeping, motivation, communication with clients – and equally consistent complaints about school leavers' performance in these areas.[40] It was also confident that, in the core-skills list, it had identified the missing elements in education-for-the-economy, and that core-skills assessment and certification were the way forward. For all six core skills, including problem-solving and personal skills, it argued, 'there is now ample evidence that these skills can be assessed with sufficient rigour for the purpose of accreditation' and that, since 'NCVQ has demonstrated the value and acceptability of assessing problem solving and personal skills, it is imperative that the momentum is maintained'.[41]

Government departments duly funded a range of studies and develop-ment projects, as well as promoting core skills in government-funded training. The studies tended to confirm both the slipperiness of the core-skills concept – few of those who claimed to have heard of core skills actually gave the same, let alone the 'correct', definition – and the combination of confusion with conviction that something important was being discussed. The Beaumont Report encapsulates this looking-glass world precisely:

> There is a widely held view that Core Skills are important but not total agreement about what they are. The literature search showed some academics felt Core Skills could not be defined ... NCVQ ... [has] developed Core Skills units ... These underpin effective performance. Employers in this country widely indicate that they require their employees to have some basic abilities; they call them 'core skills'. Critics rightly say they are not all 'skills'. Nor are they 'core' but they are essential to enable performance ... The title is not helpful. However, as it is widely used, I am persuaded it should continue to be used.[42]

Things might have limped on like this for years; but in 1996 core skills hit the jackpot – being relabelled, repackaged, and promoted as central to all post-sixteen education. Their unlikely patron was Lord Dealing, a former civil servant and Post Office chairman with a genius for chairing potentially embarrassing inquiries. Fresh from extracting the government from a National Curriculum debacle in which the testing regime for schools produced an England and Wales-wide boycott backed not only by heads but by school governors, he was now asked to review the structure of post-sixteen education.

The context of Dearing's inquiry was the situation described in Chapter 3: a huge increase in post-sixteen participation, continued dissatisfaction with highly specialized A levels, criticism of both GNVQs and NVQs, and government confusion over what to do about older qualifications' refusal to lie down and die. Ministers wanted Dearing's speciality – an apparently comprehensive reform that still left everyone happy. One way in which he obliged was by promoting and praising some pet ideas from each of the circling interest groups; and in NCVQ's case the favoured offspring was none other than core skills.

Dearing had little time for the idea that 'core skills' was a widely used business concept and that the label had therefore to be preserved. On the contrary, he promptly renamed them 'key skills'. Otherwise, however, the list he offered was straight off the NCVQ press. The key skills were, however, to come out of their vocational ghetto. The 'hard' three (number, communication and information technology (IT)) should become part of a separate award, an AS level in key skills; and key skills generally should be written into all syllabuses – vocational and academic, A level, GNVQ and NVQ alike.

Governments – first Tory, then Labour – rushed to oblige. Key-skills development was rapidly under way; after endless redrafts, a new 'Key Skills' qualification was ready to hit schools in autumn 2000, along with other Dearing-recommended reforms, and key skills also became a mandatory part of apprenticeship training on any government-supported apprenticeships.[43] As the government's official position paper explained, 'The genesis for the Key Skills ... was concern from employers in the 1980s that their young recruits did not have the general skills needed in effective employees.'[44] The new qualifications would encourage the skills employers need. They were backed by a £17 million 'support programme' to help teachers understand what to do, and a funding regime which gave colleges, in particular, a major financial incentive to enter their students.

Colleges (and many schools) duly did so. However, none of the latest batch of reforms has prevented vehement protests about the new qualification's unwieldy assessment regime, and the burden it places on teachers – or widely reported scepticism from pupils about whether employers are actually interested in the awards at all.

The core-/key-skills story marks a high point in business influence on the full-time school curriculum, as compared to vocational training proper. The idea gained currency because of and through the prestige of 'business opinion' about what education should offer, and correspondingly became protected terrain, in spite of consistent problems with implementation, official criticism from government's own inspectors, and a public assault by Chris Woodhead, at the time an apparently omnipotent Chief Inspector of Schools.[45] Is the result a genuine improvement in the economic relevance of education? Is this a case where business has got it right?

My own answer comes encapsulated in a prediction: twenty years from now, key skills will be forgotten like all the other vocational initiatives the UK has sped through in the twenty years to date. The vast majority of the population has still not heard of key skills; I would venture they never will.

But this is not a tragedy for the economic relevance of education. The core-/key-skills story teaches some interesting lessons, but they are far more to do with the nature of bureaucracies – private or governmental – than with the skills that the economy needs. It is absolutely true that employers are interested in a range of qualities and skills that are not covered by formal academic qualifications. That is why they do not generally hire people sight unseen; and why many not only interview candidates, but set up selection tasks or group discussions, and administer personality tests.[46] But the world's public education systems are huge enterprises with very clear functions, and anything they are to do routinely needs to be possible, and affordable, and generally 'fit for purpose'.

Core skills met and meet none of these requirements. The reason why schools and colleges work to fixed timetables and syllabuses is not that they are against flexibility, innovation, initiative and other such valuable qualities. They do so because otherwise no one – staff, students or examiners – would know who was doing what, when or why. Schools also live with constant staff turnover, absences and shortages, while students come and go frequently, often moving mid-year. No institutions like this can possibly devise individualized ways of developing and assessing each student's performance in different contexts as the occasion arises.

What teachers *can* do is tick boxes after some specially staged classroom event, to record that someone has taken part in a discussion, or identified a problem's solution. They can also collect together sheafs of paper on which students supposedly demonstrate their skills. Or at least schools and colleges can: trainers in a workplace understandably find even that near-impossible.[47] In any case, such laborious paper collection fails totally to meet another critical requirement of any modern education system: that assessments be consistent and reliable, treating different students in different schools or colleges the same.

Before the introduction of the new Dearing-inspired qualification, we know that what was delivered as core skills varied wildly. This was hardly surprising, given that no one involved had any real idea of what they were supposed to do. The latest attempts to make key skills deliverable and credible are actually transforming them into something far more traditional and far removed from the CBI's original vision. The formal Key Skills qualification covers only communication, number and IT; and the real determinants of success, in England, are three separate multiple-choice tests, for number, literacy and IT, which will double up as basic-skills tests for adults. In Scotland the whole affair is being finessed out of existence, with direct equivalences between key skills and component parts of school examinations and no need to do any additional work at all.

Large bureaucratic organizations, including the education systems of modern states, have their own necessary logic, as plenty of other revolutionaries have found. The moral here is not that the education establishment is antipathetic to business, but that changes which require comprehensive institutional change are doomed to fail. From this attempt at rewriting the traditional curriculum, we take away neither better skills for the economy nor revitalized academic learning – just a great deal of wasted money and, for teachers and students, a great deal of wasted time.

Policy in whose interest?

The most curious thing about core/key skills is that they were promoted by a business organization. For these skills, and the idea that they must be developed in a range of practical contexts, belong in the heartland of ideas about learning through doing, and student-centred learning, with a line of descent that stretches right back to Rousseau. This is very obvious in the published guidance distributed by NCVQ;[48] but it was not a matter of hard-headed CBI ideas being distorted by 'progressives' in government. On the contrary: CBI staff firmly believed in this approach. One of my more surreal experiences around this time was sitting in a meeting convened to help the 'Review of Most-Used NVQs' (which produced the Beaumont Report) address problems with NVQ assessment. The CBI representative argued passionately against any requirements for written tests, in case these discriminated against anyone with language and reading problems.

This was a surreal experience because, all over the Western world, when employers complain about the standard of education, it is the world of spelling tests and mental arithmetic that is in their mind's eye, not that of discovery learning. Nor is the detail of education practice top of most business people's personal agendas when it comes to government policy. Regulations, taxes and the exchange rate generally come a lot higher.

We are left with a paradox. Why have the representatives of what is essentially a lobbying organization for big business been so active in education policy, and also so curiously 'progressive' in their attitudes?

To answer this we need a short detour into something called 'public-choice theory'. Public-choice theory applies the principles of economics to situations which are not conventional markets with people buying or selling for cash, but where resources are nonetheless scarce – not everyone can get everything they want. Adam Smith famously pointed out that 'it is not from the benevolence of the butcher, the brewer or the baker that we expect our dinner, but from their regard to their own interest'.[49] To which public-choice theorist James Buchanan adds the gloss that 'It is not from the benevolence of the bureaucrat that we expect our research grant or our welfare check, but out of his regard to his own, not the public, interest.'[50]

The great insight of public-choice theory is that, to understand how large organizations work, you need to look not just at their shared or official aims, but also at what drives the individuals in them. The purpose of a national ministry of education is to provide a consistent, high-quality and morally sound education; but in explaining day-to-day policy-making you also need to remember that no individual civil servant ever made his career by advocating the closure of programmes run by his ministry, or by halving the annual bid to the Treasury. The CBI too is a large, bureaucratic organization. Its full-time employees are paid to represent members' interests; and, in a society where business and government are increasingly intertwined, that means nurturing links with government and using both formal and personal contacts as a basis for lobbying and exchange of information. But they are not business people themselves. On the contrary: they are individuals making careers, often in the general area (economics, tax law, training) where they work for the CBI.

London today boasts burgeoning ranks of policy entrepreneurs, offering ideas within the interlocking circles of institutes, think tanks, business, labour or professional associations, and government seminars and committees. Those involved have a strong interest in making a name fast – for themselves and for their organization. But there is no particular reason why their opinions and values should precisely reflect those of their organization's members or subscribers, and especially not in areas where there is no reason for the latter to have well-worked-out views in the first place.

It is hard to explain its educational agenda except by seeing the CBI as a large organization with its own life. Those involved have, in many cases, strongly held personal views and an interest in their own careers, and in their organization's general visibility, as well as in particular 'business' issues. But the question remains: Why was the CBI so successful in its *education* entrepreneurship? And here we come full circle to, first, the general global obsession with education and training and, second, the very specific British suspicion of education professionals and their supposed antipathy to sound education and high standards.

In most of Europe and the Far East, where there is no such suspicion, there is less opportunity for 'business' (or, rather, business organizations) to colonize educational policy-making.[51] In Britain, business did not even need to push at an open door: it was flung back with the red carpet laid.

Business's performance once inside, however, was no great triumph. There is nothing in the history of national targets, NVQs or core skills to suggest that business representatives have any clear answers on how to make education 'work' for the economy. Large centralized organizations (like government departments) find it easy to talk to other large organizations which claim to offer a single, national view. But, far from having an inside track on what business wants or needs, national business associations run up against the fact that, on most issues, there *is* no single view. So, while the CBI was promoting NVQs, with loud support from a few member companies, most of its other members were voting with their feet: failing to use NVQs, and often continuing to use traditional qualifications.[52]

There is, however, one education and training issue on which business people *have* had a near-unanimous view. And, while the CBI needs to be understood as a home to individuals making their own careers, it is *also* an organization with a primary purpose: to lobby for business interests. On this issue it seems to have done so quite effectively.

As the first part of this chapter recounted, the CBI's innings as a fount of wisdom on education followed a very different period. In the 1960s and 1970s a major point of contact – and friction – with government concerned the latter's determination to force business to train more, and to train better. The cross-party conviction that the key to economic success was more and more training might well have led to similar demands in the 1980s and 1990s: to new training levies and the return of 'compulsion'. Indeed, on a number of occasions civil servants proposed reintroducing compulsory requirements for companies to train and to spend on training. The CBI, however, consistently and successfully resisted such moves, insisting that they would be counter-productive and wasteful, and that individual companies were best able to judge their training needs.

Look back at Table 4.2, which reproduces different versions of the national training targets developed during the 1990s. In the first version it is not only NVQs that figure large: so too does business activity. In 1991 there were targets for business which included ambitious levels of workforce training and NVQ qualification rates: within five years, all employees were to be in training, with at least half aiming at NVQs. However, look across to 1995 and then to 1998 and an interesting gap appears. While educational targets have been ratcheted upwards, the targets for business have, by 1998, simply vanished.

Overall, the upshot of business – or, rather, business representatives' – involvement in education policy was some additional centralized policies whose impact on education and public-sector training was substantial but largely negative. Business involvement also safeguarded employers from any comparable coercion. Yet, as we have seen throughout the previous chapters, the national consensus emphasizes training as an engine of growth as much as it does formal education. Does this mean that business pressure groups are actively responsible for keeping training levels, and thereby growth and prosperity, significantly below where they should be? Or, was their analysis of company training issues far more perceptive and sensible than their forays into education? Chapter 5 looks at the training controversy, and argues that business people, like other people, should be taken seriously on the topics they know about. Their resistance to 'compulsion', and to spending more on training because governments tell them so, is perfectly well founded. Business people are no more deluded just because they are self-interested than teachers and students are. Why, then, is workplace training in Britain regarded as such an issue?

5   Why worry about training?

We need a step change in workplace learning.
Labour Party manifesto, 2001

The business sector ... has, time and again, neglected disgracefully its training responsibilities.
Baroness Sharp of Guildford (Liberal Democrat peer),
January 2000[1]

The idea that British companies do too little training has been a standard one for the last 130 years. At the 1867 International Exhibition, Lyon Playfair, chemist, MP and civil-service reformer,[2] was so shocked at British manufacturing's poor showing that he sparked off a series of official training inquiries. Thirty years on, and Sir Philip Magnus MP, creator of City & Guilds and founder of London's first technical colleges – from which Imperial College was to grow – bemoaned owners' and managers' belief that technical instruction was of 'very little use to the workmen'.[3] The governmental Committee on Industry and Trade of 1927 reported gloomily that, in industry, 'there is very little demand for staff [who are] technically trained', and that 'so far as manual workers were concerned, training was in decline'.[4] The 1962 White Paper on Industrial Training which heralded the UK's government's first direct intervention in training announced that much training 'is barely adequate and some definitely unsatisfactory'.[5] And, as Figure 5.1

illustrates, during the following decades the consensus held. Indeed, it was strengthened by the conviction that training failures were handicapping companies in an increasingly competitive global economy. Not only was vocational education promoted vigorously, as we saw in Chapter 3. Companies' in-house training of their workforce also became a governmental preoccupation.

The idea that companies do not do enough training seems, at first meeting, rather odd. Presumably, after all, employers wish to run successful and profitable concerns. So, if their workers need training, why wouldn't they train them? British commentators tend to invoke particular idiosyncrasies of British culture and attitudes in explanation. But look carefully at the evidence and such idiosyncrasies are far from self-evident. There *are* circumstances in which too little training might regularly occur – too little in the sense that firms, and therefore the economy as a whole, perform less well than they otherwise would. However, there is nothing about them which makes it obviously likely that the UK will have more of a 'training problem' than any other country.

This chapter looks at whether the factors that affect workplace training are important, one way or the other, for economic growth and productivity. We start with the theory; but to see how *much* of a problem training might be we need to look at some real cases, and real economies. It turns out, as we shall see, that neither America (the economic superstar of the 1990s) nor Germany (with which the UK is constantly compared), nor indeed the UK itself, provides any clear evidence that this country has a major shortfall in workplace training. The question that then follows is whether government policies to boost workplace training are really a sensible use of time or money. And here history suggests the contrary. Recent UK policies in this area, including NVQ-driven targets and the associated franchising debacle, have been misconceived and wasteful. Nor have they done anything to compensate, in a workplace setting, for the vocational-education failures we discussed in Chapter 3. In Britain, at least, it seems that government interventions are likely to do considerably more harm than good.

Figure 5.1 British workplace training: the twentieth-century consensus

'We need more training, . . . we need better training and . . . we have somehow to approach the record of our major competitors.' Lord McCarthy (1990)

'In Britain, in contrast to the Western European countries, training . . . has been an area of . . . failure.' Adrian Campbell (1991)

'The basic problem with . . . training in Britain is that there is too little of it.' Richard Layard, Ken Mayhew and Geoffrey Owen (1994)

'British firms offer a lower quality and quantity of training than their counterparts on the Continent.' David Finegold and David Soskice (1988)

'Our present under-trained . . . working population goes back to the beginning of the Second World War. The overall problem can be traced back to the 19th century. Our antipathy to formal training originates then.' Lord Peston (1990)

'Britain does then have a real widespread and severe skill shortage. The implications are very serious.' John Cassells (1990)

'. . . in order to maintain its competitiveness in the international market place, British business must raise the skills profile of its workforce. Insofar as other countries are already ahead, Britain will need to improve its education and training performance even faster than its competitors.' Training Agency (1989)

Sources: Lords McCarthy and Peston: Hansard, House of Lords Official Report 31 January 1990, debate on a motion on education and training; A. Campbell 1991: 164; Layard, Mayhew & Owen 1994: 11; Finegold & Soskice 1988: 23; Cassells 1990: 11; Training Agency 1989: 76.

Thinking about training

To understand current thinking about training, we need to start with 'human-capital theory', and a body of economic work which has developed over the last forty or so years. Far and away its most influential theorist is the Nobel Prize-winning economist Gary Becker. His 1960s analysis of when workplace training is likely to take place, of who benefits, and of who should pay created a conceptual scheme within which almost all later discussion has taken place. It is, for example, the reference point for much of the recent policy on skills, productivity, competitiveness and 'employability' to emanate from the Treasury, the Department of Trade and Industry, and the Department for Education and Skills.

Becker's work is concerned with anything that increases someone's skills and productivity – their 'human capital' – and not just with workplace training.[6] It is nonetheless his discussion of 'on-the-job training' which has been most influential. He does not define such training very precisely, since he is concerned with any form of learning that takes place on the job, whether formal or informal, and whether involving new skills or the perfecting of old ones. Becker argues – absolutely correctly in my view – that such learning is very important for economic productivity, and also in explaining why more experienced workers generally earn more. Of course, this was hardly a new observation: what *was* new was his formal analysis of what happens.

Becker argued that on-the-job training can be divided conceptually into 'specific' and 'general' components. Specific training is defined as training which is relevant only to a particular company or employer. It makes economic sense for employers to pay for this, just as for new machinery, rent on premises, etc., because they can expect to reap the benefit when they sell the resulting output. However, even where very specific training is involved, it also makes sense for *employees* to contribute to the costs (most obviously by accepting lower wages during training than they would be getting in other jobs). They will receive higher wages once they have acquired the relevant skills, and will be in a good long-term bargaining position vis-à-vis their employer, who needs trained workers who possess those particular skills.[7]

In theory, if rarely in practice, academics, politicians and business people agree that there is no case at all for public subsidy of this sort of training. For example, if a company develops a new way to draught-proof windows, and trains people to fit it, or an insurance company launches a new policy, and sets aside a day to explain it to the sales force, there is no justification for asking the taxpayer for a subsidy. The company (and its workforce) will reap the benefits, so why should anyone else pay?

General training is different. Becker notes that 'general training is useful in many firms besides those providing it; for example, a machinist trained in the army finds his skills of value in steel and aircraft firms and a doctor trained (interned) at one hospital finds his skills useful at other hospitals'.[8] Such general skills are actually the more common type: the number which are valuable to just a single employer are pretty limited. But the more general the skills, the less incentive there is for the employer to pay. Take, for example, Becker's machinist (we'll come back to his doctor later), or an employee who is learning accountancy or desktop-publishing skills, or Spanish or German. Suppose the firm pays for the training, and the employee then promptly leaves and gets a higher salary elsewhere as a result. His or her ex-employer is going to feel like a patsy who has been doing a favour to any and every other employer in the land.

Becker's argument is that completely general training, which is useful to all employers, should in principle be paid for by the employees (*not* the taxpayer). The person who gains the skills is the one who reaps the benefits, becoming more productive and earning higher wages. This is true whether or not trained workers go off to better and higher-paid jobs elsewhere, or stay and get higher wages from the firm that trained them, to whom they are now worth more and which therefore wants to keep them. If the training takes place within a firm, then the obvious way for the employee to 'pay' is by accepting lower wages while the training is going on. This argument is what justifies low wage rates for apprentices – and indeed, in the past, families often paid for apprenticeships with a direct up-front payment as well as accepting an indentured period of very low or no wages at all for the young person concerned.

So far, so good: Becker provides a way of thinking about the full range of on-the-job learning, and how it contributes both to individuals' 'capital' and to firms' productivity. And the common-sense proposition that learning and training pay is also borne out by the literature. Workers who receive training seem – by and large – to be paid more (though not always, or by very much). Similarly, companies which train are – again by and large – likely to be ones which also grow and profit.[9] But what has all this to do with governments? As Becker sees it, there is no need for training to involve taxpayers' money, let alone the creation of a vast government bureaucracy. Yet, in almost every country in the world, governments and public funds are more or less involved with the provision of workplace training and with trying to increase its frequency. Is this just a vast, unnecessary combination of subsidizing and interfering with what firms do? Or was Becker missing something?

Ever since Becker's analysis was published, academic economists have busied themselves trying to find new reasons why the argument is internally flawed, or only applies in special cases, or is otherwise inadequate. Their most powerful point is one mentioned above, as well as by just about every employer one talks to – namely that very *little* training is relevant to just one particular firm. Any trained worker, even one with quite specific skills, is likely to be attractive to other employers in the same sector, who may therefore poach him, leaving his old firm short of skills and feeling in all likelihood out of pocket.[10]

Talk to any firm with apprentices and an active training programme, and it won't be long before its own personal poaching experiences come up. Nor is it only other *companies* that are blamed. In February 2000, Yorkshire electronics companies could be found furiously criticizing their local regional development agency for offering sweeteners to tempt Korean companies into Yorkshire. 'I object to inward investors being financed by taxpayers' money to go into competition with us,' complained the chairman of Filtronic plc, whose own skill needs have led him to provide direct support for a Leeds University Ph.D. programme. Pace Micro's chief executive agreed: 'We have invested heavily in developing skills [and] sponsoring students . . . it seems we are going to allow inward investors to siphon off all this hard work. It is completely wrong.'[11]

Of course, the stories one hears are always from the good guys, who train notwithstanding. No employer ever admits to being a bad guy in this scenario. Academics and civil servants, on the other hand, tend to doubt whether all firms are public-spirited. Instead, they suspect that, in the absence of government action, *market failure* will ensue. In other words, less training will take place than should, from an economic point of view. Employers will hold back from training, because they think their trained workers will be poached, and will instead put time and effort into trying to lure away ready-trained workers from elsewhere in the system. Since there are not likely to be many of these (because every other employer is behaving in the same way), the result will be general inefficiency and a 'low-skills' approach to production across the sector.

A different problem arises when employees are effectively tied to their current employer. This may be just because of the difficulty of finding a new job, and then probably having to move house to take it, or because they work in an occupation where only one employer exists. Take Becker's second example of someone with general skills: a doctor. British doctors (in common with most of the world's teachers) are effectively state employees. Their salaries are what the state decides to give them, and they are correspondingly less willing, likely and able to contribute to their own training costs than are their American counterparts, who can charge much higher fees.[12] Another labour-market 'imperfection' which may have similar effects, and has attracted a lot of attention in the UK, is the level of apprentice and youth wages. If these have been negotiated at very high levels, because unions fear that apprentices are being used to undercut jobs and adult wages, employers may cut back dramatically on training – coping in the short term, but storing up economic trouble for the future.[13]

All these arguments are rehearsed regularly by people arguing that less workplace training takes place than is 'optimal' – by which they mean that, with more training (and more skills) the economy could grow faster, even if nothing else changed. In 2001 a major (pre-election) ministerial speech on 'The Role of the DfEE in the Economy' stated the standard argument perfectly. 'The government should intervene where the levels and types of training produced by the free market will be sub-optimal,' it argued. 'Left to their own devices firms and individuals will not engage in an optimum amount of training.' Consequently, we have a clear 'economic rationale for government intervention'.[14]

But, before accepting that there is, in the same document's words, 'systematic under-investment in training', and that all governments therefore need to involve themselves, fast, two more questions need asking. First, is the problem actually a terribly important one? Even if, for theoretical reasons, we suspect that 'too little' training is going on, does the empirical evidence suggest that it is far too little, and that increasing it is a serious priority? Second, and even more important, is there anything that *can* usefully be done? Does history, or the experience of other countries, encourage the belief that government action might actually work? Or is this a case where the cure more often than not turns out to be as bad as the disease?

How much training is enough?

Many Western governments consider that workplace training needs taking in hand; but, as we saw above, the British believe that their problem is a particularly bad one. During the relative economic decline and crises of the 1960s, 1970s and early 1980s, people were, not surprisingly, looking desperately for explanations of failure. However, as we have seen, this particular preoccupation goes much further back, with commentators being convinced of UK companies' inadequacy for almost a century and a half.

One obvious way to decide whether your country trains too little is to look at other countries as well: more specifically, to look at some which are an undoubted economic success. At the beginning of the twenty-first century, where better to start than the United States?

Looking to America for training advice is not, in fact, a common practice. Although its general influence on UK policy is enormous, in education and (by extension) training the United States is often dismissed as the one developed country whose pupils can be relied on to do even worse in international comparisons than the British. It is the home of the despised multiple-choice test, and the butt – at least until our own recent university explosion – of jokes about degrees in hamburger-flipping and creationist studies.

Moreover, as Chapter 2 described, Americans themselves maintain a level of anxiety about their education which can make the British seem positively apathetic. For example, in 1982 the US federal government created a National Commission on Excellence in Education, because of 'the widespread public perception that something is seriously remiss in our educational system'. The Commission agreed. 'Our Nation is at risk,' it concluded. The 'educational foundations of our society are presently being eroded by a rising tide of mediocrity that threatens our very future as a Nation and a people. . .If an unfriendly foreign power had attempted to impose on America the mediocre educational performance that exists today, we might well have viewed it as an act of war.'[15]

Later governments and policy-makers have concurred. The Clinton administration's flagship legislation, the Goals 2000: Educate America Act, set up a National Education Goals Panel and a list of goals designed to promote 'coherent, nationwide, systemic education reform'. There needed to be 'valid and reliable mechanisms for . . . building a broad national consensus on American education reform', 'high-quality, internationally competitive content and student performance standards', 'certification of opportunity-to-learn standards', new 'high quality assessment measures', 'occupational skill standards', comprehensive school-improvement plans in all localities, and moves to make 'every major American business . . . involved in strengthening the connection between education and work'.[16] To which the response becomes, 'If you're so dumb, how come you got so rich?'

During the 1990s the American economy enjoyed a period of extraordinary growth and innovation. Both GDP per worker *and* GDP per hour worked are comfortably higher than in any other of the major industrial economies, and are combined with some of the highest average employment rates in the developed world, achieved through rapid job creation at a time of record immigration. Nor is it just the basic economic statistics that impress. Levels of productivity growth[17] surged in the 1990s after fifteen years of falling well below those of Japan and the main European economies,[18] and currently stand more than 40 per cent higher than in the UK.[19] Even more impressive is the way in which American firms have reasserted their position as world leaders in innovation and development. The period of extraordinary growth halted in 2001 with the belated deflation of a classic stock-market bubble centred on Internet stocks. However, regardless of how severe the eventual downturn becomes, the growth, innovation and jobs created by American companies in the 1990s were a real and major achievement – and one that was very largely the creation of the US-born and the US-educated. It is not just a case of Intel, Sun, Cisco, Microsoft and other high-tech West Coast creations. US pharmaceuticals companies, for example, now dominate that sector; they include all three of the world's largest such companies, instead of just one as in 1981, and all three boast market shares far higher than any companies in the sector did two decades back. Similarly, the huge accountancy and audit firms which now boast global networks, such as Price Waterhouse Cooper, or Ernst & Young, are American creations.

How did America do it? As we saw in Chapter 2, it wasn't by having the highest classroom maths scores. And it wasn't by direct government intervention in pursuit of a high-skills workplace either. To an overseas onlooker, one of the striking features of the US scene is the lack of support for government training subsidies, either from policy groups or from business organizations themselves. American government (federal, state and local) certainly intervenes in the market in a thousand obvious and not so obvious ways, but company training is not one of them. Whatever fuelled the acceleration of American productivity and growth, it was neither huge employer-funded workplace training systems nor government policies to counteract market failure in training.[20]

American companies do train, of course, both in-house and externally. Among adults with a job (which in the contemporary USA is almost everyone), over half take some sort of formal education course in a given year, typically in a community college; and over half of those – i.e. more than a quarter of the workforce – are being partly or wholly sponsored by their companies. Equally, new workers entering a company – whether it is a brokerage house or bank, a retail company or hotel, or a huge automobile plant – will receive some sort of organized training, just as they do anywhere in the world. But apprenticeship is virtually non-existent, and there is nothing approaching the structured-training culture of Germany, or the centralized national systems of vocational awards which exist in France and half-exist in the UK.

The absence of a centralized system for promoting training tends to horrify activist observers. In some cases we get the absurdity of the USA being described as a 'low-skills' economy, doomed by the absence of 'skill-formation' policies to the sort of 'low-skills' equilibrium that Finegold and Soskice diagnosed in the UK.[21] And an absurdity is what it is. Of course, the USA has many low-skill jobs. (That is one reason why it also has far lower unemployment than Europe.) But the growth of the last decade has meant that *more* of the workforce is now in 'good', middle-class and skilled employment than ever before.[22]

Back in 1984, as we saw in Chapter 3, the UK's National Economic Development Office and the Manpower Services Commission published their influential report on *Competence and Competition* (see above, p. 69) which compared the UK's training and education system with the systems of its three most economically successful competitors. The three were Japan, Germany and the United States – chosen for their shared 'effective response to changing markets and a rapidly changing economic environment', and because they all see 'education and work competence as a key to their economic success'.[23]

The writers praised the United States for its enormously high rates of adult participation in 'work-related education and training', and Japan for a 'broad based education . . . in harmony with the labour market' and an enormous volume of flexible and informal on-the-job training. In the end, though, and predictably, it was the German model which won the authors' and the policy-makers' hearts. The 1980s generation of British policy-makers and politicians was no different from its predecessors since the mid-nineteenth century in its preoccupation with German training and the links between German industry and education.[24] Hence the attempt to emulate German approaches that culminated in the ambitious and now forgotten YTS scheme for young people.

What is it about the German system that invites such admiration? For, while the British have been preoccupied with Germany's approach for much the longest, we are certainly not alone. In recent decades the American, Korean and French governments have all seen it as an inspiration to emulate.[25] Does German practice tell us something useful about how much workplace training people ought to have in a highly productive economy, or, for that matter, about the role that govern-ments should play in securing such training?

Because the German system has been so influential, and is seen as so exemplary, I have described it in some detail in an appendix to this chapter. That appendix describes the key features of a system which is often misunderstood outside Germany; but readers who are mostly interested in the general arguments about training can skip over it with a clear conscience. However, there are three key points to emphasize. First, when people talk about the German system they are more or less invariably referring to Germany's *apprenticeship* system – a formal system of initial training for young people which is only a very small part of what Becker was referring to. Second, this is only to a very limited degree a governmental system at all. And, third, a major reason why training analysts get so excited by the German model is precisely this lack of governmental contribution. German employers seem to spend large amounts of money on apprenticeship in spite of the possibility that their workers will get poached. In other words, they seem to be 'successfully correcting the market's inherent tendency to lead to under-investment in workforce skills'.[26]

Around two-thirds of a given cohort of German young people still go through an apprenticeship, although increasing numbers combine this with higher education in the universities or polytechnics. This means that they spend, on average, three years with an employer, working and studying for very low wages. At the end, almost all achieve skilled-worker status, awarded on the basis of examinations by the local Chamber of Commerce. Some of their time is spent working under the supervision of older skilled workers, but all apprentices must also continue their general education, in publicly funded schools: hence the use of the term *Dual* to describe the system. Government spends directly only on the general-education component of an apprentice's life. Otherwise the system is genuinely both funded and run at local level, by the employers, by companies' works councils and by the Chambers of Commerce, but *not* by public officials.

German apprenticeship is impressively well organized and good, highly unusual,[27] and also very expensive. So why isn't there wholesale poaching, followed by wholesale withdrawal by employers? Why, for that matter, are so many young Germans willing to devote three years, at low wages, training for what often seems too specific a trade for a fluid modern economy?

The system works quite differently for small and large companies.

While even the small firms have to follow a very detailed training programme, they can also be quite informal and fit the workplace learning into the slow parts of the day or year.[28] Many small employers therefore make a net profit over the length of the apprenticeship as a whole, so their participation is fairly easy to understand.[29] For larger companies, however, the net cost is substantial. Many use apprenticeship to select good, life-time workers, and many probably recoup their costs during the early years of a young worker's life, while he or she is still receiving relatively low wages. But apprentices *don't* all stay, or want to stay, with their training company; and the large companies spend a very great deal on training facilities.[30]

The critical factors in keeping things afloat are therefore probably first and foremost the employer associations and the Chambers of Commerce, and, second, the power and importance of the German unions. German Chambers and employer associations have a formal role in regulating entry into trades which is enshrined in law: they are not purely voluntary, in the fashion of their UK (and US) counterparts. Nonetheless, they are valued and also trusted *because* they are business-controlled. And one of the things in which companies have confidence is that other companies will, like them, continue to maintain the training system – because of informal pressures, and through the Chambers' quite substantial arsenal of incentives and rewards. (When the German subsidiary of a big US manufacturer announced its intention of baling out of the Dual System, it took a matter of weeks to bring its management to heel.) The unions are also directly involved because the legally constituted works councils play a role in running the system, and they have a strong incentive to maintain high-quality, high-cost provision. Apprenticeship offers a very thorough training, but also a *Beruf* – a vocation, an identity. The training helps maintain skills, status and pay for workers who have completed it, and the identity tends to include union membership as part of the package.[31]

This institutional framework explains company involvement; but it is also something which evolved gradually, and without any grand plan to create an all-embracing national training system. But what about the apprentices themselves? Why are young Germans willing to be poorly paid apprentices, generation after generation? British analysts frequently point to high apprenticeship wages as a factor in the decline of apprenticeship numbers and of high-quality workplace training in the UK. Less often considered is why Germany gets away with paying so little. Imagine yourself as a German eighteen-year-old, with a fair grasp of local reality. It is obvious why you might want an apprenticeship in a high-tech fast-growing company. But a well-known wisecrack in Germany is that the largest employer of bakers is the BMW assembly line. So why take a bakery apprenticeship? Why not go straight for the pay packet?[32]

If you were convinced by my earlier arguments about why rational teenagers shun vocational schools, you can probably guess the answer to this one too. Rational German eighteen-year-olds don't go straight into the labour market because German employers – rationally or otherwise – figure that anyone who does that isn't worth hiring. So there is a self-reinforcing cycle: you go on to an apprenticeship because not to do so is to label yourself as incompetent and unreliable. It doesn't follow that you wouldn't much rather be at university, or in a bank, than apprenticed to a baker.

So what does all this tell us about the importance of workplace training for economic growth? First of all, the Dual System certainly produces a very highly skilled industrial workforce. Bob Bischof, a German who is a long-term resident in Britain, executive chairman of a marketing company (McIntyre & King) and chairman of an engineering company (Boss Group), argues for its continued importance, noting bitterly that 'I know what it means to run British companies with workers who have "on the job training" instead of proper apprenticeships.'[33] Equally, the skilled labour force produced by this system certainly contributed to post-war German growth and prosperity – albeit with a host of other factors, including, in particular, the international competitiveness forced on German companies when the Erhard reforms of the 1950s broke up the old cartels.

Second, though, and critically, the system is about high-quality initial training for the young. Much of the content of a three-year apprenticeship isn't about specific vocational skills at all, or even about instilling the sort of timekeeping, customer-service and general work habits which employers slaver over. It is about initial general education. So the system doesn't have much to do with the bulk of workplace activity and learning. All other levels of German workplace training, during people's forty-odd years of post-apprenticeship employment, remain largely unregulated and unrecorded, dependent on individual workers' and firms' willingness to fund and undertake them – similar, indeed, to those of many other countries, and presumably just as susceptible to 'market failure'.

The third point is that, while the Dual System involves a huge number of different apprenticeships and sectors, one cannot argue from this that other countries are obviously under-training at the initial level. The industries best suited to apprenticeships – engineering and machine tools, cars and shipbuilding, plus the traditional 'crafts' – are a small part, and a shrinking one, of any modern economy. In fact Germany is unusual in still having a relatively big manufacturing system, which demands large numbers of highly skilled workers with specific vocational skills. The rest of the world can usefully enjoy (and pay for) German machinery: it needn't, and anyway can't, imitate Germany's industrial structure. Look at the rest of the German economy and the 'optimality' of so many long-term apprenticeships isn't so obvious – or at least not the economic optimality. As a number of people have pointed out, it is not obvious that the Dual System produces a workforce which overall is hugely more productive than the workforces of countries with very different systems.[34] On the contrary: the pay gap between skilled manual and managerial/professional workers seems to be almost identical in Germany and the USA. It seems just as plausible to argue that a system which takes three years to train a shop assistant is doing too *much* training, and that a lot of what goes on is a deadweight cost for the economy, even though it has major social benefits in giving an identity to the young people involved.[35]

Two of the world's economic stars: two hugely different approaches to workplace training. Neither the USA nor Germany seems to offer any general lessons about whether 'market failure' in this area is a serious problem for economies, let alone any obvious pointers for advocates of more training elsewhere. At the same time, everyone in the UK does seem to agree that workplace training is something that Britain does badly.[36] So, if we can't find a simple blueprint for how things ought to be done, can we at least be clear that in the UK more training is badly needed?

UK workplace training: market failure found at last?

We all know that too little workplace training goes on in Britain, because we have been told it so often and for so long. As we saw at the start of this chapter, politicians and educators have been criticizing British employers' attitudes to training for almost a century and a half.[37] Recently, the attacks have been redoubled with particular reference to the influential argument that countries can get stuck in 'a low-skills equilibrium, in which the majority of enterprises staffed by poorly trained managers and workers produce low-quality goods and services'.[38] It is an *equilibrium* because it is self-reinforcing: companies concentrate on products with low skill requirements, and so generate neither a workforce which could operate in high-skill, high-quality environments nor any incentive for people to acquire (and be paid for) high skills. High skill levels, and firms operating with high quality thresholds, generate a quite different self-reinforcing equilibrium.[39] Britain, in this analysis, is the low-skills economy par excellence.

But how well do the facts about workplace in-company training bear this out? Is there evidence of under-training serious enough to provide, in the then Secretary of State's words in early 2001, an 'economic rationale for government intervention'?[40] Can we find clear links between training practices and economic failure and decline? And can we identify where firms should be forced to act?

It turns out, first, that Britain does not obviously train at below-average levels at all. On the contrary. Looking at the period since 1985 shows

- *first*, that in the mid to late 1990s Britain's training levels were well above the OECD average (see Table 5.1);[41]
- *second*, that since 1985 there has been a marked increase in the numbers of UK employees who report participating in formal training.

Table 5.1 *Percentage of adults aged twenty-five to sixty-four participating in job-related training during 1994–5*

Australia	30
Belgium (Flemish)	14
Canada	30
Ireland	16
Netherlands	24
New Zealand	38
Switzerland (French and German)	27
UK	40
USA	38

Source: International Adult Literacy Survey

Recent figures show that, in the autumn of 1999, 15 per cent of the UK workforce reported receiving job-related training during the last month, compared to less than 9 per cent in 1985.[42] Over a quarter – 28 per cent – of UK employees stated that they had received formal employer-provided training in the thirteen weeks before they were surveyed; 39 per cent had done so in the year leading up to interview. Among firms employing five or more people, the majority were providing formal off-the-job training in any given year (though not necessarily to all employees)[43] – and of course none of this includes the unrecorded on-the-job training that also increases 'human capital'.

Perhaps, however, the problem is the *sort* of training that occurs. After all, the reason why commentators have, for so many decades, bemoaned UK companies' training record is the belief that training raises productivity. If we look in more detail at what is going on, will we find that the problem is not a simple question of quantity, but that too little of the right sort of training is being done?

What is this training business?

In fact what you find when you dig around a bit is that we know extraordinarily little about what 'training' actually consists of, let alone whether it is the wrong sort. If we leave aside traditional apprenticeships and look at workplace training for the adult workforce in the industrialized world, it is all very murky. Discussions of training are almost always illustrated with shots from manufacturing industry, with photogenic people doing things with machines, or possibly computers. But we have no idea how much of our and other countries' 'training' bears any resemblance to this at all.

We do know about typical British training *patterns*: namely some reasonably intensive and sometimes moderately lengthy induction training at the start of a new job, followed by occasional short training sessions. In 1999, those UK employees who had received formal (off-the-job) training from their employer in the last three months had done so for an average of eight and a half days.[44] Labour Force Survey data indicate that 44 per cent of employer-funded training lasts for less than one week. This suggests a marked drop in average length since 1985, when only 26 per cent of training courses were that short.[45] At the same time, a substantial amount of training lasts much longer: the same recent Labour Force Survey data show that 17 per cent of training lasts from six months to three years, and 28 per cent lasts either more than three years or is 'ongoing'. Long-lasting training includes apprenticeship and training leading to initial professional qualifications, such as banking and accountancy qualifications;[46] but we don't know how much of what is reported belongs to one or other of these categories, or what other types of training are included.

And that more or less sums it up. We simply don't know what most training involves: how much of it, for example, is driven by legal requirements – general health and safety, or requirements for particular occupations to undergo regular training and updating (as, for example, GPs, financial advisers and teachers all do). We don't know what is covered; what people learn; how it relates to the details of their jobs. And when it comes to informal learning at work we simply haven't a clue.[47]

What we do know is that formal training is not randomly distributed.[48] Not only in Britain, but all over the world, the highly educated and those in professional or technical jobs are far more likely to receive such training than people with lower-level qualifications or in manual jobs.[49] Grouping people by their wages also shows stark contrasts. Over a five-year period, 80 per cent of those in the highest UK wage quintile, but only 40 per cent of those in the lowest, report that they have received workplace training.[50] Training is also very often directly associated with promotion and pay rises for the trained. For example, recent British data show that 70 per cent of men and women who have been promoted have also received employer-provided training in their current job, compared with 46 per cent of men and 31 per cent of women who have not.[51]

It is these patterns which convince so many people that 'training pays', and that the way to upgrade the productivity *and* incomes of the low-paid is to give them the same training opportunities as high-income workers receive. After all, if one group, in one firm, is earning so much more after training, why not repeat the trick in another firm down the road? Train the workers, upgrade their skills, the firm will do better, and everyone will earn a lot more.

But you can't make this simple jump – even less, in fact, with training than with the educational qualifications we discussed in Chapter 2.

First of all, a lot of 'training' doesn't involve discrete free-standing skills which can get added to any employee's repertoire. Instead, it involves and continues from what was learned in full-time education. Accountancy and accountancy-technician training, a huge amount of which is part-time and employer-sponsored, is of this type. Doctors' salaries advance upwards alongside their exposure to regular, short updating courses; but those courses would not be much use to anyone else. So in many cases prior education and training are inextricably entwined – not because employers are prejudiced, or even because the more educated may be quicker and more efficient to train,[52] but because the content of one may depend directly on what was learned in the other.

What little we know about training practices suggests another scenario as well. Training is more frequent for those higher up the hierarchy;

but perhaps much of it *follows* from success at work, rather than causing it. It may not be about adding skills with a general economic pay-off but rather something that comes with certain jobs. For example, some research I have been doing recently shows that interviewing skills are a very common topic of in-company training for managers.[53] Companies take these courses very seriously, partly because they want managers to make effective hiring decisions, but mostly because they are terrified of ending up before an employment tribunal. Attending such courses is part and parcel of promotion, and so is very likely to be associated with success and higher pay; but it is training that tags along with a successful career, rather than training that leads to one.

If a significant amount of training follows from, rather than causes, people's career success, this would certainly explain some puzzling findings. Remember that a major reason to expect systematic under-spending on training is fear of poaching. Employers supposedly train less for fear that trained employees will be snapped up (for higher wages) by other companies which didn't incur the training costs. Yet in practice individuals who receive training are *less* likely to move than those who do not, and the pay-off to training appears, on the whole, to be higher when you *stay* with the employer who provided it.[54] (One clearly documented exception to this is foreign-language training, especially since the rise of English as a world language.[55] Employers who pay for their employees to do intensive language learning may well find them moving on to better-paid jobs elsewhere.)

If a lot of formal company training isn't about providing new general skills, but about legal requirements, or procedures attendant on a job for which the trainee is already prepared, these findings make much better sense. They may also help explain why company-based training and training paid for by employers consistently appear to have much more impact on future earnings than training which people undertake for themselves. This is true even when formal qualifications are involved. For example, a vocational qualification obtained on an employer-provided course seems to be worth almost twice what it would be when obtained off the job, without any employer involvement.[56]

So far, nothing in the evidence suggests a major shortfall in the training of adult British workers – either in absolute terms or compared to other countries. And yet, not only are many people convinced otherwise, they also believe that more training could have a major impact on economic growth. From this perspective, raising workforce skills 'improves organisation performance through increasing productivity, increasing employee commitment, enhancing adaptability to organisational and technological change; encouraging process and product development; improving relations with suppliers and customers; improving quality and stimulating moves to high value added goods'.[57] David Blunkett, as Britain's Secretary of State for Education, was convinced that 'Spending [on training] benefits both firms and their workers . . . [given that], other things being equal, even short periods of training appear to raise people's wages by about 5% over quite long periods of time.'[58] If this is indeed the case, and UK employers are systematically failing to realize it, then perhaps the government does need to intervene; and never mind that other countries are currently just as bad as we are.

What makes people convinced that training offers so much? Partly it is that the higher paid are presumably more productive, and definitely more trained. However, as I have just argued, moving from this statistical link to a causal relationship leaves one on pretty shaky ground. There are also studies that suggest that the fastest-growing firms train more.[59] The trouble here is that the training may be just as much a result of success as its cause. Firms that expand, innovate and change will certainly be training old and new hires: the reverse scenario doesn't obviously follow. Finally, a tiny number of studies have actually looked in detail at people's wages before and after training. Some of these (*but by no means all*) come up with huge apparent returns to in-company training, with average wage gains as high as 20 per cent.[60] Surely we should take these seriously?

Actually, I think one should be pretty sceptical – certainly about seeing these returns as reflecting increases in substantive skills, and, therefore, general productivity. Remember, for a start, how short most training courses are. If such tiny segments of learning are really equipping people for the high-skills, high-productivity economy we all crave, they must be the most efficient teaching and learning experiences in history.[61]

The more closely one looks at the data, the harder it is to see them as justifying wholesale expansion of training as a route to growth. In one of the very few (and therefore constantly quoted) research studies with information on the types of training that people were given, it turns out that 'technical' training is associated with *far* lower wage gains than 'economic/administrative' training.[62] The Dutch researcher who examined the results leaps from this to arguing that 'participants in technical training would have received a larger wage gain if they had participated in economic-administrative training'.[63] However, this isn't really obvious at all. If you see training as tied up with career promotions, or with issues like company-wide restructuring, or government regulation, the difference in apparent pay-offs looks less odd. But not only does it not follow that everyone would have been better off if the companies had scrapped the technical training and given everyone administrative training instead. It also doesn't look like much of an advertisement for training as the proverbial route to a high-skills manufacturing economy, German or Silicon Valley style.

In spite of such limited evidence, many people continue to believe that, because we can mount a case, from first principles, for market failure existing somewhere, it follows that governments need to get involved. That brings us to my second question. Even supposing there *is* major under-investment in training, is there any reason to suppose that governments can do anything useful about it?

Can governments improve on the market?

In the very late 1990s, some colleagues and I studied education and training developments across the European Union.[64] In doing so, we found a striking increase in the degree to which adults were being offered vocational training rather than general-education courses, because of government policies promoted through coercion, subsidies or both. The motives were the same as those fuelling recent UK policy: worries about growth and productivity, a belief in courses tailored directly to economic 'needs', and, evidently, a belief that governments could indeed improve on what individuals and firms would provide if left to themselves.

Perhaps some governments, somewhere, are indeed doing a superb job in improving training (albeit in the absence of any clear information on what training, where, will pay). However, the experience of recent years certainly gives one little faith in British governments' ability to fine-tune workplace training, and so achieve those desired spillovers into a high-skill equilibrium. In evidence, let us first return briefly to NVQs.

We saw in Chapter 3 how NVQs were expected to revolutionize young people's choices, and how utterly they failed. However, they were also designed to transform the whole nature of workplace training following the UK's short-lived experiment with industrial training boards.[65] The idea was that, because NVQs were so directly relevant to industrial needs, workers would have strong incentives to obtain them, and employers would find them an excellent way to organize and improve their own in-house training. The latter would become more effective and increase productivity, more and more companies would follow suit, and a virtuous circle of high-quality training would develop.

In the early days, NVQs were greeted with real enthusiasm by many employers, not just by the CBI. One of the enduring problems with formal vocational qualifications everywhere in the world is that they very quickly become both out of date and bogged down in academic paperwork.[66] The promise of new 'competence-based' awards, with close and immediate links with 'real' work, seemed hugely appealing. While it was the government that poured money into the development of occupational standards and NVQs, many businesses and sectors also contributed resources on a substantial scale. Only as the original ideas hardened into a rigid bureaucratic orthodoxy, generating even more paper than ever before, did the reaction set in.

In Chapter 3 I criticized NVQs as far too narrow and specific a preparation for young people entering a fluid and changing labour market. But their approach was (and is) also quite at odds with company practice. NVQs basically involve ticking off a very large number of separate activities, with assessors confirming that the employee (or trainee) has done the requisite tasks. However, even in larger firms, the common pattern is one of frequent job changes and job redefinition: as employees move, so the match between their work and a particular

NVQ evaporates. In small companies, often with a niche specialization, job changes simply compound the fact that employees don't *do* most of what a particular NVQ demands.[67]

Because the government was so keen to promote workplace training, companies were both exhorted and subsidized to adopt NVQs. Money was funnelled through the now defunct Training and Enterprise Councils, and by the mid to late 1990s the vast majority of employers had certainly heard of NVQs. However, only 14 per cent were offering them to 'one or more' of their employees,[68] and at then current take-up rates and trends it would have taken until 2091 to achieve the original national target of half the workforce working for an NVQ.[69] Since then, with falling numbers of NVQ registrations, the date has receded yet further.

Of course, NVQs did 'work' in some cases. In a few industries where there were a few dominant companies (like the water industry), awards fitted fairly tightly into companies' own training policies; and as we saw earlier, these companies were willing to back the CBI's line on NVQs. In the public services, especially the care industry, NVQs now also provide a vehicle for new government regulations and quality-assurance requirements. But revolutionize the quantity, quality and productivity of training? Hardly.[70]

If this story says little for governments as training advisers, the policy which came hard on its heels says even less. The franchising saga was partly a result of governmental panic over the lack of NVQ take-up, but it also reflected a more general concern that employers were sponsoring fewer part-time FE courses for their employees than in the past. It certainly channelled government funding into training departments up and down the country; but it also led to waste, fraud and large-scale bankruptcies that devastated many people's lives.

The history of franchising was short and exciting. It began in 1994, when the Further Education Funding Council (FEFC) introduced new rules allowing colleges to enrol, and be funded for, people who were trained completely outside the college. An employee who never left the employer's premises could become a 'student', for funding purposes, of a college which might be 5, 50 or 250 miles away. By registering for a franchised course leading to a qualification, that student entitled both his employer and the college to receive public funds: the employer for the training (funnelled through the college), and the college for the cost of assessing, 'verifying' and processing the qualification. (The funding regime made NVQs by far the most attractive option for franchisers, so that is what they normally were.)

The only surprising thing about the result is that anyone was surprised. Franchising exploded. While many colleges were cautious, some saw it as an opportunity for meteoric, profitable expansion. They signed up students by the thousand – or, rather, they signed up the employers and the students came too. Companies involved in franchising included huge firms such as Tesco, Sainsbury's and Railtrack, and the vast brewery group Scottish & Newcastle. While there were certainly a few cases of outright fraud, the real question is how far franchising simply provided money for activities that firms would have undertaken anyway. 'To a considerable extent' is almost certainly the answer; but in the short term nobody minded – and the NVQ count rose.

The most ambitious college of all, Halton, claimed that it was on track to be the largest college in England on the basis of franchising. By 1996 it had 28,000 students on franchising arrangements, and almost half its income was bypassing its bricks-and-mortar home base. Another franchising leader was Bilston, which ran a conference for other colleges on 'How to Increase Your Units' (the funding mechanism), and managed to double its own; in 1996/7 it had a bid for extra units, based on projected demand, equivalent to the whole budget of the City of Liverpool Community College (which covers all of Liverpool).[71] While many colleges were involved at some level, 58 per cent of franchising was run by 7 per cent of colleges – and dominated by four or five 'entrepreneurs' who also showed a pathological faith in the stability of government policy.[72]

Cynical observers muttered that the students would be hard put to find their colleges on a map, and noted that, since what was funded was qualifications, colleges were increasing their incomes but barely maintaining their numbers of normal on-site students.[73] However, what finished franchising, curiously enough, was neither the dizzying expansion of the leading colleges nor the diverting of funds from mainstream FE to FTSE-100[74] companies and the training of bar and supermarket staff. It was scuba-diving.

Table 5.2 *Estimated expansion and activity levels of selected 'top' FE franchisers: 1996/7*

| College | Increase in funding allocation from central government compared to the previous year | |
	Increase in £s	Increase as percentage of 1995/6 allocation
Halton	1,978,000	18%
Bilston	1,625,000	13%
Clarendon	1,494,000	12%
Handsworth	1,345,000	11%

Source: Adapted from Gravatt 1997

Fairly early on, both colleges and the sports industry realized that franchising could easily be used to support specialized sports centres offering qualifications in the coaching of particular sports – an area which, perfectly reasonably, has been under the control of sports governing bodies. Sports-qualification awarding bodies tumbled over themselves to get their awards on the list approved for FEFC funding. (At one point, they made up 20 per cent of the total list.)[75] Colleges and sports centres now seized the opportunity offered by franchising. Within a year of the scheme's start, one Cornwall college was franchising 38 scuba-diving centres and bringing in almost £1 million – most, but not all, of it being passed through to the scuba centres.

When news of this bonanza, and the fact that British taxpayers would finance your scuba-diving course, reached the world of backpackers' magazines, franchising's days were numbered. In general, further education funding methods are like the famous Schleswig-Holstein question. Three people understood it: one is dead, one is mad, and the third one has forgotten. Scuba-diving on the taxes, though, is the stuff of a tabloid dream and a spin doctor's nightmare. Rules were tightened, hit teams were sent into the colleges, and franchise claims were disallowed. By 1999 the biggest franchisers were bankrupt: 147 of Halton's 'normal' teaching staff were made redundant because of policies devised by their senior managers, and Bilston College had been formally dissolved and closed, its staff sacked and its students sent elsewhere.

So business may not train optimally – but nothing in recent experience suggests that governments know any better. Nor is it a question of UK governments being uniquely incompetent (instead of, or as well as, our companies). Many other countries have also been convinced of the need to boost training, 'correct market failure' and encourage adults to acquire relevant workplace skills. None of their experiences suggests that governments are actually well placed to fine-tune training expenditures or improve on companies' and organizations' own training decisions. The Koreans, for example, as mentioned earlier, made an effort to create a German-style 'Dual System' by government fiat. It failed. And the USA, in the middle of the economic boom of the 1990s, offers a perfect example of governmental ambition and failure.

In the late 1980s and early 1990s many US reformers became convinced – like the UK commentators quoted earlier – that, without more workplace training, the American economy would be on its knees, failed by its despised education system. A group of writers and researchers, associated with think tanks such as Jobs for the Future and the National Center on Education and the Economy, campaigned for change and had a major role in persuading the Clinton administration to make better workplace training one of its 'goals'. This would be achieved by developing occupational 'skill standards' to structure and improve workplace training, and by promoting and subsidizing apprenticeships for young Americans. The latter were supposedly modelled on what one of this group characterized as the 'highly successful European . . . systems for skill preparation' and the 'high status, earning power, and . . . responsibility' of (all) young Europeans as compared to the 'high unemployment, low status, [and] lack of access to jobs in the primary labor market . . . of most American 16–19 year olds'.[76]

Political campaigning groups such as the Eagle Forum feared that these programmes heralded a 'national industrial policy dictated by government czars'.[77] They have done no such thing. A National Skills

Standard Board laboured to agree occupational standards with industry, unions and business groups; after eight years, and in near-total obscurity, the first set went out for consultation just as Clinton left office, and just four others are in development. There is no national apprenticeship culture either. Expensive federally funded 'school-to-work' programmes have made barely any impact on either education or the labour market. Like their UK and their German counterparts, American teenagers are well aware of what sort of labour market they are entering. Top German firms in the USA, like Siemens, signed up to 'school-for-work' schemes in the hope of attracting the type of young people who clamour for apprenticeships in their home waters. They never got them, because these sorts of young Americans already have multiple opportunities in a labour market which values frequent job changes, an appetite for early entrepreneurship, and a college degree. Youth apprenticeships, coaxed into life by the federal government, seem bound to disappear some time now, along with the tax dollars that sustained them, and leaving not a trace behind.[78]

Conclusion

So where does this leave us? First and foremost, agreeing with the CBI. Workplace training is not a core concern for governments, and their aim should be to stay away from it. Whether organizations be public or private, their training activities are inherently bound up with a host of decisions on other matters and with the whole way in which they plan, hire, promote and innovate. Not surprisingly, attempts to treat training as a bolt-on which can be 'fine-tuned', augmented or even run from outside lead consistently to waste and failure.

Moreover, from the viewpoint of economic growth, companies' training activities aren't really that important. I have argued throughout this chapter that even an unimpeachable theoretical argument for the likelihood of 'market failure' does not mean either that the failure is very serious or that it justifies the cure. Recent history bears this out.

No one, to my knowledge, has yet suggested that the UK's recent economic turnaround has resulted from huge improvements in the quantity and quality of workplace training. What it does suggest is that company training failures cannot, after all, have been a very important drag on growth. Geoffrey Owen, in his fascinating case-by-case analysis of post-war industrial failure and revival, concludes that, except in one case – mechanical engineering – his industry studies 'do not indicate . . . that an inadequate supply of workforce skills was a central element in the industrial failures of the early post-war decades . . . [D]eficiencies in the training system do not appear to have been a major cause of the productivity lag behind Germany and France in the first thirty years after the Second World War, nor did they prevent the productivity catch-up which took place in the 1980s.'[79]

The other lesson of governments' training interventions – in the UK or elsewhere – is the need to understand the local labour market. The most unmitigated failures in public training policy occur when governments, inspired by some other country's apparently efficient approach, attempt to transpose this approach wholesale. The favourite subject of such expensive and abortive transfers has been the German Dual System – an apprenticeship system which grew organically, which is run primarily by the companies themselves, and which, as we have seen, rests on a distinctive and complex network of labour-market institutions. In summarizing the German system, this chapter has also emphasized that it is about initial training – and education – for the young. Adult workplace training in Germany offers the same complicated and fluid picture as elsewhere. And this brings me to my final point.

Providing a high-quality general education for the young is a core duty of modern governments (for economic as well as for other reasons). The importance of this type of education is a major reason why we should be worried about governments' ever growing educational ambitions and activities, for the latter swallow up funds, energies and attention which are all in finite supply.

Although apprenticeship tends to be discussed in the context of workplace training, it is actually much better understood as a form of initial vocational education for the young. Thus German apprenticeship produces high levels of skill and expertise in large part because it includes a lot of very general initial training and education, much of it done off the job. You *can* do all of this within the formal education sector: as we've seen, the USA has no real youth-apprenticeship system, and nor have a number of other highly successful economies, including Japan and Sweden. On the other hand, in many areas learning in a work environment has huge advantages over learning in any full-time education institution. The equipment is state-of-the-art; the people around you are in touch with current market conditions; the environment gives you experience of dealing with multiple demands, and is not subject to the artificial divisions of a timetable and syllabus. Aristotle expressed the value of the practical over the theoretical over 2,000 years ago, when he wrote that absorbing knowledge intellectually is not enough. If you are going to use it, knowledge 'must be worked into the living texture of the mind' through practice and application.[80]

This is the huge benefit that apprenticeship offers: the chance to practise and learn in a real environment. On the other hand, in a modern labour market, apprenticeship is not an obvious way to educate and train large proportions, let alone the whole, of an age cohort. As we saw in Chapter 3, young people's realism about the world explains their rejection of narrow vocational programmes in favour of general education; and is why, even in Germany, smaller proportions enter apprenticeship than in the past, and more and more apprenticeships are linked to higher education. But to say this is quite different from arguing that apprenticeship has no role at all to play anywhere, and that where it exists we should kill it off. It is particularly suited to certain sectors and occupations, with specialized skills that need to be practised in an authentic setting – engineering and the traditional crafts are the obvious examples.[81] And, as Paul Ryan has documented, where it has survived it *can* be strengthened. This has happened recently in a number of countries – notably Ireland and the Netherlands – which have adopted a gradualist approach confined to a limited number of occupations.[82]

As we also saw in Chapter 3, apprenticeship in the UK has proved surprisingly tenacious, but in spite of government policy, not through it. The antagonism to 'time-served' apprenticeships which underlay the 1980s New Training Initiative led to years of neglect and to the promotion, instead, of YTS, NVQs, TECs and a host of other short-lived initiatives. Companies like Rolls-Royce and JCB nevertheless went on offering apprenticeships, because they needed and wanted highly skilled young employees and could see no other way to get them. They found it increasingly necessary to offer a package that included sponsorship through higher education as well; but recruit they nonetheless could, because in the UK a 'good' apprenticeship was still valued by parents who had never learned the new acronyms tumbling through the revolving door of government policies.[83]

Now the latest round of relabellings has brought fashion full circle. Everything, including the lowest-status government training, is to become an 'apprenticeship'.[84] In typical centralist style, current policy envisages apprenticeships spread evenly across the landscape, in proportion to the number of jobs in a sector, and irrespective of different sectors' structure and needs. Despite all the usual rhetoric about high-status vocational routes, the policy is also clearly aimed at lower-, and indeed lowest-, achieving young people. The real risk is that this belated recognition of apprenticeship's currency as a respected term will, in the UK, kill by kindness what has survived years of neglect.

Firms are not social-work agencies, or colleges, or charities. We cannot expect them to redress the inequalities left by schooling through some vast remedial training programme funded at shareholders' expense. If we knew that the training would be hugely beneficial to the individuals who receive it there *might* be an argument for paying companies directly to train their more disadvantaged workers.[85] But not only is that likely to interfere with companies' own productive activities (and invite fraud): it is also the case, as we have seen, that we don't actually know when, or what sort of, workplace training would actually be worthwhile.

As this whole book documents, the philosophy driving modern British education policy is one of education-for-growth. In this context, exhortations to business to take on low-achieving young apprentices for public-spirited reasons provide an ironic subtext. Schools, colleges and universities should make wealth creation their priority; meanwhile, those organizations that are actually in the productive sector should apparently stop putting profit first. But a subtext is all this is. Education policy doesn't really pay much attention to the lowest-achieving young, or to the long-term-unemployed adult: it is far more concerned with the mainstream institutions that are seen as major contributors to wealth and productivity. Up to now, we have been looking at the first set of policies which governments have backed as winners in this context: namely vocational education, business advice on qualifications and the curriculum, and workplace training. None of these, I have argued, has lived or can live up to expectation. In the next chapters we turn to contemporary governments' other economic favourite: a vastly expanded higher-education sector. Are policies here any better conceived? Is the quest for economic growth through university expansion really doing the world's economies any favours? And what is it doing to the UK's, and other countries', universities?

Appendix: German apprenticeship training

As the previous chapters will have made clear, the German training system – or what people think is the German training system – has had an enormous influence on other countries' policy-makers. This appendix, while optional reading in relation to the main argument, descibes the system's key features in some detail.

Apprenticeship training, or the 'Dual System', is the core of employer-based training in Germany, famous, and constantly discussed throughout the industrialized world.[86] It is so called because it combines two separate elements: namely training in companies (most of them private), which is funded by the employer, and vocational and general education delivered in public vocational schools. All German apprentices are involved in both parts of this system.

Around two-thirds of a given cohort of German young people go through an apprenticeship, although increasing numbers combine this with higher education in the universities or polytechnics (with fast-track apprenticeship programmes being developed for this group). Apprentices spend an average of three years with an employer, at the end of which almost all achieve skilled-worker status, awarded on the basis of examinations by the local Chamber of Commerce. Dropout rates are low, as are failure rates in the final examinations. Company-based time is spent partly working under the supervision of older skilled workers who have achieved the demanding *Meister* qualification, allowing them to train apprentices, and partly in workshops, classrooms or laboratories which are in the employer's workplace or sponsored by a group of employers.

The system is very large: in the late 1990s there were about 1.65 million apprentices, each training for one of 350 different occupations. It is also both highly decentralized and highly regulated. Its key characteristics were codified in the Vocational Education Act of 1969, although there has been additional legislation since. Young people and companies can enter into training contracts only for occupations which are recognized and approved, and for which full training ordinances exist. These are extremely detailed, and lay down the precise content of a training programme and the examination requirements.[87] Their development is the responsibility of the federal government, in collaboration, at all points, with the 'social partners' – the employers and unions – while the state governments have responsibility for the vocational schools. The key development and coordinating role in monitoring and updating vocational training falls to the Federal Institute of Vocational Training (BIBB – Bundesinstitut für Berufsbildung), where apprenticeship-based occupations are defined (and redefined) and training ordinances are developed. At this level the system is genuinely tripartite – involving business, unions *and* government.

Implementation of the Dual System is similarly highly regulated, but also strictly local, with government's role confined to the public-education component, funded by the state (*Land*) governments.

A whole literature exists to explain how it is that German employers are willing to support the enormous company-based element – and it needs explaining, because it is very expensive. The critical institutions are first and foremost the employer associations – notably the Chambers (of commerce and industry, crafts, agriculture, and the professions) – and second the unions and the company-based works councils. German Chambers are themselves 'public-law corporations' – unlike, say, the Chambers of Commerce in the UK and USA, which are strictly voluntary affairs. They have clear responsibilities for vocational training in their member companies, including checking company capabilities and running the final examinations. At the same time, they are *employer* associations, not governmental ones. They provide advice and services which are directly valuable to their members, and they are trusted by employers because they are under companies' control.

The central role played by the local Chambers is important in understanding how the Dual System maintains itself. It gives participating employers confidence that other companies will also continue to participate – partly because informal pressure can be exerted through the Chambers and associations, but also because of a variety of quite substantive incentives and rewards that the Chambers can use to keep people on side. German employers thus 'own' the system in a way quite different from the situation in countries such as Britain or France, where business provides 'representatives' on central vocational-training committees which are essentially government-created and government-owned.

The other key players in the German system are the employees, who are involved through company-based works councils, and the unions. The works councils (on which the unions will normally provide the employee members) play a direct role in running apprenticeship within a company, and the unions are guaranteed representation on the Chamber-based organizing committees. Both works councils and national unions are hugely supportive of the system and, within a company, will generally provide strong support for high-quality (and high-expense) provision. Relationships between works councils and managers are usually good at firm level, with most employer–union animus centred on annual national wage-bargaining.[88] Employers' desire to maintain those good relations at firm level provides another strong force in support of the apprenticeship status quo.

Nonetheless, German employers are not obliged to participate in the Dual System. Indeed, a good many of them do not, and pressures from local Chambers and unions are not an adequate explanation of why so many do. One other important factor is the German labour market, which is very different from that of the UK or USA. In both the latter, young workers change jobs very frequently in their early years of employment – and do so whether they are well or poorly qualified. In Germany the pattern is overwhelmingly one of long-term employment: people tend to stay with their employer for a very long time. Firms don't *have* to take on apprentices if they are to have any chance of obtaining good, stable adult employees, because many apprentices do not in fact take their first full jobs with the firms where they train. On the contrary: over half leave as soon as they qualify, and almost three-quarters have moved on within five years. So companies can and do hire the qualified young, whether or not they are involved in training themselves. But it is nonetheless true that for a good number of companies, including the largest and most high-tech firms, apprentices are an important source of lifetime employees. By taking on apprentices, and keeping only some of them, they can cream off the best from a pool of candidates.[89]

It is also important to understand that the system – and the costs it imposes – is quite different for small and large companies. The very low wages paid to German apprentices, and the length of the apprenticeship, mean that many small employers make a net profit over the length of the apprenticeship as a whole. (They also train a disproportionate number of apprentices, as this might lead one to expect.) By the end, the apprentice is making a real contribution. Moreover, while even the small firms have to follow a very detailed training programme, as laid down by the ordinances, and must release the apprentices for substantial periods of formal education and training, it is often quite easy to fit this into the slow parts of the day or year. But these apprenticeships in small companies – and especially the traditional craft ('handwork') ones – are also those with the highest numbers of graduated apprentices not remaining with the company.

For the larger companies, analysts agree that apprenticeship training involves some very substantial real costs. It does so even though fewer apprentices leave – only around half, and from the very largest firms less than a quarter – and many companies are probably able to recoup costs during the early years of a young worker's life, while he or she is still receiving relatively low wages. But, for all that, the net cost is substantial – less in wages than in the major overheads associated with large training workshops, permanent training staff, extra payments to the qualified shop-floor trainers, and lost production. It is not likely that the chance to select good employees, or to recoup costs during the early post-apprenticeship years, outweighs the substantial outlays. Nor is it surprising that, during economic downturns, the supply of training places shrinks and government agencies agonize over whether they can match supply to demand.

Overall, the system seems to be maintained by a range of interlocking incentives and pressures – including those which encourage young

Germans to become poorly paid apprentices, year after year. British analysts frequently point to high apprenticeship wages as a factor in the decline of apprenticeship numbers in the UK; less often asked is why Germany gets away with paying so little. It is obvious why a young German would want to be accepted on to a high-tech apprenticeship in a large and growing company, or for a banking one with the possibility of university and management jobs thereafter. But if, at the end of a craft apprenticeship, you are going to end up on the local assembly line anyway, why not go straight for the pay packet? The answer, of course, is that anyone who doesn't even complete an apprenticeship won't be seen as worth employing in any capacity – added to which, far more jobs in Germany than in the UK are open only to the properly qualified, with the right skilled-worker certificate. Equally, young Germans and their parents maintain a high respect for the system: acquiring the identity associated with having a *Beruf*, a vocation, is an important component of becoming an adult.

Starry-eyed foreigners talk a great deal of nonsense about the German training system. Many people believe that German parents are indifferent to whether their children enter apprenticeships or go to university – which is not true – or that one result of the system is that German skilled workers enjoy relatively greater economic benefits than their counterparts elsewhere – which is also not true. The country as a whole (and therefore its citizens, including its skilled workers) may benefit from its training investment. German apprenticeships are very different from the highly specific task-based training programmes associated with, for example, English NVQs. Hence a young ex-baker or former shop assistant has spent two days a week in continued general education, as well as learning how to plait dough or operate a credit-card machine. But the average earnings *gap* between those with vocational and those with academic qualifications is pretty much identical to that in the USA or the UK.[90]

For all its highly organized and regulated current state, the Dual System was far less a product of deliberate government strategy (just as its practice is much less governmentally controlled) than many foreign observers apparently believe. Its institutional bulwarks – for example the legal requirements for work councils, the insistence that only the qualified can practise many trades, and the formal responsibilities and powers of Chambers – were hardly created as part of a grand plan to further skills creation and workplace training. Ironically, the power to license people to practise trades (and so, indirectly, to plan apprenticeships and award certificates) was given to many of the modern associations in the nineteenth century – when they were still 'guilds' – because Bismarck was worried about the political effects if skilled craftsmen were proletarianized.[91] And today's works councils were set up after the Second World War as a watered-down version of union demands in a post-Third Reich atmosphere of violent union hostility to the employers.[92]

For many years the German apprenticeship system could do no wrong in foreign eyes: the British, French, Koreans and Americans were among the would-be imitators. In recent years the world has fallen out of love with the German economy, and its ardour for apprenticeship has also waned. Instead of being seen as self-evidently the basis of Germany's economic success, the Dual System has come in for a hammering. Apprentices may be learning a lot, but, since many of the skills won't be used even by those who stay in their apprenticeship trade, it can all look *very* expensive to observers inside and outside Germany. Moreover, it is the bedrock of a system whereby skilled workers, whose wages are tied to their recognized qualifications, maintain their high wages by restricting entry. As a senior German civil servant remarked to me, 'If I were a German construction company, I'd be after Polish and British bricklayers too.'

The Dual System undoubtedly produces extremely skilled and well-educated workers, as well as providing a very effective system for socializing young people and organizing the transition from school to working life. And it does appear to involve greater levels of spending on initial training by private employers than other countries manage. It is admirable; but it is not, and never has been, a perfect system. And the most important lesson for other countries may be that, like many national institutions, it is so bound up with a host of other detailed practices and traditions, many of them quite accidental in origin, that it simply cannot be copied and exported wholesale to foreign climes.

6 The tyranny of numbers and the growth of the modern university

> **For the state ... higher education has become a crucial asset.**
> Lord Dearing, 1997
>
> **World class higher education ensures that countries can grow ... It is therefore at the heart of the productive capacity of the new economy.**
> David Blunkett, Secretary of State for Education and Employment, 2000[1]

Looking for a large, global industry combining a long history of sustained and rapid growth with excellent prospects for even more to come? This is harder to find than you might think. Internet companies *may* make profits, one day in the future; but five years ago hardly any of them even existed. The giants of the early twentieth century – mining, shipbuilding, steel – are shrunken vestiges of their former selves. The car industry has massive excess capacity worldwide; agriculture, however productive, is in crisis as an industry, with farmers leaving the land in their thousands as incomes plummet. Entertainment is vast, growing and global, but definitely for those with roller-coaster tastes: of the companies that created the American film-studio systems in the early twentieth century, just two entered the twenty-first as major players.

And then, on the other hand, take higher education. Take any country, anywhere in the world – developed or developing; capitalist, ex-Communist or Communist still – take the Americas, Europe or the Pacific Rim, and the story is one of meteoric expansion. Higher education has become, over the last century, one of the few truly global industries. The university sectors of the twenty-first century are of a completely different order of magnitude from those of a century before. They have also been completely transformed in a way which most adults (and almost all politicians) have not yet fully grasped, since they either remember a long-vanished university world or never knew that world at all.

For believers in education for growth, this must be good news. Successive UK governments have made university expansion one of their major policies, alongside the campaigns for vocational training analysed in Chapters 3, 4 and 5. A Conservative Secretary of State, launching a national higher-education inquiry during the Major government's closing years, explained that 'Higher Education has a vital role to play in raising the levels of the nation's skills and competitiveness and thus enhancing our capacity to generate wealth and improve our quality of life.'[2] Her Labour successor promoted his government's goal of 50 per cent of young people undertaking higher education by explaining that universities are 'powerful drivers of technological and other changes . . . critical to local and regional economic development . . . They are the seed bed for new industries, products and services and they are at the hub . . . of the knowledge economy.'[3]

The CBI, representing the country's large businesses, would cavil only at the speed of progress. Throughout the 1990s it argued for 40 per cent of the young to participate by 2000, and 50 per cent by 2010. 'Higher education is a prime source of highly skilled people, a key contributor to a dynamic economy and central to the future competitiveness of UK business,' it argued. '[Participation] levels continue to lag behind the achievements of some of the UK's major international competitors and the gap must be narrowed to avoid losing competitive advantage.'[4]

Universities are, indubitably, central institutions in modern societies. It would be hard, if not impossible, to find someone who denied their importance, whether in imparting skills or in research: some of it immediately relevant to the economy, some the source of future, unguessed at, transformations. But that is quite different from concluding that more means better, that we are short of graduate employees, and that economic growth in the future demands more university students now.

As we saw in Chapter 2, most labour-market specialists think our economy currently has an over- rather than an under-supply of graduates. This chapter looks in some detail at whether the growth of universities can nonetheless be explained by economic change and the need for higher skills. It concludes that these are not the dominant forces driving current university developments, and that there is no economic imperative justifying ever greater enrolments. It also argues that such conclusions are actually irrelevant, since nothing can stop, let alone reverse, the stampede into higher education. Here is why.

Elite to mass to universal? The growth of higher education

The 1880s are a good place to start exploring today's higher education, because by then the modern university was already taking shape. The first women's colleges in England had been established in Cambridge and Oxford in the 1870s, and, instead of the small provincial colleges of the university-extension movement, cities such as Manchester, Leeds, Birmingham, Newcastle and Bristol now boasted fully fledged universities. German higher education was achieving world renown for its scientific research. Japan had created its first flagship university, the University of Tokyo, and had done so on an essentially European model. In the United States, the foundation of Johns Hopkins and Chicago had forced the old leading colleges of the east coast to take research and research students seriously; while throughout the American West new higher-education colleges were multiplying on the back of Land Grant Act funding.[5]

Yet the apparent familiarity of this university scene masks an enormous difference: the tiny scale of all this activity. In 1881, Somerville

College – the Oxford college that would later produce the first female prime ministers of India and the United Kingdom, as well as the UK's sole female Nobel Laureate, Dorothy Hodgkin – had a *total* of eighteen students. Corpus Christi College down the road, three and a half centuries Somerville's senior, admitted just fifteen new students that year, while the whole University of London encompassed just 700 students. In Germany, student numbers were rising slowly; but this meant that, whereas in the 1860s only around 1 per cent of the male cohort – and no women – attended university, by the turn of the century this had almost doubled. In other words, at most, one young man in fifty was able to enrol for higher education. The Italian situation was much the same. In France, even fewer attended.

The contrast with today is overwhelming. Figure 6.1 juxtaposes total enrolments in the late nineteenth and the late twentieth centuries for the three largest European countries, including the UK. Some of the increases reflect population growth rather than changes in access rates, but the changes are essentially the result of huge increases in the proportions of young people – of both sexes – who attend universities and other forms of higher education. Set beside today's enrolments, those of 1900 are almost invisible.

Higher-education enrolments in each of the large European countries are heading for the 2 million mark: Rome's La Sapienza University alone enrols over 150,000 students. Korea has over 1.5 million higher-education students, Japan 4 million, while the huge US university sector entered the twenty-first century with over 14 million students on its books. The Oxford colleges, where 1880s student numbers were so tiny, have themselves expanded hugely – Somerville by a factor of twenty, Corpus by a factor of seven, since the 1880s. But they are nonetheless totally atypical – the tiny, intimate corner of university life in a system which, in the UK, has grown 150-fold in the course of a hundred years.

A moment of take-off

The change in higher education has been dramatic and also sudden. This has been no slow, steady expansion: quite the contrary. This is shown in Figure 6.2, which maps the pattern of university attendance

Figure 6.1 *University enrolments at either end of the twentieth century*

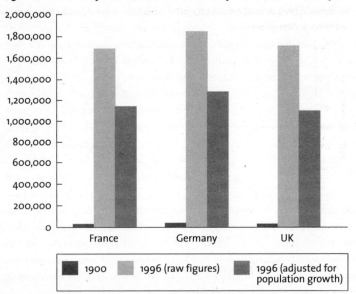

Sources: OECD 2000; Windolf 1997; Board of Education 1900

in the world's six largest economies over the last 100 years. These graphs represent not simply a revolution but a hugely rapid one, whereby university attendance moved, within a generation, from being relatively uncommon to the pretty much normal pattern for young people.

For decades, from the late nineteenth century on, advanced secondary schooling and higher education expanded – steadily, but also very slowly. In 1938, on the eve of the Second World War, there were still less than 2 per cent of Britain's young people, 2 per cent of Germany's, 2 per cent of France's enrolled for a degree. Twenty years later, in the late 1950s, numbers were only a little higher. Then participation rates took off.

In former West Germany in 1960, 6 per cent of young people completed the *Abitur*, the academic school-leaving certificate that gives

Figure 6.2 *Participation rates in higher education: percentage of age cohort entering higher education directly from, or within a short period after, upper-secondary education*

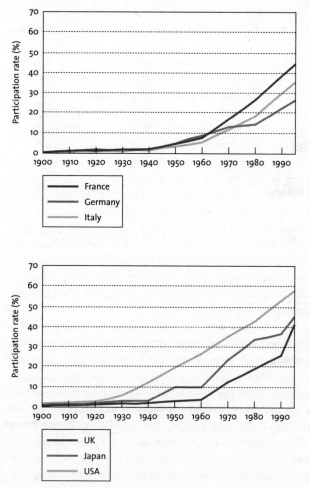

Sources: National statistics from relevant Ministries of Education

access to university. By 1997 the figure was 37 per cent. This more than sixfold increase almost exactly parallels the growth in university and polytechnic (higher-technical) students. In the USA, take-off came earlier, but just as steeply. Japan, Italy, the UK – all show the same pattern of slow growth and then a sudden surge. The parallel shape of the curves underlines that what we have here is an international phenomenon not a particular national one.

Chapter 3 described how teenagers the world over are now rejecting specialized vocational courses in secondary schools in favour of more general academic ones that keep their options open. One of these options, and an increasingly important one, is university study. In France, as in Germany (or Italy, or the UK), the expansion lines for general secondary and higher education run parallel: a doubling between 1980 and 1995 in the numbers completing a *baccalauréat* programme is followed by a near doubling over the exact same timescale in the numbers of university students. Behind every one of those exploding university enrolments is a comparable explosion in academic secondary education. We thus arrive, first, at the sort of society which now characterizes Western Europe, with over a third of the age group following academic routes into higher education, and traditional vocational schools in headlong decline; and then, not so long after, at the situation of the modern United States, where not one-third but two-thirds of the age cohort enters college.

How does this happen? Not (though governments hold the purse strings) from any conscious international agreement or resolution. And not because of any simple growth in the economy's 'need' for graduates either: there was no dramatic change in late-twentieth-century occupations that can parallel the surge in student numbers. Rather, enrolments take off because and when things reach a point of no return: at a certain level of participation potential students are destined – or doomed – to join in. That is what I mean by 'the tyranny of numbers' in the title of this chapter, and it is why student numbers, first in academic upper-secondary and then in university programmes, will continue to grow.

To understand why, imagine yourself to be a sixteen- or seventeen-year-old, or the parent of one, back in 1953. In the England – or France,

Figure 6.3 *Employers' views of where the formally qualified are to be found*

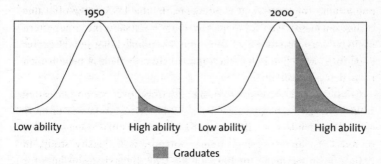

Graduates

or Australia – of this time, less than 5 per cent of the age cohort attends university. So prospective employers all know perfectly well that the vast majority of able employees are to be found in the non-graduate pool. It is very enjoyable to be an undergraduate; it may, indeed, be a necessary route to some – not all – elite positions. But for most people, in most jobs and families, university, and undergraduate life, are simply irrelevant. As a teenager in 1953, you look for an apprenticeship or a job in an environment where the vast bulk of people – from army officers, business managers and nurses, through to skilled craftsmen, secretaries and manual workers – lead their lives without any reference to university at all. And, as a 1950s parent, you discuss your children's future, and tap your contacts for that first job in an office, a shop or a shipyard, again without any reference to universities and degrees. Look at the obituary columns of today's newspapers and it is striking just how many people who have died in their nineties, eighties and even seventies made major careers without going to university.

To understand why things are so different today, we need yet another diagram. Figure 6.3 shows two examples of what many people will recognize as a normal distribution or a bell curve. With anything that has this sort of distribution, you find a few cases which have very high values attached to them – the cases out on the extreme right – and also a few with very low values – the ones on the left. The vast bulk of cases register values somewhere in the middle.

Many things seem to be naturally distributed in this way: people's weights and heights for example, where a few individuals are considerably taller (or shorter) or skinnier (or fatter) than average, but most people are clustered together within a few inches or a few stone of each other. More important, in this context, is how often human beings, rightly or wrongly, *perceive* things as being normally distributed. We find it very easy to distinguish very good and very bad cases. Think, for example, of being a child deciding whom to include in a playground sports team. There will be three or four players who will dominate the game (and who have to be split up if there is to be anything approaching a game at all), and three or four others whom all the captains would really like to exclude from the game altogether. Between them, though, is a large group of children who are of pretty much the same ability, and where choices depend as much on friendship as on sporting ability. Similarly, if you have ever been a teacher or an academic you will know that student work generally follows a similar pattern. You tend to find an 'obvious' top and bottom, and then a large group in the middle – that large hump in the curve – where it is much less easy to differentiate students and rank and mark them precisely.

For young people, the ubiquitous normal distribution has profound consequences, because the things we perceive in this way include intelligence, ability and achievement. Look again at that world of the 1950s, where only about 3 per cent of school leavers go on to university, and only a few more take A levels or their equivalent, and imagine being an employer in that world. Your view of the labour force is represented in the left-hand curve in Figure 6.3. The small shaded segment shows those with a university degree, because by and large you will reckon that the tiny academic elite belongs out there, at the top end of the ability distribution. However, you will also know both that these people are going to be very hard to get hold of and hire, because they are so few, and that the remaining vast bulk of the distribution, the unshaded part where people have not got degrees or higher certificates, is bound to include some very able individuals. So you will be happy to look for employees without degrees, and to see them as potentially high-calibre, high-achieving people.

But what happens when the numbers going to university start to move up fast? Suppose we move to a situation where three-quarters of the young population are staying in school to age eighteen and acquiring senior secondary qualifications, and where a quarter to a third are attending university and getting degrees? Suppose, in other words, that we are back in the present day. With this many degree-holders, the graduate population is bound to include plenty from that large middle hump of the ability distribution. When that happens, perceptions, and actions, change radically.

Now in theory it is perfectly possible that many or most of our new graduates don't belong at the top end of the distribution in terms of 'real' ability at all, but are instead scattered all over it. (Some may come from the very low end of the ability spectrum.) However, this isn't a very obvious or plausible conclusion for an employer or anyone else to reach. It is much simpler to perceive what has happened as having produced the right-hand side of Figure 6.3. What this shows is a situation where, as qualification rates have increased, the cut-off between qualified and unqualified has moved in a straight line from right to left along the curve. In other words, the increase in the qualified population has all come from the upper end of the distribution. And this is exactly the simplifying assumption that employers do make. They hire the formally qualified: those with A levels and *baccalauréats* and, increasingly, with degrees.

Now put yourself in the shoes of a rational seventeen-year-old, or his or her parents. Seventeen-year-olds are in competition with each other, all the time. They are self-conscious and image-obsessed, more or less consciously projecting themselves as desirable not only socially and sexually but also to the gatekeepers who control opportunities. Each time there is an increase in the proportion of teenagers with a given qualification, who are consequently perceived as belonging to the top end of that ability/achievement distribution, the pressure on the others increases. So long as only a small proportion have the given tag, the pressure is not very great. But when you move into a situation where the numbers with an upper-secondary qualification, or a degree, have moved well into that big middle bulge, then the pressure suddenly ratchets up. If you don't get that qualification, then what you are effectively saying to the world is that you belong in the left-hand tail.

And in that case employers will have no reason to look at you, because they have plenty of people on the right-hand side to choose from.

That is the reason for the sudden accelerations in university participation rates which we saw above. At a certain point in what had been a steady, slow expansion, large numbers of people started to feel that they really had better get a degree, because not doing so would be such a bad move. That first wave set off another, and so on. And their parents were very likely to agree. Of course, your child *might* be Richard Branson, and make a fortune without going to university at all; or Bill Gates, and make a far bigger one after dropping out. But the likelihood is pretty tiny. As Chapter 2 explained, graduates, on average, earn far more than non-graduates, which means that for every Branson or Gates there are thousands of people who would have done better with a degree to their name. If nothing else, they could apply for that growing army of jobs which once were open to non-graduates but now are 'graduate entry only'.[6]

The exact speed and scale of university expansion are affected by a number of other factors. Costs do matter, especially to poor students. Nationalized, public systems of higher education mean that governments can control the supply of places. University entrance procedures can be tied to formal qualifications which represent substantive hurdles to students. But, compared to the underlying pressures that are created by expansion, these are small beer. In the medium, never mind the long, term, no democratic government will hold out against the combination of voters' and potential voters' demand for higher education – and particularly not when it is also convinced that competitors with lots of universities are thereby stealing an economic march on it.

We have already seen how closely the expansion rates mirror each other in the Pacific Rim, in the states of the European Union, and in North America. Among Western European countries, Switzerland, with a strong tradition of apprenticeship, held out longest against a huge increase in university attendance; even so, it now has 15 per cent of school leavers registering – almost double the level of just five years ago. Meanwhile the former Soviet Union includes some of the most unregulated education sectors on the planet, as private schools and colleges have been set up in reaction to the total state control of the

Communist era. In the Republic of Georgia, for example, (population 5.4 million, GDP per head $930 in 1998, and number 139 in the world in GDP per inhabitant at purchasing-power parity) half of school leavers now go straight into higher education. Another third enter tertiary vocational training, but largely as a possible back door into university. Since 1991 over 200 new degree-offering institutions have sprung into life alongside the old state universities. With half the registered adult unemployed holding degrees, it may seem obvious that Georgia is 'over-educated'. But look at it the other way: if it is so hard to get a good job with a degree, what hope is there without one?

Onward and upward?

The recent surge in university enrolments is, of course, the flip side of the rejection of vocational courses, discussed in Chapter 3. But where next? Will it continue until absolutely everyone goes to university? Will tertiary education soon be as universal as primary? And, economically, would that be a good idea?

Extrapolation is always risky and almost always wrong; but American enrolment rates have generally run several decades ahead of Europe's, and suggest that there is still a long way to go. In Germany, with its uniquely important and effective apprenticeship system, the 'best' apprenticeships are increasingly taken by young people who have chosen the academic route at school and obtained their university-entrance diploma. They then enter an apprenticeship in which their employer also sponsors their university studies – not because university is a necessary part of the training, but because otherwise the company won't get the quality of apprentices it wants. Large UK engineering firms, as noted in Chapter 5, report the same trend. The promise to sponsor an apprentice through a degree is now a standard part of their recruitment package.

Some of the recent growth in university enrolments reflects underlying changes in the labour market, and the increase in managerial, professional and technical jobs. (If the increase had instead been in skilled manual openings, trends might look quite different.) But, as we saw in Chapter 2, growth in 'top' jobs, while substantial, falls well short of the explosion in university attendance. Surely this means that the average amount extra that a graduate earns will start to decline. And since attending university is costly even when the state pays the fees – at the very least, in earnings forgone, and often in living costs too – won't real expense and declining returns soon mean that demand tapers off?

Well, up to a point perhaps – but not so you'll really notice. For governments who are paying the bulk of the cost of higher education, as everywhere in the world they do, the question of whether we 'need' a given quantity of graduates is a real one. From the individual's point of view this isn't the issue at all. What matters is how much more pay someone personally can expect with a degree (or at least some college education) than without one. And that involves not just how much graduates are paid, but also the average salaries of *non-graduates*. It is quite possible for the average pay of graduates to be stagnant or declining at the same time as the gap between that and the average pay of non-graduates is increasing. This happens when non-graduates are, relatively, losing ground, and this is exactly what has been happening in the United States, most markedly for those with no college education at all. It is also exactly what one would expect, other things being equal, when college enrolments reach the point where employers see non-attenders as a minority rump.

It is less than forty years since the Robbins Committee on Higher Education issued what was seen, at the time and ever since, as a clarion call for mass higher education in Britain. Just a generation or so on, its concept of huge expansion falls almost comically short of reality. For example, its report cites research which concluded that 'even at the most optimistic estimate, it seems unlikely that the proportion of those in a position to make an application [to a university] could rise beyond about 8 per cent of the population'.[7] The report's authors themselves are rather more sanguine. If their recommendations are accepted, and the country goes for growth, they estimate that 'the percentage of the age group entering full-time higher education . . . will reach 15 per cent towards the end of the first quarter of the twenty-first century'.[8] In the year 2000, the figure in Britain was almost 40 per cent; the government's 50 per cent goal beckons well before 2025.

In Britain, then, just as in the USA or ex-Soviet Georgia, the question becomes less 'Does a degree pay well?' than 'Can I afford not to have one?' At the moment, with under half the population starting (if not finishing) full degrees, and students bearing very little of the cost, attending university in most developed countries still looks like an investment with enormous returns. But go far enough up that participation curve and universities could start to operate more like part of basic education, to be endured before you are allowed anywhere near the bulk of the labour market.

Fortunately for governments desperate to reduce the higher-education bill, and pass more of the costs on to students themselves, this is not how most people will see it. Human beings are incorrigibly optimistic about their chances in life, and indeed about the general likelihood of good things happening, such as winning the Lottery. (They tend to over-estimate the chances of a good number of unpleasant things happening too, but failing a degree isn't one of them.)[9] Even if ever more 'graduate' jobs are routine and not very well paid, the very best jobs, in a university-educated world, are going to belong to graduates. That means that degrees are perceived by young people as the way they get a shot at the good life, and even the very top, rather than just a form of imposed time-serving that permits them, at twenty-two, to do jobs their parents did at sixteen or eighteen.

A little piece of recent educational history shows how these calculations affect people's behaviour, and with it the whole shape of higher education. In the 1970s the French government created the IUTs: Instituts Universitaires de Technologie, or university technical institutes. Their creation was a response partly to growing demand for university places, but also to government concerns over the increased time that people were taking to complete (or not complete) their degrees, and the growing preference for arts and social sciences over the 'hard' science and technology which the economy was thought to need.

The IUTs would, the government claimed, provide an education closer to 'the aspirations of contemporary youth and the demands of the modern world' than did the traditional universities. They offered students the chance to acquire technical skills in intensive two-year courses, with significantly higher spending per head than in the crowded university faculties,[10] closer ties to industry and commerce, a higher likelihood of obtaining a diploma successfully, and lower costs (because of the shorter timescale: French students do not pay fees, but mostly do not receive maintenance grants either). The official forecast was that within eight years of their establishment the IUTs would be educating 21 per cent of all the students in higher education. In fact it was a bare 7 per cent – from which it has crept up, over a quarter-century, to just a little under 9 per cent today.

What makes this even more peculiar at first sight is that the *average* salaries of university and IUT graduates are the same (so on a straight rate-of-return analysis the IUTs would come out looking much better: their shorter courses mean you forgo less income while studying). But, as the eminent French sociologist Raymond Boudon pointed out in an analysis of the government's thwarted hopes,[11] the *pattern* of salaries is very different. IUT graduates' salaries are all very similar to each other: university graduates' are far more variable, but it is in this second group that the high-flyers and high-earners are found. And there lies the clue.

If everyone did two-year degrees, then from an individual's point of view the whole IUT idea would be a great one – lower costs, and fewer exams all round. But everyone doesn't do two-year degrees, and at present the best jobs virtually never go to the IUT graduates. Eighteen- and nineteen-year-olds in Lyons or Brest may not know the exact salary statistics, but they have a very clear idea indeed of how institutional prestige stacks up, and of how different qualifications label people in employers' eyes. Table 6.1 sets out the options they face, and for most students universities come out clearly ahead. Certainly there is no guarantee that, by choosing the university route, they will do well. They may actually end up worse off than by choosing an IUT: the higher variability in university salaries reflects lower earnings as well as higher ones. But, being human, they do not assess that chance very highly. Conversely, university at least gives them a chance of getting to the top, rather than the certainty of being stuck well below the ceiling. The result: only a tiny proportion of French teenagers from the academic stream (taking the 'general' *baccalauréat*) enter IUTs.[12] Even among 'technical' *baccalauréat* students, who are generally less academically able, far more enter university than an IUT.

Table 6.1 *The student's dilemma: which course to choose*

	A full university degree offers . . .	*A short technological degree offers . . .*
Upside	Some chance of very high rewards	Low cost; secure reward
Downside	High costs; possibly low rewards	No access to top careers and salaries

The French experience underlines young people's sensitivity to labour-market possibilities, and the fact that their choices will not necessarily accord with government ideas about economic 'needs'. There are some obvious lessons here for the UK government's current policy of encouraging 'foundation degrees': two-year tertiary-level qualifications, largely offered in further education colleges rather than universities. These new degrees are developed in collaboration with employers, and the idea is that they will be 'targeted upon higher level skills shortages in growth areas of the economy'. Holders will, in the words of the Secretary of State for Education (at this point David Blunkett), 'contribute their full potential in all sectors of the labour market, so meeting the needs of employers'.[13]

Foundation degrees are meant to help meet targets for participation in higher education, but by steering new students with lower academic credentials into the intermediate qualifications which the economy 'needs' for growth. The policy is, at least, realistic about who might take these degrees, since the clear lesson from France is that short courses recruit only to the extent that would-be students are squeezed out of longer ones, and that the squeezed-out students are the less academically qualified.

What is a lot less clear is why any student would enrol other than with the express intention of going on to a full degree (with a university label) later. This will be possible. Indeed, automatic access to full degrees for successful students, and with almost no extra study time compared to 'regular' undergraduates,[14] is what distinguishes the new policy from previous failures. In the 1970s the government established two-year specialist Diplomas in Higher Education – an initiative which was launched with uncannily similar rhetoric but, at its height, managed to enrol a total of only 4,000 students, or less than 2 per cent of the then undergraduate population.[15]

The government's idea is that most foundation-degree students will stop there, because that is how the aim of producing 'intermediate' skills for highly specific 'growth areas' will be realized. Perhaps they will; although, if (unlike in France) the new venture also achieves its aim of costing less per student than the universities, it is doubly unclear why either students or potential employers should see foundation degrees as anything but second-best. It seems much safer to predict that 'foundation' students will mostly be en route to a full, and more general, degree and will show their usual disregard for governments' vocational rhetoric. Given the nature of the modern labour market, this is sensible of them; but how much will the result have to do with economic growth through higher education?

The S-curve in the grass

In the second half of the twentieth century, upper-secondary education, often continuing to age nineteen, has become virtually universal in the developed world. I have argued that higher education is far from reaching its limit yet; but is it really conceivable that it too will become universal?

A century from now, who knows? But in the shorter term there are good reasons to think not. Instead, I predict that we will reach a plateau, perhaps at a level much like that in the USA today. To understand why, suppose we take another look at those normal curves that appeared earlier.

Imagine this time (Figure 6.4) that virtually everyone has a degree (or at least some sort of higher diploma). Employers then have to select from an almost completely shaded area: there is no simple cut-off between the formally qualified and the unqualified that they can use to

Figure 6.4 *Employers' perceptions of the labour market: 2050?*

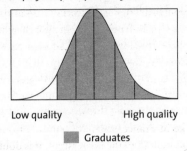

Low quality   High quality

■ Graduates

divide applicants into sheep and goats. On current trends, moreover, this is a world where, although professional jobs are expanding, a large section of the labour market remains low-skilled, low-paid and unlikely to change. (If you look back at Chapters 2 and 5, you will see that what the hype about the 'knowledge economy' ignores is that unskilled jobs are a pretty stable part of the employment scene. If you want someone to wheel you down to hospital X-ray, or to have your post delivered, or your office cleaned, then you had better hope that these jobs don't totally disappear.)

When everyone, or almost everyone, has a degree, employers will obviously become more and more picky about the type of degree they want, and, justifiably or not, will create new dividing lines: right subject, right result, right institution. (These correspond to the vertical lines added to the curve in Figure 6.4.) Imagine, at that point, being somewhere near the bottom of the academic heap at school. The way things are going you'll be hard put to complete the upper-secondary courses needed to enter higher education – and even if you make it you are only going to get into the lowest-status courses. It is hard to persuade yourself that you are ever going to get a shot at the really good jobs; and if, at the end of the day, you are going to end up with only a low-paid one anyway, then the results of the cost calculations start to look pretty negative. Better to just give up on the academic stuff and get a paying job now. Repeated across the country, your decision means that participation finally levels out.

A couple of years ago I showed graphs of higher-education participation rates like those in Figure 6.2 to a couple of eminent economists.
To this audience they looked just like classic S-curves – the sort of shape
you get for ownership of new consumer goods like telephones and
televisions (in the past) or mobile phones and PCs (today), or for the
adoption of effective new techniques in agriculture or in a particular
manufacturing sector. At first there are a few pioneering users; then,
generally by word of mouth, more and more people start to see the
point; and suddenly you are on a steeply rising gradient. With consumer
goods, the benefits of ownership tend to rise with more widespread use:
the more people have telephones or email, the more useful these are as
a way of contacting people. With production techniques that work (or
seem to), it is more that people feel confident, or even obliged, to fall
in with the change once evidence for its usefulness has spread. But in
either case, at the end, the curve flattens off again – usually somewhere
short of saturation. Some people just don't want a PC, and some just
don't see the point of a particular process or technique.

In higher education we can already see how levelling off will happen
and create that S-curve where not everyone enters college. In upper-
secondary education, every country has a small group of teenagers –
varying in size but always present – who reject school and academic
work, and who are the subject of national agonizing over 'social
exclusion'. Young people who do badly at school and leave without
qualifications are also much more likely than their peers to earn less,
be convicted of crimes, be unemployed more, have worse health, and
experience family breakdowns. So, while the S-curve can be benign
enough when we are talking about voluntary PC ownership, in people's
lives it represents something quite different.

However, it is not at all clear what governments can actually do
about this. Young dropouts are often behaving quite as rationally as
their more successful peers. If you are fourteen or fifteen and well
behind academically, your chances of catching up start to look very very
slim. And if you are not going to improve your relative position much,
even if you change your whole lifestyle, then why not give up on the
academic competition completely? It is likely to be better for your self-
respect and, at least in the short term, not obviously worse for your other

prospects: time spent in school when it isn't going to improve your job opportunities, and you don't enjoy the work, is just time wasted.

Thus, exactly the same sorts of calculation that impel most young people towards higher education make it perfectly rational for others to bale out. It seems unlikely that we will reach university for everyone in the near future. Just where and when the curves will flatten, and for how long, will depend largely on how young people and their elders perceive the job market. But it will also depend on how much governments go on subsidizing provision through direct funding of universities, or student aid and loans, and on how far they control supply (directly or through entrance qualifications). On past form, we can be fairly sure that it won't reflect occupational demands or skill needs in any very precise or direct way. Whether the result may nonetheless be good for growth is a question we return to below.

Counting them in *and* counting them out: the new inequalities

In one very obvious sense, the huge increase in university enrolments means an expansion of opportunity. Societies in which around half of an age cohort can expect to enter higher education, either straight after school or during adult life, cannot also be places in which universities are the preserve of a tiny upper-class elite. Nor are they. Not so long ago – back in 1983 – Tony Parker wrote a vivid portrait of people on a large south-London estate, 'Providence'. According to the head of the local eleven-to-sixteen school, 'Very few of the girls think much further than leaving, getting a job for a few years and then settling down into marriage and children. The boys' thoughts run mostly along practical lines . . . being wage-earners rather than salaried people . . . Schooling . . . is largely regarded as a necessary evil . . . life begins . . . when you're old enough to leave school. Nearly everyone is waiting impatiently for that moment.'[16]

No London head – perhaps no British head – could talk like that today. University is something real and conceivable across all social classes, just as marriage is less and less guaranteed, let alone a likely lifetime career. But, while universities have genuinely been opened up to families who had never previously considered higher education, there is a worm in the apple of opportunity – and a rather large one.

The major beneficiaries of university expansion have been and remain the middle and upper middle classes. These are the dominant groups of our modern societies: the 'ABs' of the advertising agencies, whose readership delivers far higher advertising rates to their favoured papers and journals than are commanded by tabloids with larger circulations. They are the 'Class I and II' of government statisticians, the people who manage and administer, who belong to professional associations, and who value and live by formal qualifications.[17] No matter whether you look at the United Kingdom or the United States, at France, Germany, Italy, Japan or New Zealand, the picture is the same. The children of these middle classes now go on to higher education almost automatically. The issue is not whether, but merely where. Meanwhile, children from poor and unskilled backgrounds only trickle in. And, while the absolute chances of entry, and absolute numbers, may have improved for families at the bottom of the heap, on some measures the gap in opportunity has actually widened.

To see what has happened, take a look first at Table 6.2, which shows the proportion of English young people from families of different occupational groups or classes who entered higher education at various points in the post-war period. In each case, we can see that there have been huge increases. Roughly twelve times as many eighteen-year-olds with fathers doing unskilled or semi-skilled manual jobs entered higher education in the mid 1990s as in the 1950s, while for 'Class II' – families headed by teachers, middle managers, social workers and the like – the chances increased fourfold.

If, however, you look down the columns of Table 6.2 rather than along the rows, a rather different picture emerges. It was arithmetically impossible for the chances of Class-I children to increase fourfold, let alone twelvefold, in the great late-twentieth-century expansion: they were too high already. But they could and did increase enormously nonetheless – to the extent that it is the middle- and upper-middle-class children of Classes I and II who are the major beneficiaries of expansion rather than their less advantaged peers.

Table 6.2 Participation in higher education by class of father: percentage of English and Welsh young people entering higher education[18]

Class of father	Participation rate (%)				
	Early 1950s	1960	1977	1991	1994–5
I (professional, higher management)		33	33	55	79
II (middle managers, teachers)	16	11	18	36	45
III (non-manual)		6	11	22	31
III (skilled manual)	4	2		11	18
IV (semi-skilled)			4	12	17
V (unskilled)	1	1		6	12

Imagine that you have 100 children from Class-II families – so not from the 'top' professional families, but rather the 'middle middle' classes – and 100 from Class V, all together in a large school hall. Those who are going to university are told to climb up on a stage, or go into the playground – somewhere where they're easy to count. Do this in 1960 and 11 middle-class children and just one single child from an unskilled manual worker's home will be selected for the count. Now fast forward to 1995. This time 12 unskilled manual workers' children will be chosen as future university students, but so will no fewer than 45 of their peers. In other words, there will be an increase of 34 children from the middle-class group and only 11 more from the unskilled-manual-worker group. As for Class-I children, the figures indicate an

Table 6.3 *Chances of attending university by parental class: actual entry rates compared to rates if entry were equally distributed (full-time undergraduate degrees, UK)*

Class of father	Attendance rate (%)	
	1974	1994
I (professional, higher management)	2.7	3.3
II (middle managers, teachers)		2.2
III (non-manual)	0.5	0.7
III (skilled manual)		0.5
IV (semi-skilled)	0.2	0.5
V (unskilled)		0.3

Note: The calculation shows share of higher-education acceptances relative to population share: 1974, universities only; 1994, all HE.

Sources: 1974 – population estimates from the Labour Force Survey; 1994 – estimates from the General Household Survey

absolute increase of 46 children per 100, as university education becomes more or less universal for families of their type. The middle-class increases swamp, in absolute terms, the numbers coming through from semi-skilled or unskilled workers' homes.

While major changes over a generation are quite clear, it is much more difficult to calculate precise figures year by year.[19] However, relative inequalities seem to have changed surprisingly little in the recent past – that is, in the period in the late 1980s and 1990s when enrolments took a huge upward leap. While all groups ended up as much more likely to send their children to university than before, the relative chances for children from Classes I and II remained not only far higher than for those from Classes IV and V, but higher by about the same ratio.

Table 6.3 takes another angle on this picture. It uses the best estimates I can find not only of students' class origins, but also of the changing class structure of Britain, which, as we saw in Chapter 2, has become considerably more middle class overall as managerial and professional jobs have expanded. From these, one can compare the reality of university recruitment with what would happen if your chances bore no relationship at all to your family background – for example, if entry were allocated by a random lottery. What this shows is that, in the 1970s (before the growth of the polytechnics), middle-class children were almost three times and working-class children about one-fifth as likely to go to university as if chances were randomly distributed: in fact one group had almost fourteen times the chances of the other. And twenty years later, although the absolute chances for all groups were much higher, the relative chances remained ten times as great for upper-middle-class children as for the children of the unskilled.

So, while universities in the UK are far more numerous, as well as far larger, than just a few decades ago, in one key respect they remain amazingly similar to those of the recent past. They are overwhelmingly middle class – and not just because society itself is increasingly so. Well before university entrance, family background starts to tell. In England and Wales, A levels remain by far the largest and most important qualification for university. As we saw in Chapter 3, the proportion of the age cohort sitting them has risen fast; yet no less than 80 per cent of these examinations are taken by students from non-manual family backgrounds. Even among those sitting BTEC Diplomas and Advanced GNVQs – the 'vocational' sixth-form courses which also provide for university entrance – middle-class families are heavily over-represented.

The British preoccupation with comparing independent- and state-school results tends to obscure the key fact that, while students from independent schools make up a far larger proportion of university students than of their overall age group, the same is true of the middle-class state-school pupils who make up the bulk of their university companions. Independent-school pupils account for 7 per cent of the school population and 18 per cent of the university one, while students from Classes I and II account for 27 per cent and 61 per cent respectively (see Table 6.4).

Table 6.4   *The family origins of UK students (percentages of first-year undergraduates from different occupational classes)* [20]

| | First-year undergraduates (%) | | |
Class of father	1960	1991	1999
I (professional, higher management)	19	18	15
II (middle managers, teachers)	42	47	45
III (non-manual)	13	12	14
Subtotal: non manual	74	77	74
III (skilled manual)	19	14	17
IV (semi-skilled)	6	8	7
V (unskilled)	1	1	2

Sources: UCCA/UCAS; Reid 1989

Being in step with the world

British commentators (and politicians) are prone to believe that any aspect of society that they dislike is totally different elsewhere, and that other countries do everything better. They believe this passionately with respect to vocational education and training, as we saw in earlier chapters. They also tend to believe that we send fewer young people to university than our main competitors, and that this is a bad thing economically. Indeed, this predilection for overseas comparisons is one reason why university expansion has been such a plank of UK government policy of late. When talking about universities, politicians draw their invidious comparisons from different countries from those used to compare vocational training, so it is typically the USA which is emphasized, rather than Germany. But the underlying logic is the same: other countries educate more, other countries are richer, so clearly we need to educate more in our turn.

In fact, as we have just seen, British universities have expanded in almost exactly the same way, and to comparable levels, as those of the

Table 6.5 *Social origins of students in Japanese universities*

	Percentage of students from families in the top 40 per cent of income: national universities	*Percentage of students from families in the top 40 per cent of income: private universities*
1961	44.7	72.1
1976	59.9	76.1

Source: Based on Windolf 1997

societies we resemble. (Our *graduation* rates are actually well above average, though our dropout rates are now starting to converge on others' too.) The continuing domination of British universities by the children of the middle classes is also fully in line with what happens in the rest of the world. Historically, in fact, the UK's universities have been relatively open to working-class children compared to those of other European countries, and the most recent data suggest that on this measure of access the country comes pretty much in the middle of developed countries as a whole (a set which includes Australasia, Japan and North America as well as the European mainland).[21] Just as these countries have all experienced huge increases in university enrolments over the last few decades, so too have they seen the middle classes take up the bulk of these new student places.

Japanese universities, for example, tripled in size during the 1960s and 1970s. In the process, the student body's social origins developed as shown in Table 6.5 with the middle classes taking ever more of the places both in the 'merit entry' national universities, with their lower fees, and in private universities.

In Germany we find that, between 1975 and 1996, students from blue-collar homes increased in absolute numbers, but actually fell as a proportion of the student body – from 18 to 14 per cent. German universities are free; but if we want to see how little this phenomenon has to do with fees, or their absence, Australia provides the evidence. Abolishing fees in the early 1970s – they have now been reintroduced – had virtually no impact on entry patterns: in Australia, as elsewhere, the 1970s and 1980s saw huge increases in participation from the top third of the income bracket, swamping those from families lower down the scale.[22]

The United States remains the country with the largest college enrolment rates as well as the oldest mass higher-education system in the world. If you look back at Figure 6.2, you will see the participation rate there taking off for the stars decades before any European one. The USA had a quarter of a million students in college in 1900; a million and a half on the eve of the Second World War. Today it has 14 million. Moreover, after plateauing in the 1970s, enrolment rates took off again in the 1980s and 1990s, so that two-thirds of high-school graduates now go straight to college.

Obviously any move from one-third to two-thirds participation rates will involve thousands (maybe millions) of students from poorer homes. But in the USA too the striking change is the continued increase in students from middle-class families. Table 6.6 shows what has happened to participation rates for young people from the lowest and the highest income quartiles: in other words, from large swathes of the managerial and of the unskilled/manual classes. Between the 1970s and the 1990s, participation rates for both increased by the same number of percentage points. The 'bottom' 25 per cent of families started the period with less than half their children continuing to college, and a six-point rise still left the rate at under 50 per cent. For the rich, a six-point rise took them from very high to even higher – near universal – entry.

Is the continued huge gap in access between the wealthy and the poor, the professional classes and the unskilled, important? Perhaps, from an economic viewpoint, it isn't. If the primary function of education is to increase economic efficiency and growth, then we want higher education to go to the most able, and the potentially most productive. Suppose we were now close to the utopia described by Michael Young in his superb satire on *The Rise of the Meritocracy* (1958). If that were the case the middle classes would enjoy their positions by virtue of their superior brains and have, on average,

Table 6.6 *Percentages of US young people entering college*

	1972		1992	
	Low-quartile income (bottom 25 per cent)	High-quartile income (top 25 per cent)	Low-quartile income (bottom 25 per cent)	High-quartile income (top 25 per cent)
All	42.0	85.1	48.9	91.3
Lowest-quartile school achievement	31.2	57.9	35.9	77.3
Highest-quartile school achievement	69.7	94.6	77.6	96.7

Source: US Department of Education 1997: figures for enrolment in higher education within two years of scheduled high-school graduation

intellectually superior children; also, the minority of clever lower-class children would be identified in school and would make their way appropriately upward through the meritocratic ranks. Which would be just what the growth rate needed, and would produce the sort of differential patterns of access that we have just described.

But we are not anywhere near that state (regardless of its desirability). We know that children's achievements are affected not just by birth and family, but by the schools they attend and by their peer group. We also know that, among groups of equally high achievers, family background still matters. If you look again at Table 6.6 you will see that for high-income young Americans who were also high achievers (top quartile in school), college was already pretty automatic by 1972: almost 95 per cent of this group already went into higher education by then. For high-income but low-achieving eighteen-year-olds, however, the figure in 1972 was much lower – 'only' 57.9 per cent attended college. In fact in 1972 clever poor kids were actually a lot more likely to attend college than dumb rich kids were. By 1992 all this had changed. Now 77.3 per cent of low-achieving but high-income eighteen-year-olds were going straight on to college. The chances for high achievers from poor families also increased in these two decades, but by nothing like as much. By 1992, as Table 6.6 shows, their chances of college were no longer higher, but instead just about level with those of richer kids with far worse academic records.

While we don't have equivalent data for Western Europe (or Japan), the huge recent increases in middle-class university attendance suggest that a very similar pattern would emerge there too. This is not to deny that, as universities have grown, opportunities have opened up. Only four generations ago the novelist Thomas Hardy described how 'Jude the Obscure', his village schooling completed and apprenticeship served, faced the total impossibility of ever achieving a university education. Though intelligent and scholarly, he could never hope to win a scholarship in an 'open' examination against the well-taught products of established schools, and never earn or save enough to pay the fees himself. An Oxbridge college head's response to his request for advice was that he would be better off 'remaining in your own sphere and sticking to your trade. That, therefore, is what I advise you to do.'

No equivalent of Jude would face such barriers in a 'First World' country today (or, indeed, die at age twenty-nine as Jude did). Large numbers of children from working-class homes do attend university; hundreds of thousands of adults have been able to change their lives and improve their job prospects by enrolling as 'mature' students. But it is worth belabouring the extent to which expansion means the worldwide middle-class colonization of mass university systems, because this highlights how imperfect the link is between university growth and economic 'needs'. What is driving current expansion is far more the correct perception by individuals of where their or their children's own self-interest lies than any close relationship between overall student numbers, the particular subjects they study, and the requirements of the workplace. That is why the USA has moved from one-third to two-thirds participation in higher education at a period when the growth in managerial, executive and professional jobs has been far more modest: from just 23 per cent to 33 per cent of the whole.[23] It is why estimates of 'over-education' in the graduate workforce in 1980s Britain – *before* the last great expansion – consistently suggested that a quarter or more were in jobs for which their degrees were not necessary.[24] It also explains why more than half the 'graduates-only' job advertisements do not specify a subject: the degree requirement is as much about screening, and screening out, by general ability as it is about specific skills.[25]

If our huge university sectors are not, after all, 'needed', might not everything suddenly change? Certainly it would be foolish to predict that universities' current importance as gateways to the job market will automatically continue for ever – just as I argued earlier against extrapolating from the last two decades to a future of universal higher education. Universities *have* collapsed in the past, as we can see in Figure 6.5, which depicts the history of student enrolments in a national system and (separately) in one of its elite institutions: a giddy rise, and then a precipitous fall. Could that happen across the developed world?

The answer must be 'Yes, in theory': but not imminently, in any plausible economic or political scenario. What Figure 6.5 shows are the rise and fall of the universities of Castile (and of Salamanca specifically) during Spain's Golden Age and its later economic and political collapse. Over that 250-year period, the society moved first to being one of the most (if not the most) highly educated in Europe and then to one in which hardly a single family deemed it worthwhile to send its sons to any of the surviving institutions.[26] Just as in the developed world today, Spanish families for many years saw universities as the way to make a career – ideally in the royal administration and upper clergy; otherwise in law or medicine. New universities sprang up all over Spain, substantially over-catering for the actual demands of Court or Church. But what killed the universities was not this, but a total change in the way in which offices were distributed – not on merit, or by degree, but tied increasingly to particular families or sold directly to the rich. Spanish universities, like ours, were highly responsive to labour-market signals, though hardly an engine of economic prosperity. As the labour market atrophied, and the economy disintegrated, so did they.

Figure 6.5 *Student enrolments – a system's rise and fall*

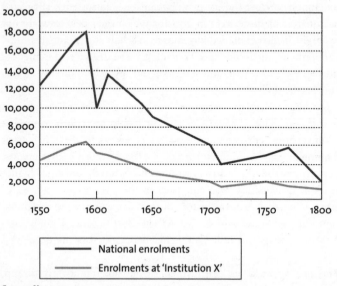

Source: Kagan 1975

It was, however, economic catastrophe that shattered this historic symbiosis between university studies and advancement. I personally find it quite impossible to conjure up a plausible scenario in which, during the next half-century at least, the best jobs in society go largely to non-graduates rather than graduates. And as long as university remains the best, and in many cases the only, way of getting a crack at desirable occupations, then enrolments will stay buoyant no matter how badly paid some university graduates are. Middle-class families now perceive degrees as a necessity for their children; more and more of a government's key voters consequently have a stake in maintaining the value of acquiring them. And, as the fuss over student fees has shown, many of those same key voters are convinced that the state ought to foot the bill.

None of this makes it likely that a modern democratic government will prune its university sector. Yet it is not only the case that current expansion has little directly to do with the demands of the economy. It is also, as Chapter 7 will discuss, that this hectic expansion – fuelled by individual self-interest, and by politicians' quest for growth – may actually be doing more harm than good, to the economy as well as to other of our universities' fundamental concerns.

7 Pyramids and payments: the higher-education market

> The expansion of higher education ... has been a major success story ... More resources must be found ... to enable the system to continue to expand.
> Confederation of British Industry, 1994

> I don't want a qualification that everyone can pass.
> Kent accountancy student, 1996

> Being first is everything.
> Global advertising slogan, 2000[1]

In the last half-century, as Chapter 6 described, higher education has exploded in size. In the process, it has also changed profoundly: the system that enrols 33 per cent of the age cohort is not just the one that enrolled 3 per cent, grown larger. This chapter looks at the two most striking results of this transformation: namely an increasingly differentiated and hierarchical university sector, and one which is in more or less permanent financial crisis. Both are inevitable adjuncts of a mass system, and of the role that university studies now play in the labour market. And, since neither situation is set to change, we can expect further stratification, more competition between countries in a global education market, and continuing pressure and controversy over university budgets and costs.

Will this be good or bad for economic growth? As we have seen, governments have promoted rapid increases in student numbers because of the supposed importance of these to the economy. They have got the increases, too – but for reasons that have a great deal more to do with individuals' own economic prospects than with national economic 'need'.

However, this doesn't mean that universities play no important role in the economy. On the contrary, they can make two vital contributions. The first is as educators and trainers, which they have always been: of priests, lawyers and doctors, and more recently of engineers, research chemists, teachers, physiotherapists and designers. That role remains critical, even if we don't need more and more of all these professionals. And university study – especially in 'generalist' disciplines – has always been regarded as something which has a discernible effect on people's cognitive skills. Graduates have been assumed to be better at arguing, analysing and evaluating, with skills based on, but not confined to, the particular subjects they have studied. The main rationale for such study was not, in the past, its direct contribution to GDP. But, unless our ancestors (as well as we) have been completely deluded, these skills are distinctive, and do make some contribution to economic life.

Universities' second economic role is as a generator of scientific and technological ideas with direct commercial relevance. This is also not new: the research of its nineteenth-century universities was central to the development of Germany's chemical industries, and associated economic growth. In recent years, however, governments have become increasingly aware of and excited by the potential of universities as growth 'incubators'. The main inspiration has been the United States: first the North-East, where many high-tech companies grew up around Boston, often with the direct involvement of academics from MIT and other universities, and more recently Silicon Valley, linked symbiotically to the research cultures of Stanford and the University of California campuses.

As we saw in Chapter 6, governments' higher-education policies are a response as much to voter demand as to their own ideas about promoting economic prosperity (let alone theories about the broader purposes of education). How else to explain the worldwide surges in student numbers? Nonetheless, government policies do have an enormous impact on universities' development. In every country, government is the major source of funds; in many, almost the sole one. With the money come strings, often in the form of highly centralized directives and controls on how universities operate. Governments' policies make a great deal of difference to the nature of their university sectors – both to their education and training and to their research functions.

As we shall see, governments' recent record is not very encouraging, even if we stay focused on growth and ignore any wider university remit. The following pages discuss the way in which global trends are fomenting both university hierarchies and budgetary pressures, and how governments are responding. In this context the recent history of Oxford and Cambridge, also described here, encapsulates the pressures facing universities and their government paymasters, and shows why politicians, who so passionately believe in the economic potential of higher education, find it so hard to follow policies that might actually promote it.

Universities and the winner-take-all society

> We class schools, you see, into four grades: Leading School,
> First-rate School, Good School, and School.
>
> Evelyn Waugh, *Decline and Fall* (1928)

As the university sector has ballooned, simply having been to university no longer serves as much of a distinguishing mark. There have always been differences in prestige and focus between universities: now the rigid hierarchy of preparatory schools faced by Evelyn Waugh's would-be teacher in the quote above is increasingly echoed within higher education. For more and more employers, detailed information on degrees starts to matter – where you went and what you studied, as well as whether you finished your studies. Students scrutinize higher education as more or less well-informed consumers, and universities behave as, and feel themselves to be, competitive enterprises in a far larger and more volatile marketplace than ever before. In this new environment, institutions can have everything to play for and almost everything to lose. Everyone dreams of belonging to a leading university, and everyone also dreads relegation to the unlabelled bottom of the heap.

As university attendance increases, ambitious parents worry obsessively about whether their children are getting into the right university. Ambitious young people who feel that they have a chance of getting to the top perceive the 'top' universities as the most useful first step, and perhaps even a necessary one. A recent series of Dow-Jones advertisements in quality newspapers presses home the message that only being top will do. 'Pierre Le Something, France's second fastest World Superbike racer.' 'Andrew So-and-so. The second man to go round the world by balloon.' 'Some horse that came second in the Grand National.' And the punchline: 'Being first is everything.'

Of course there have always been 'top' institutions (just as there are prestigious addresses and were once fashionable army regiments). But we are now in a world where hundreds of thousands of families are involved, and where their reference point is increasingly global. They are right to think that the university attended matters, because top people today indeed tend to be not just graduates but graduates of top institutions. In Japan, graduates of Tokyo and Kyoto dominate the elite; in France, graduates of ENA and the Polytechnique. In the UK, the university you attend directly affects your post-graduation earnings.[2] In the USA, graduates from the top selective colleges earn more than their contemporaries with equivalent family backgrounds and high-school records.[3]

In this environment, the old-established institutions start with a big advantage – so that at first glance one might think that, for them, nothing has changed. Higher education can be portrayed as a haven of stability, with Harvard, Yale and Princeton at the top of the US pecking order both in 1900 and in 2000. Similarly, France was and is ruled by the graduates of a few tiny *Grandes Écoles*; while, in the UK, Oxford and Cambridge (Oxbridge) continue to occupy a class of their own. In Japan, Tokyo University was and is the most desirable university to attend, as is Peking University in China (its self-confidence asserted in its retention of 'Peking' rather than the newer government-approved 'Beijing' transliteration).

But in fact things are not the same. None of these institutions does, or can, take its position for granted. Their top administrators and academics worry constantly and publicly about *positioning* and *funding*, the topics of this chapter.[4] They are right to do so. Universities can and do fall (Salamanca, the Sorbonne) and rise (Berkeley, Cornell, Warwick). They are in constant competition not just for funding and faculty, but also for the choices of the able and ambitious young.

Take a tale of two Florida universities – Florida State University and the University of Florida – both of them public (state-funded) institutions, and traditional rivals. Back in the 1970s, university administrators in the United States surveyed with gloom the coming demographic dip: a big fall in the number of eighteen- and nineteen-year-olds, which they feared would hit enrolments, especially in the large state campuses. Florida State decided to open itself up: to lower its admissions standards and have fewer prerequisites for particular degrees. The University of Florida did the opposite: instead of lowering, it raised entrance requirements, insisted on foreign-language studies, and announced that course standards would be tougher. The result: a big increase in applications for the 'difficult' University of Florida, and an equivalent fall at Florida State, which had so visibly attempted to devalue its brand.

Pressures on students and institutions are greater today, not just because of mass higher education, but also because they are increasingly international in context. Higher education is part of the 'winner-take-all' society, itself in part spawned by globalization, and vividly portrayed in a book of that name by Robert Frank and Philip Cook.[5]

Compared to most of recorded history (or, indeed, most poor societies today), developed industrial countries have relatively equal distributions of income and wealth. But in the last twenty years there has been a general increase in inequality, reversing trends since the Second World War.[6] Most striking is the way that the top earners, especially in the USA and the UK, have pulled away from the median, and the emergence and visibility of the superstar salary. For example, in the

USA the group that has done particularly well in this period, in both real and relative terms, is those in the top 1 per cent, whose real incomes doubled in the boom years of the 1980s and 1990s. Silicon Valley millionaires in their twenties are the stock-in-trade of newspaper features. But so are the stratospheric sums paid to top opera singers, top athletes, top film stars, top lawyers (especially top barristers), top traders, and top investment-fund managers. In the UK, the average earnings of solicitors for the year 2000 was £41,000; but a small group at the top earns well over £1 million a year.[7]

Most of these situations are classic winner-take-all – meaning that the gap between the very top, where people can command almost any sum they want, and everyone else is huge. They also tend to be situations where people's performance can be ranked more or less objectively. What is important, and what generates this enormous cash advantage, is that the winners are just that little bit better than the rest.

Of course at one level there is nothing new here. Top performers always got paid a lot; ditto top lawyers. But a number of things have been happening which intensify winner-take-all effects. One, as Frank and Cook argue, is the rise of global communications. The whole world can watch the same movies and sports, listen to the same music, and read the same best-selling books. Since the number of hours in the day hasn't changed, and we are each of us reading or watching much the same amount as before, this means a far smaller number of best-sellers than when each country had its own largely insulated market – and a comparable pulling away of the top earners.[8]

More generally, the increased speed of international travel, a global telephone and email network, and the growth of English as a global language have all tended to create one market where multiple national ones existed before. Chief executives of major companies often have careers that span continents. Since their average time in post has also shrunk, today's examples are gone tomorrow; but, at the time of writing, chief executives of top UK companies in the FTSE 100 included an Argentinian who came to England via the Netherlands, an Irishman who made his career in Canada, a Belgian who worked in six countries before the UK, and a dozen or more Americans, Australians, Europeans, Indians and Chinese.[9]

The income inequalities in our societies make many people angry, and many others highly uneasy. Does a chief executive's contribution to company profits really justify a multi-million-pound annual salary? Is it really so much more likely that you will win a libel case with the top lawyer pleading for you (at £6,000 a day) rather than one who is good but not the top (at £600)? Isn't it just that top managers are making cosy deals at customers' expense? Or that we have lost all the moral constraints which curbed greed in the past?

Certainly, attitudes to wealth have changed – especially compared to the mid twentieth century – and have done so unevenly. In some cohesive and generally small societies (such as Sweden), extreme inequalities of income are still deeply frowned on. But, like Frank and Cook, I don't think it plausible that the business people, footballers, lawyers and film stars of the 1920s or the 1950s were simply far less grasping than today's. Nor does a change in values explain the way a few 'winners' pull ahead, as opposed to a more general increase in the relative wealth of, say, the top 5 or 10 per cent. Some other explanation is needed.

We can find it in the changing dynamics of how salaries are set and fees paid. Start by thinking of a board of directors choosing a new chief executive. They need to stay ahead of fierce international competition, but are afraid of taking too great a risk. Someone who adds even a little extra growth to the company will be worth far more than his or her (huge) salary. Equally, the wrong choice can be disastrous – not just in the longer but in the short term, if institutional investors and the stock market look askance. So the best candidate will be someone with an already established reputation and track record.

Purchasing managers investing in IT systems face the same sort of pressures, which is why, throughout the 1980s and 1990s, they all tended to make the same expensive but safe choices. (No one ever got sacked for buying IBM.) In fact the human equivalent of an IBM is what most boards are after. But you can't clone a good track record the way you can mass-produce a computer or a database. Instead, in a move first from local to national marketplaces, and now from national to international ones, we find more and more people interested in the same small groups of individuals. The result is a runaway bidding race which drives up top salaries.

Substitute a football team for a FTSE-100 company and the dynamic is exactly the same – hence the constant shifts between teams and countries and the vast transfer sums paid for successful European footballers. Or imagine you are a patient facing a quadruple bypass operation. If it's within your power, or bank balance, to secure it, won't you always want the very best, and fly to Harley Street or New York to secure it? Isn't even a small increase in the odds of success worth grabbing?

But what has this got to do with higher education? Well, put yourself in the shoes not of the board of directors, but of a company's middle manager, or senior personnel officer. You need to hire some young high-flyers. You want the best you can get; but also, and quite as powerfully, you don't want to be dumped on internally for making a poor choice. Your best (as in safest) policy is one which will probably net some good employees and which also can be defended if things go wrong. So what do you do? You go for people whose MBAs are from top business schools, or who, earlier still, went to the best universities. So salaries for those graduates pull ahead of those from other institutions: success breeds success.

This sounds very much like the flip side of the process by which more and more young people feel that they *have* to go to university. And so it is – but with an extra twist. In this case employers are perfectly aware that not all the brightest, most capable young people went to the top universities, or vice versa. But they do feel that the probability of finding 'the best' is higher if they hire graduates of selective institutions with a global brand. For all the occasional rhetoric of politicians, no one in the post-war West has ever been sacked for habitually hiring graduates of Tokyo or Cambridge, or picking MBAs from INSEAD, London Business School or Harvard. On the contrary: what boards of large companies habitually request from their human-resources departments are profiles of the universities that recruits attended – and what they want are plenty of recruits from the top.[10]

Frank and Cook chart the way in which increasing proportions of prize-winning high-school students in the USA now migrate to just seven 'top' universities (almost all private), and how, within the eight campuses of the (public) University of California, the highest-prestige one, Berkeley, has hugely increased its share of California students with the highest scores in the SATs (Scholastic Assessment Tests – the machine-scored maths and English tests available nationally and used by selective American universities as one of their main admissions criteria). The same process explains why entries for the difficult, multi-subject US 'Advanced Placement' tests have exploded. Once taken by only a few very academic high-school seniors, who received college credit in return, they now attract over 10 per cent of the age group, all taking them with a view to getting into competitive and therefore desirable colleges.[11]

The same pressures explain why so many French children spend an extra two years in high school cramming for the *Grandes Écoles* entrance exams even though they have passed the *baccalauréats* which offer university entrance. (Eight per cent of *baccalauréat* holders enter these entrance-examination classes, though less than half of them can hope to gain a place in the *Grandes Écoles*.) They are also why Japanese parents worry about getting their child into the kindergarten which will lead to the elementary school which will lead to the high school which will lead to Tokyo or Kyoto University. As Ron Dore has explained, this is far less about education than about providing the world's most 'enormously elaborated, very expensive, intelligence testing' – and elite selection – system.[12] The self-same dynamic explains why British families, scouring schools' promotional literature, hone in on the number of Oxbridge places won, and why schools always list these separately. Clearly, entering an elite institution can do great things for any individual. But does this increasingly visible status hierarchy do anything for the economy?

One way in which it might do so is by sorting out people more efficiently, matching them better with job openings. Suppose, for a moment, that the amount a job pays closely reflects the job's economic importance and its contribution to national output. Then, if the most academically able students are filtered and ranked efficiently, with the best going to the best universities and on to the top-paying jobs, we should also increase the nation's economic efficiency and income. Granted that, as we saw in Chapter 6, getting to university depends on your family and school, as well as your own brains. But with 40 per cent of the UK cohort university-bound (and two-thirds of the American), perhaps we are sweeping most of the most able young people into university and then sorting them into order for the greater economic good.

Well, perhaps. Certainly the increasing stratification of universities helps employers make sense of what would otherwise be a huge mass of more or less undifferentiated graduates. But, if you want to make a case for big gains in economic efficiency, you have to do a good deal of supposing. First, as we saw in Chapter 2, wages may be the best measure we have of individuals' productivity, but they are an enormously imperfect one. This is just as true for individual superstar payments as it is for whole occupational categories such as doctors, lawyers or teachers. Second, academic ability has some relationship to success, whether in business, medicine, government or journalism, but this too is a very long way from a perfect match. Lots of skills and qualities are very important later in life that have no connection at all with whether your grades get you into a top university (or whether you leave it with a good degree). Finally, if some occupational areas boast huge salaries that have only a little to do with economic productivity, *and* use 'top' academic credentials to recruit, they are likely to attract more and more high-achieving young people towards them at the expense of other occupations. The result isn't likely to be optimally efficient, or anything close to it.

Figures on university access also undermine the idea that university stratification is promoting anything close to a pure meritocracy. Back in Chapter 6 we saw that the major beneficiaries of university expansion in general have been the middle classes. Look at who goes where in these huge new university systems, and the importance of family background again comes through loud and clear. As water flowing down a rocky hill finds the best channel, so middle-class children are steered and find their way into the 'best' higher education.

France is an interesting example because, as noted earlier, the universities are not the main route to top French jobs. Instead, this honour falls to the *Grandes Écoles* – small, highly specialized institutions which set their own joint national entrance examination and have their own clear internal hierarchy. Candidates' scores decide not merely whether they win a place in the *Grandes Écoles* as a whole, but also exactly where in the pecking order they are offered it.

Table 7.1 *Family background of ENA students (selected groups only)*

	1952–8	1978–82
Workers and artisans	12%	1%
Professions	15%	15%
Senior civil servants	9%	19%

Source: Bourdieu 1989

The 'career open to all the talents' is a phrase that English has lifted from France, and as an ideal of success through intellect alone it is central to the history and self-image of French education. The reality, however, is rather frayed. Pierre Bourdieu, France's best-known sociologist, is himself a *Grandes Écoles* product from a lower-middle-class provincial family. He has investigated what has happened over time to the student body of the ENA (École Nationale d'Administration), which trains the top bureaucrats and many of the country's top politicians and business people as well. The story, as Table 7.1 shows, has been one of an increasing concentration of upper-middle-class students, and the virtual disappearance of students from the poorest homes.

As French higher education has expanded, it has become steadily more stratified – from the 'senior-technician sections' at the bottom to the *Grandes Écoles* at the top – and the class origins of students mirror this hierarchy. Pierre Cam, director of a research centre on higher education, points out that for entry to the very top – École Normale Supérieure, École Polytechnique – 'most students . . . come from just a dozen or so *lycées*'.[13]

What of the USA, which sees itself as the land of opportunity? Here too, as we saw in Chapter 6, the middle classes have taken the most advantage of expansion; but huge numbers of young people from all backgrounds do enter college. Moreover, the top American universities have been getting a very good press in the UK recently because of their ability to offer scholarships and financial aid to students from low-income backgrounds.

Table 7.2 Proportions of college students from different family income groups attending public/private colleges (of all types): 1997

	Private colleges	State-funded (public) colleges
Low-income families	18.9%	81.1%
Upper-income families	35.3%	64.7%
Richest families	51.0%	49.0%

Note: Family annual income: low <$20,000; upper $100,000–$200,000; richest >$200,000
Source: McPherson & Schapiro 1998a

But, in a country with almost 300 million citizens and 14 million students, ten or even a hundred poor students entering Harvard are hardly what define the university system. Higher education in the USA involves large numbers of private and public institutions. Some offer undergraduate and graduate degrees; others (including some of the most prestigious) are devoted to undergraduate education only; while in others – notably the community colleges – the 'associate' degree (equivalent to the first half of a bachelor's) is the highest award. At the top of the tree are some private universities (such as Harvard and Stanford), a few highly selective and private four-year colleges (such as Amherst), and a few highly selective public universities (such as the University of California, Berkeley).[14] At the other end, public community colleges are open-entry, and many of the huge state university campuses are also, in effect, open to any holder of a high-school diploma with the relevant minimum course credits.

Who goes where is pretty much what you might expect. The richer your family, the more likely you are to go to a highly selective, private four-year university. And the poorer your family, the more likely you are to go to the local community college.[15] As Table 7.2 shows, for all the exceptions to be found at either end – the poor, clever kids at Harvard, and the rich (and generally dumb) ones staying at home – family income plays a major role in where you attend college. And,

Table 7.3 *Percentage of students from low- and high-income families attending different types of HE institution*

	1981	1997
(a) Highly selective private universities		
Low-income	0.4	0.9
Upper-income	5.1	5.4
Richest	9.6	10.9
(b) Highly selective public universities		
Low-income	2.2	2.7
Upper-income	6.3	8.6
Richest	5.1	8.6
(c) Two-year colleges (largely non-selective)		
Low-income	44.6	47.1
Upper-income	20.4	16.3
Richest	13.2	12.0

Note: Family annual income: low – 1981 <$10,000, 1997 <$20,000 (inflation-adjusted on 1981 base); upper – 1981 $50,000–$100,000, 1997 $100,000–$200,000; richest – 1981 >$100,000, 1997 >$200,000
Source: McPherson & Schapiro, 1998a

while not all private colleges are good and prestigious, most of the highly selective institutions are also private.

Moreover, as Table 7.3 shows, entry to a selective university is not only much more likely for the rich: the gap between rich and poor is actually widening. This matters even more than the figures suggest, because attending a top university makes it much more likely that you will actually graduate. Thomas Mortensen, an American analyst, calculates that in 1979 a student from a family in the top quartile of the US income distribution was four times more likely to have actually completed a bachelor's degree by age twenty-four than one from the bottom quartile. By the mid 1990s, changes in participation rates plus the huge differences in speed and completion rates between college types had widened that difference from four to *ten* times.[16]

Table 7.4 *The social make-up of UK universities: proportions of first-year full-time undergraduates from social classes I and II at institutions from either end of the distribution: 1998*

Cambridge	80%
Oxford	79%
Bristol	77%
University College London	71%
Edinburgh	71%
Durham	70%
Newcastle	70%
St Andrews	70%
Leeds	69%
Exeter	68%
University of North London	33%
Thames Valley University	33%
North East Wales Institute of Higher Education	32%
University of East London	31%
London Guildhall University	31%
Bolton Institute of Higher Education	26%
University of Central Lancashire	21%

Source: UCAS web site: http://www.ucas.ac.uk/figures/index.html

Finally, and predictably, Table 7.4 shows parallel outcomes for universities in the UK. UCAS – the central clearing house which manages university admissions – collects statistics on the family origins of new UK-domiciled students, including the proportions from families in social classes I and II. Shown here are these proportions for the universities which had the highest, and lowest, representation of such students in 1998. There are no surprises. Middle-class teenagers are most over-represented in the selective universities, and least in evidence in the large-city ex-polytechnics and in the colleges of higher education which lack full university status.

Making it as a name brand

> I don't think one 'comes down' from Jimmy's university.
> According to him, it's not even red brick but white tile.
>
> John Osborne, *Look Back in Anger* II.i (1956)

As the previous section showed, the increased stratification of universities has a huge impact on young people because it affects the relative attractiveness (and market value) of different university studies. The results *may* also be increasing the efficiency with which firms recruit young graduates (and so the way in which higher education feeds into the economy); but, on the evidence above, they are just as likely to be introducing new biases and barriers to opportunity.

What, however, of the impact on universities themselves? They are also deeply affected. A situation where more and more of a country's highest-achieving students concentrate on applying to just a few universities creates a winner-take-all syndrome at institutional level too, with those students concentrated together in a self-reinforcing way. Just as students want to enter the best university they can, so a university wants to be as close to 'top' as it can manage, and at all times to be moving up rather than down the ladder. Even for the most prestigious institutions, none of this can be taken for granted. Modern universities eye the quality of their applicants nervously year on year, because the ability to attract the best students is an immediate indicator of their market reputation. It is also an important influence on the quality of academic activity: good staff want to teach and to benefit from teaching good pupils.

For many years a country's universities operated as pretty much a closed system, recruiting students and staff nationally, and supplying a national elite. Today's university world is increasingly global – in the reference groups of its increasingly specialized academics, as well as in recruitment of students and staff. This means that the competitive forces we are describing affect everyone – though not necessarily to equal degrees. It is perfectly possible for governments to resist the global tendency to stratify universities, and to do so with real success; but, if they do, it is also at a real cost, both in terms of their own favoured goal of economic growth and from a wider viewpoint. Before exploring the possibility of resistance, however, let us look at where competitive stratification has been given the most free rein: namely the United States.

The American university system depends indirectly and directly on huge amounts of public money,[17] and is subject to a great many laws and regulations. But education is not a federal responsibility, and the country's multiple state universities operate under quite different sets of conditions from each other. In addition, the system boasts 2,000 or so private universities and colleges. The net result is as much of a marketplace as that enjoyed by most industries in our age of regulations and controls. Many, if not most, American universities and colleges are effectively free to set their own salary levels. They adopt different product mixes aimed at different parts of the student population.[18] Unlike many of their European or Asian counterparts, the main activity of administrative staff is not item-by-item budget negotiations with state bureaucrats. Rather they are concerned with devising different financial packages to keep student numbers and quality up, with publicity and marketing, with searching for new high-quality members of staff, and with raising money from alumni.

Competition among universities is far more evident in the United States than anywhere else on earth. So, predictably, is wide inequality in salaries, and the emergence of the academic superstar. America's million academics have, on average, done fairly poorly over the last two decades, with real increases in earnings well below those for teachers, let alone lawyers. But professors at the top of their field have drawn further and further away from the pack. At the institutions which have an immediately recognizable 'name brand', and cater almost entirely to young, full-time students at both undergraduate and graduate levels, salaries are far above average for all levels of academic post – almost twice the level found at the lowest end of the private college market, and half as much again as in the big public universities.

Universities at the top want to stay at the top; universities not at the top want to move higher; and academics want to be in the top institutions. This last is partly a matter of status – working for a top institution bestows an aura. More concretely, clever students are more enjoyable to teach. Colleagues who are at the head of their field are stimulating. Research funds accumulate faster: a huge proportion of federal funding for research goes to just a few top universities. This reflects merit, but also that same safety-first principle we met among employers: a grant or contract to a top-class institution isn't likely to go completely to waste. Success breeds success – but only to a point. Grow complacent, and hungrier (often younger) institutions will be snapping at your heels.

Take a top US Ivy League university like Harvard, and it is clear how hard it works to stay ahead. Yes, it scours the country for clever students, and offers financial aid packages to all who can't afford the $24,000 fees;[19] and, yes, this is partly philanthropic. But it is also just as much about attracting the cleverest students because they add lustre to the university, provide first-class recruits to graduate programmes, *and* are set fair to become highly successful adults who will remember the university with affection, and with large and regular gifts. Harvard's recruitment drive may be efficient. Its system for keeping its alumni in constant touch with it (and with each other) is little short of staggering. Regular reunions are first and foremost exercises in successful, organized fund-raising.

One way in which alumni are kept sweet is by preferential entry for their offspring.[20] If a major result of being plucked from obscurity to Harvard, and making it in the world, was that your children could never attend the place, university finances would receive a serious blow. But family preferences don't have any real impact on the average academic achievement of entering students. Ivy League alumni tend to be clever and successful, so they tend to have children many of whom are also clever and almost all of whom are well schooled.[21]

Alumni gifts are important because staying on top is expensive. Aid to students isn't the half of it. Top universities need top faculty, who need to be paid top rates. Leading scholars need to be bought in, from other US universities and from across the world; your own best staff need to be kept happy in the face of counter-offers. The other side of paying for the best is ruthlessness towards the slightly less good. Junior academics who aren't making the grade are heading for contract termination, not nurture and protection.

But for those who make it to the top it does increasingly look like a classic winner-take-all situation. Harvard's endowments in 2000 were about $13 *billion*, which was about $3 billion more than a decade before. The university boasts thirty-eight Nobel laureates on its faculty, and pulls in over $300 million in federal government research funding alone in a typical year. Take a look at the web sites of any of Harvard's very few current rivals: Chicago (academically superb – seventy Nobel laureates among alumni and staff – $2.5 billion endowments, and $24,000 undergraduate fees). Or Yale – alma mater of George W. Bush (Al Gore went to Harvard): also rich ($7 billion endowments), also successful, and also hunting for the best students, the best faculty, and the grants and gifts that will help it to stay ahead.

Nationally, the results in research terms are vividly displayed in Table 7.5, which shows how, during the twentieth century the USA came to dominate scientific Nobel Prizes, and how it dominates scientific publishing. Some of those prizes were won by native-born Americans who were well educated by their home universities and have stayed at home. Many more, however, were won by scientists born and either fully or partially educated elsewhere who did not stay at home. Instead they followed the resources – material and intellectual – offered by an increasingly attractive American university sector: a process which has signally failed to occur in the reverse direction.

Many overseas politicians are entranced by the technological and economic spin-offs from America's top universities, and long for a Silicon Valley or a Microsoft of their own. In understanding how universities relate to the economy, however, perhaps the most interesting point is that there was a previous period when one country's universities seemed to have the secret of generating growth. They were, as noted earlier, the German universities of the late nineteenth century, and the similarities with the American situation are very striking. German universities also competed vigorously with each other, backed by rival localities and regional authorities intent on securing the best research professors for themselves. They produced the best science of the period, and for a short time were hugely influential – not least because of their perceived and genuine importance in the development of German industry: any ambitious budding scientist or engineer learned

Table 7.5   The growing scientific dominance of the USA [22]

US share of world population	5%
US share of scientific publications (refereed journals) in 1980s	37%
Number of science Nobel prizes gained by top seven US institutions:	
pre-1945	11
post-1945	96
Number of science Nobel prizes gained by top seven non-US institutions:	
pre-1945	35
post-1945	47

Sources: B. R. Clark 1995; Nobel Prize information web sites

German in order to read the literature.[23] The interwar years, culminating in Nazi rule, destroyed the universities' internationalism and their quality. Post-war they became, like most other countries' systems, largely inward-facing and protected, training their own national elites in a fairly self-contained way.

It would be foolish to conclude from this that only a competitive, and so stratified, university sector can generate economically relevant research. France, for example, has a highly successful economy. It separates the teaching of its elite (in the *Grandes Écoles*) both from mass higher education in the largely undifferentiated universities and from research, which takes place in a separately constituted state-run organization, the CNRS.[24] Japan managed almost a half-century of dramatic economic growth with virtually no university research centres to speak of. It depended instead on company-based developments, although recent work[25] does suggest that it has paid a heavy price in the narrow range of its successful sectors and the total absence of, for example, a successful chemicals industry. Contemporary German politicians and academics alike bemoan the state of their universities – the teaching, the facilities, the research. Again, though, we find a network of well-funded separate research institutions,[26] firm-based R & D, and an economy which has been the powerhouse of Europe for decades.

What contemporary experience and history do both teach, however, is that there are clear preconditions to be met if governments want *universities* to be vibrant generators of new research (with or without immediate economic relevance). That is important, because one of the major planks in the current educational consensus is the importance of *universities* to the 'knowledge economy' and the consequent need to expand the higher-education sector. If governments are serious in wanting this, then they have to accept competition among universities, and differentiation.

In theory, most countries are currently in favour of such a development. Intellectually at least, governments are aware that, in a world where at least a third of a cohort enters university, it simply is not feasible to have your whole university system at the top of some worldwide league table. So your choice is between following the American route, with ever greater differentiation, and hopefully some world-class winners (but probably some world-class stinkers too), and opting for more or less homogeneous mediocrity. You accept inequalities of provision and prestige as a way of stimulating creativity, innovation and efficiency, or you resign yourself to across-the-board second-class status.

I say 'intellectually at least' because, so far, much of the policy discussion has run into the sand. Many countries' systems remain startlingly different from the US model. Stratification may be proceeding apace in a global context, but many national systems remain distinctively national, not to say insular – neither obviously having adopted nor moving towards the competitive, international and differentiated model I have just described, and which has emerged so clearly in North America.

The reason is simple: that education remains one of the last great nationalized industries. At university level this means, in most European countries, that academics are effectively employees of central government. Their salary structures are set by the state; once they obtain a full appointment, they have complete civil-service-type job security; and the whole system of appointments and promotions is itself determined not by individual institutions, but by centrally set and regulated civil-service procedures. University heads will normally be state appointments, and budgets will also be set, in detail, at central level.[27]

This pattern can be compatible with high levels of academic freedom, in the sense of tenured, senior staff being allowed to teach and write what they please. What it precludes are variety and competition. In some countries, such as the Netherlands or Italy, there is a deliberate government policy of maintaining approximate equality among all universities in terms of not just resources but also prestige. In others, this is not so much the prime objective, more the recurring result. The fewer the courses for which universities can restrict entry, and the more that possession of a secondary diploma offers automatic access to any institution (or even any faculty), the harder it is for any one university to distinguish itself from another. And in many faculties, in many countries, this open access remains the rule.

When this type of system is combined with a huge rise in enrolments, the result is that a country's universities are not just much of a muchness: they are also all much of a mediocrity. Individual academics may still conduct first-class research. Others will offer first-class teaching. Nonetheless, for a whole institution to break away from the mass and distinguish itself, to become a general winner, is well-nigh impossible in this sort of centralized, controlled system. Very few countries indeed now have universities with the sort of global brand name that automatically attracts the world's top academics, students or recruiters. Those that do include the UK (for the moment) but virtually no others in the whole of Europe.

Whatever their specific ideological position, and however strongly they believe that 'world-class' universities are important for the economy, democratic parties face common constraints. They find it politically unpalatable to have very wide gaps between top and bottom in *public-sector* institutions – which is what almost all the world's universities are. Equally, whatever their ideology, governments are instinctive centralizers and are naturally most comfortable with centrally set, national pay scales for the public sector and centrally set rules for how courses and exams should be run, rather than freeing up individual institutions to set their own rates of pay and spend money as they see fit. When it comes to their own lives, politicians (and ruling elites generally) are masters of the benefit in kind: the car, the official house, the expense account and entertaining. Very high and visible pay, let alone highly unequal pay for civil-servant professors in nominally equivalent positions, is altogether more problematic.

The result is that university systems around the world are changing only very slowly. In Italy, for example, as Giliberto Capano points out, the government proclaims itself in favour of reform and modernization of the university sector. In theory, there is to be 'provision of an increasing share of public funds according to an assessment of the universities' actual performance'.[28] The reality is something else. Allocation is 'geopolitical': a combination of spreading provision out geographically (every city deserving its own university), political firefighting, and pork barrel. Only tiny amounts can be added to academics' centrally fixed salaries; promotion procedures continue to be laid down by national statutes; it remains official doctrine that universities 'are supposed to offer a similar standard of teaching', so that students need not worry about whether their school preparation is adequate for any particular university or whether a university is up to their school's standard. In Italy (as in many other countries) 'The state refuses to use the basic instrument of the differentiation of universities . . . a university ranking system.'[29] And in a centrally regulated, publicly funded system no other mechanism exists to create that differentiation.

At national level, governments have a choice. They can opt – consciously or by default – for egalitarian funding or minimum change, and out of the global race. Or they can opt into a system of differentiation, competition and, they hope, some institutions with a global profile. What they cannot do, however, is opt out of global pressures altogether. Because, while they can largely control how the universities within their borders operate, they cannot control all their potential students *or* potential researchers, teachers and professors.

As we have seen, for the top prizes recruitment is no longer national, let alone local: increasingly it takes place across the developed world. That means more people chasing the best graduates of the best universities, not within but across countries; and more universities chasing the best researchers and academics too. The process is hastened by the advent of a new world language, English, which is learned and spoken by a far larger proportion of humanity than predecessors such as Latin, French and Arabic. The elites of the most prosperous nations are themselves increasingly closely in contact: speaking that same world language, reading their own parish newspapers (the *FT*, the *Wall Street Journal*), following careers which routinely involve moves between countries – and entering these careers via the top universities and business schools. The latter are now *global* gatekeepers, and their league tables (like the *FT*'s annual business-school tables) are correspondingly global too.[30]

If a country's own system is inadequate, the results are predictable, if expensive for the individuals concerned. Helmut Kohl, Chancellor of West and then of united Germany for over fifteen years, prided himself on his German persona: a love of German food, holidays spent in German spas, not speaking French or English at international meetings. But he was also a parent, with a parent's usual ambitions, and his sons went to university not in Germany, but at Harvard and MIT.[31] Conversely, since education is itself a traded, global commodity, an attractive university system attracts foreign students and their fees.[32] Some of the biggest purchasers of overseas higher education are the 'tiger' economies of South-East Asia. Their governments sponsor thousands of students to study abroad – but only in a limited number of institutions. To appear on their approved list, a university needs to demonstrate high quality. That can mean a high position in official lists (like the ones the UK government creates for 'research excellence'), or in rankings by subject or professional associations, or in the influential media listings of US colleges. The larger the higher-education sector becomes, the more important international rankings and league tables are likely to be. In a world suffering from information overload, brand names become ever more critical, and imply a fiercely competitive university sector.

The United States arrived at its current position as much by default as by conscious government policy, but now feels itself to have benefited enormously. A few other countries are embracing the US model, or hover on the brink, unable to decide between this system and one of tight government control and egalitarianism. The UK is one that has the choice and is hovering – which brings us to the fragile equilibrium of British higher education, and in particular the likely fate of Oxford and Cambridge, the UK's two current global name brands.

Can Oxbridge stay in the premier league?

One day in 1999, a young man who had dropped out of his own degree course visited another university to see an old friend who hadn't. They went out drinking, and came back to the friend's room to talk and maybe drink some more. It was hot; the window was open. The visitor leaned backwards on the sill, fell to the street below, and was killed on impact. A simple, tragic accident, but it made the evening-paper placards and morning front pages across the country. Not because the dead man was famous – he wasn't. Not because there was foul play suggested – there was not. Simply because the window he fell from was in an Oxford college, and his friend was an Oxford University student.

In recent years, as British higher education has expanded, the public's fascination with Oxbridge has actually increased. League tables now get produced and published for research, for supposed teaching quality, for facilities, for postgraduate numbers, and for anything else the government and press can devise; and Oxford and Cambridge are always at or near the top. But they are not in solitary state: others, like Imperial College, the London School of Economics, Warwick or Bristol, come equal or close on many counts, including the indicators of international-calibre research and research funding. So this Oxbridge obsession might at first seem odd.

Discussions of it within Britain tend to come back, time and again, to class and British perceptions of it. The 'Brideshead factor' is a hardy perennial, referring to the idea that Oxford is full of languid young aristocrats of the type portrayed in Evelyn Waugh's 1945 novel about pre-1939 England, *Brideshead Revisited*. Certainly the press loves pictures and stories which feature students from well-known families, preferably in evening dress, and preferably either drunk or stoned. Certainly, too, Oxford and Cambridge are amazingly and distinctively beautiful: Imperial, with all the brick and plate-glass charm of (for example) MIT, can never compete in this respect.

But this misses the point. Oxbridge is in the news not because it is haunted by upper-class sots, or because it is beautiful. Rather, because Oxbridge is already news, stories about it which also figure a Cabinet minister's son, drunken parties, beautiful buildings, or ideally all three, are double value. And Oxbridge is news because of all the factors discussed earlier in this chapter, which create not merely national but international 'pyramids of prestige'.[33]

The globalization of high-status education is instantly obvious in the numbers of overseas students. At undergraduate and postgraduate levels, the numbers of these at Oxford more than doubled between 1978 and 1998: to 1,108 (around 10 per cent) at undergraduate level and 2,944 (or well over half) at postgraduate level. Many overseas undergraduates have actually come via overseas universities rather than direct from school (in line with the Rhodes Scholar tradition of completing a second undergraduate degree in a compressed time frame). But, if you look at the new students matriculating at a random selection of individual colleges in the 1950s, in the 1960s and now, a new phenomenon is also clear. Forty years ago the sprinkling of overseas undergraduates was confined to Britain's old colonies – one from Jamaica here, a couple from India there. Today, alongside far more students from Singapore, there are some quite different and novel 'home' institutions listed – Athens Tutorial Colleges, Wilhelm Hausenstein Gymnasium in Germany, Marselisborg Gymnasium in Denmark, and even the occasional French *lycée*.[34]

Their students came because Oxford and Cambridge are not just the top for would-be members of the British elite, but up in the global league as well. And that is why the universities, and their students, are news. Of course the glamour, the history and the physical environment help to keep them there, and helped to give them that invaluable asset of 'global brand recognition'. But their newsworthiness ultimately reflects their continuing effectiveness, in the eyes of parents and students, in boosting graduates' chances in the competition for prestige, money and power. If that bonus goes, so too will the media's fascination. And name recognition alone won't keep them in the global league. Who, now, dreams of sending their children to Giessen[35] or the Sorbonne?

Universities at the top of a pyramid spend and receive more. Extra funding may not automatically deliver global success, but it is certainly a necessary condition for it. In the UK, governments straddle, with growing unease, policies that pull them in different directions: the path of least resistance, implying across-the-board more or less equal funding for everyone, versus the desire for top institutions. How is a university to pay higher salaries than the national average if it doesn't also have more money? You can't equip the whole vast sector with state-of-the-art research laboratories; so, again, is it to be low-grade facilities across the board, or higher funding levels for the favoured few? Equal access and equal funding appeal as fairer; but the £1.5 billion entering the UK economy from overseas-student fees will vanish if quality too visibly drops. Also, the next generation of doctors, engineers, chemists and designers has to be equipped with up-to-date skills, because university isn't just about putting young people in rank order – or at least not yet. And ever there beckons the vision of Silicon Valley, and the contribution not of America's vast state campuses, but of its very best selective graduate schools.

The UK's compromise response has been to distribute *some* funding selectively, but in a way which supposedly ring-fences it for research (and so treats all students equally for teaching purposes). The 'Research Assessment Exercise', established by a Conservative government under Margaret Thatcher and continued by Labour, is actually very unusual for a nationalized[36] and centralized system, because it directs significantly different levels of funding to different universities. This is done on research rankings, and technically any department or institution can change its ranking and make it to the top. In the short run, though, rankings tend to be stable and predictable: a university at the top should be able to stay there unless it is criminally ill-run, since success breeds success for all the reasons discussed in the previous pages. Oxford and Cambridge have done very well from the 'RAE' though so have a number of other top 'Russell Group' universities.[37] And of course money doesn't come in watertight compartments, so students in the top-rated universities tend to benefit accordingly in terms of facilities, and in the effect of extra funding on faculty recruitment.

However, Oxford and Cambridge have also had special treatment, and this, up till now, has maintained and even strengthened their attraction. For the last fifty years the government has, through the 'college fee', provided significantly higher levels of public funding per student to Oxford and Cambridge than to other universities. This was something that most students (even Oxbridge ones) and many academics in other universities were quite unaware of until the education ministers in the 1997 Labour government decided that its day had come. At this point, passionate appeals were made to the Prime Minister – himself an Oxford graduate – and, while unwilling to overrule his ministers, Blair nonetheless tempered the blow.

Some Oxbridge colleges have large endowments, dating back over centuries (and share them out a bit with poorer colleges).[38] This has also helped maintain the distinctiveness of Oxbridge: individual college libraries, college sports clubs, better staff–student ratios. But Oxford and Cambridge nonetheless operate within an essentially nationalized industry, with national, centrally set pay scales, and share an egalitarian ethos which has made many academics deeply reluctant to engage directly or self-consciously in the game of market positioning, aggressive fund-raising and star salaries. British academics are far more 'left' than others of similar occupational class *or* class origin: even academics educated in public schools include a majority of Labour voters, whereas in the country as a whole public-school-educated professionals vote overwhelmingly Conservative.[39]

As a result, the universities and their constituent colleges have poured money into benefits in kind rather than higher pay for professors, research stipends, or even research facilities. Oxbridge money has gone to a very large extent on building or maintaining subsidized housing – for staff, but also for students. This architectural bonus has in some cases enhanced the cities' beauty, but is hardly a way to secure a global intellectual future.

Academics conditioned by periods working in North America have tended to find attitudes in the UK incomprehensible and infuriating. Robert Stevens (Oxford-educated, holder of senior posts in various US universities, and, at the time, head of an Oxford college) expostulated against his colleagues' inability to face up to, or handle, 'the relationship between excellence and equality'. An article in Oxford's alumni magazine, *Oxford Today*, attracted his especial scorn. 'It is a healthy sign that the proportion of MPs educated at Oxford is in decline,' the magazine proclaimed, following the May 1997 election, in which a smaller proportion of elected MPs were Oxford graduates than in any previous twentieth-century election. No US university, Stevens complained, would have produced this 'ludicrous' response. The *Yale Alumni Magazine* would have seized on some other set of laurels to report, such as 'that one third of the members of the House of Lords had been to Oxford'.[40]

Today, the Oxbridge reluctance to embrace global marketing, American-style fund-raising, and lengthening academic hierarchies is disappearing fast in the face of competition and financial pressure. But the political context remains the same: a nationalized, politicized higher-education system, and one where, far from fading, central planning is *increasingly* the order of the day. I have already mentioned the Research Assessment Exercise – which provides differential funding, but also exerts huge influence over academics' activities and priorities, and over the way in which institutions allocate resources and deal with staff. Equally significant, however, is the Quality Assurance Agency (QAA), set up in 1997 to ensure 'quality' in higher education. This organization is almost a caricature of modern governmental bureaucracy, but it encapsulates the government's belief that it can combine a vital, 'world-class' system with ever-tightening central control.

The QAA describes its role as being 'to promote public confidence that quality of provision and standards of awards in higher education are being safeguarded and enhanced'[41] – a definition that, by concentrating on public perceptions and 'confidence', neatly sidesteps any serious responsibility for addressing standards in any substantive way. The definition sits well, however, with the Agency's real obsession, which is with paperwork systems and 'audits', at which it worries away in repeated visits. Universities get 'guidance' on each and every aspect of their affairs (168 rules and 11 codes of practice at the last count), but have also been receiving individual subject-related visitations which involve every single department in the land. These audits of 'teaching quality' each culminate in scores out of 4 for a list of 'quality' indicators.

The indicators themselves focus overwhelmingly on paperwork and procedures: very little teaching is ever observed, and the one thing on which every visited institution agrees is that the process has essentially been a farce – albeit a very time-consuming, expensive and stressful one. As time has gone by, and everyone has got better at guessing what will be wanted, so the QAA scores have risen upward, clustering at the top of the scale. ('Quality', presumably, is increasing too.)

The visible paper mountains, and the mistakes that inevitably occur in such a large-scale exercise, have generated protests, legal actions, and a more or less continual process of 'consultation' about how to improve QAA. None of this, however, affects the underlying principle: centralized political control of a sector, all of whose members are treated as equivalent – and equivalently endowed. Indeed, in nothing the QAA does is there the slightest suggestion that universities might not all have been created equal. On the contrary: the QAA has now developed 'benchmark standards' for all UK degrees, using a twenty-two-subject framework into which virtually the whole 172-institution, 2-million-student-strong sector is to be shoehorned.[42] These are designed to guarantee common minimum standards, whether the degree in question is taken at Cambridge or Luton, Aberdeen or Plymouth, Oxford or Wolverhampton. Figure 7.1 reproduces a few of these standards. They are so vacuous that it would be hard *not* to meet them (though the resultant paperwork will no doubt impose heavy costs), but that doesn't matter, because the meaning of this exercise does not reside in these standards. It is about uniform processes and treatment across a public sector.

At present, entry standards for UK degrees in most subjects – mathematics, engineering, foreign languages, history – cover a huge range: from a minimum of three A grades at A level for a place at one university, to one or two E grades (and then not necessarily in the subject studied) at another. If it were really the case that, at the end of a three-year degree course, students at all these institutions were reaching the same basic standard, it would be a major scandal. It would mean that, in the most selective institutions, some students were effectively learning nothing in the time they were there – something one would think that they (or their parents) might notice. Alternatively, other

Figure 7.1 Sample 'benchmark standards' – demonstrated compliance with these is to be required of all UK degrees

Graduates who have studied **English** should be able to demonstrate (inter alia)

- knowledge of literature and language, which in the case of literature should include a substantial number of authors and texts from different periods of literary history
- appreciation of the power of imagination in literary creation

and will have acquired skills which include

- ability to articulate knowledge and understanding of texts, concepts and theories relating to English studies
- the capacity for independent thought and judgement
- competence in the planning and execution of essays and project work.

Graduates who have studied **History** should be able to demonstrate (inter alia)

- The appreciation of the complexity and diversity of situations, events and past mentalities
- The ability to read and use texts and other source materials, both critically and empathetically
- Intellectual independence
- Marshalling of argument
- Structure, coherence, clarity and fluency of written expression
- Empathy and imaginative insight.

Source: QAA 2001

institutions would be achieving genuine miracles: tapping undiscerned talent, making up completely for previous academic failures, enabling students to learn far more than their better-prepared peers in far better resourced universities. Again, wouldn't someone have noticed? Wouldn't employers be beating a path to at least some of these doors?

The answer, of course, is that nothing of the sort is happening (at least not on a country-wide basis). No one really believes that degree standards are the same across the whole of this vast higher-education sector, or that they could be.[43] That is why a good many major graduate-recruitment schemes now specify minimum A-level point scores as well as a class of degree. But it isn't possible to admit this publicly. So long as universities are public-sector producers, controlled and run by Whitehall, no government wants publicly to tell students (and voters) that some of them are getting a better product than others. Vacuous benchmark standards maintain the myth that all degrees are the same 'quality' product.

Which brings us back to Oxbridge, and to the Laura Spence affair. This erupted in the spring of 2000, when I was first drafting this book. Spence, a clever student from a northern comprehensive school, was competing with many other highly qualified eighteen-year-olds for a place to read medicine at Oxford. She failed to win one; her head teacher went to the papers with the story; the Chancellor of the Exchequer weighed in, accusing the university of elitism; and the whole of the British media let fly on one side or the other. Meanwhile, Spence herself accepted a place at Harvard, with the usual income-dependent financial-aid package thrown in (part loan, part scholarship), occasioning another major round of column inches. Echoes of the Laura Spence affair reverberated well beyond these islands (as I discovered on a lecture tour of Australia), as well as gripping just about every parent in the land. That it did so tells us a lot about higher education at the turn of the millennium.

First, Oxbridge remains, for the moment, the promised land. Every year, independent and state-school heads scrutinize their pupils' experiences and write angry letters to the press, convinced (depending on their provenance) that selectors are discriminating against, or in favour of, independent- or state-school pupils. They show no such anxiety over Warwick, or Imperial, or Edinburgh, because other UK universities, however good, lack that magic branding.[44] Second, the struggle for entry is overwhelmingly *within* the middle class. No one who has read thus far will be surprised to know that Spence's own family, though not rich, was definitively middle class. Those state-school and independent-school pupils clambering to the top of the university pyramid have family backgrounds that are, for the most part, highly alike.

Third, students in Britain (and elsewhere) are increasingly sensitive to global, not just national, prestige. Spence wasn't short of offers from other UK medical schools, but she chose Harvard, even though it meant starting off with a biochemistry degree and not with medicine. (In the USA, medicine is studied entirely at postgraduate level.) If she wanted global cachet, this decision was definitely the right one. Fourth, both the Chancellor's intervention and Oxford's response underlined how political and politicized mass higher education has become.

The Chancellor, Gordon Brown, saw an attack on Oxford elitism as an effective political stroke because university entry – and *which* university is entered – now matters so much to so many people. Oxford's response – in which righteous anger, detailed factual rebuttal, and a strong undertone of panic were mixed – reflected the university's awareness of that same politicization. The future of British universities and the continued existence of Oxbridge (and indeed the Russell Group) as we know it depend on the behaviour of politicians whose recent actions have all inclined towards more control, more direction, more government planning. Sure enough, the most immediate concrete result of the affair was a further piece of central direction. Later in that year it was announced that £20 million – amounting to 20 per cent of the whole funding increase for higher education in a bumper spending year – was to be directed to combating 'elitism' in admissions to top universities.

There is one final lesson to be drawn from the Laura Spence affair. It generated such enormous publicity not just because it hit so many middle-class nerves, but also because the future of universities was already in the news. As we have seen, the UK operates an uneasy halfway house between a US-style hierarchy and state-enforced uniformity. Oxbridge's survival depends on movement towards the former rather than the latter; and that, in turn, means maintaining, and indeed increasing, the financial resources of those universities at the top of the pyramid. What was increasingly obvious, even before the Spence affair broke, was that the opposite was happening. Instead, the other characteristic of mass higher education was making itself felt – ongoing financial crisis.

Pile 'em high, sell 'em cheap

Individuals and institutions follow their individual and institutional interests. There are constraints on them, of course, including many imposed by governments.[45] But, as we have seen throughout this book, this perfectly rational behaviour explains much of the past, and indeed predicts the future, of the education system and education policies. In the case of universities, the result has been an increasingly competitive hierarchy of institutions. However, what is bad (or good) for a given university isn't necessarily economically good (or bad) for a country as a whole. To see how well our evolving university system may be contributing to growth, we need to look at the sector as a whole: not just its segmentation, but also its size and its total resources.

As anyone who works in the field will tell you, everyone knows about education because everyone went to school. Most of our politicians went to university too; but even those who went somewhere other than Oxbridge have memories (and preconceptions) of university life that bear decreasing resemblance to today's mass higher education. One indication of that gap between perception and reality is how often the Robbins Report of 1963 is cited as the precursor of large-scale higher education in the UK. It did indeed lead to the foundation of new universities, but it took total numbers to just under forty, compared to today's 170-odd members of the Committee of Vice-Chancellors and Principals (or 'Universities UK' as they have renamed themselves). The immediate post-Robbins foundations were on green-field sites near ancient towns and for full-time young and non-working students. The optimal size for a student body was thought to be around 3,000.[46]

Of course, even at the time there were observers who felt that this was untenable. Oxford's A. H. Halsey, a leading analyst of UK universities, recounts two anecdotes, both involving Americans who had not merely seen but were living something close to our future. On the new University of Sussex campus, 'built for the admiration of the peasantry without regard to their public pocket', Martin Trow, then president of the University of California (and past chancellor of its Berkeley component), 'gazed sceptically at [the] low-density, high-cost architecture' and observed that 'Neither we nor you can afford to build like this for a mass system.'[47] And Halsey himself, visiting the building site that was to be yet another University of California campus, at La Jolla, met the architect of a university designed to house 27,500 students.

> **The architect was delighted to see us. 'You people are from Oxbridge? . . . You have colleges there. We are thinking along the same lines. Tell me, how many guys do you put in these colleges?' . . . I guessed that Christ Church at Oxford or St John's Cambridge would be among the biggest, about 500 each. 'Yeah,' smiled the architect, 'That'll be the faculty, but how many students?'[48]**

Trow was, of course, right. No one can afford to build Oxbridge-style universities for a twenty-first-century university sector. The expansion of higher education which every developed country has experienced has also, in every case, meant an explosion in total spending. But in the process there has been constant pressure on salaries and spending at the per-student level. The UK was a relatively generous funder of institutions and a very generous funder of students, offering free tuition and generous income-linked maintenance grants throughout the post-war period.[49] During the 1980s and 1990s, however, there was a relentless decline, as Figure 7.2 displays.[50] The amount of money available *per student* from government funds virtually halved.[51] Not that the government chooses to describe it in these terms. In the *Brave New World* language of modern higher education, cuts in spending are announced as 'efficiency gains', while the students themselves are now 'units of resource'.

During this period, student numbers rose, numbers of university staff rose, student–staff ratios rose – and academics' market position

Figure 7.2 *Real public funding per student in UK universities (1976 = 100)*

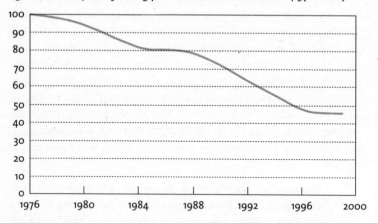

Sources: National Committee of Inquiry into Higher Education 1997; Universities UK 2001

plummeted. For students, universities might offer a financial bargain in terms of future income and employment. For staff, they were increasingly a financial wasteland in which they were trapped by decisions made in the good years before the lean.

To be a professor in 1905 was to be part of a tiny minority whose salary range of £500 to £1,000 a year put one within the top half a per cent of the population. As late as 1935, the total academic staff of UK universities were still a small elite, numbering 3,670 in total. The professors among them averaged £1,094 a year and the lecturers £471 at a time when £2.50 a week (£125 a year) was a good wage for an adult manual worker and when a family with small children on the dole would get about £80 a year. And for the first twenty post-war years, as higher education expanded gradually, academic staff largely maintained their position. The bottom end of the professorial range of salaries put those who received them in the top 2 per cent of earners, while those at the top clearly fell into the highest 1 per cent of earners both in 1949 and in the mid 1960s. Lecturers in the 1960s all had salaries that put them within the top quintile (20 per cent) of direct-income earners, while the top of the salary range fell within the top 5 per cent.

These people staffed the sort of university sector that most politicians and newspaper editors remember. But by 1999 there were as many historians alone working in the UK university sector as the total number of university staff seventy years before.[52] Paid on a fixed scale set through central pay-bargaining, they were certainly no longer a part of an income elite. Across the university sector, many professors, far from qualifying for the top 1 per cent, were now just scraping into the top quintile; basic-scale lecturers were now firmly down in the second quintile of the income spread.[53] Year on year, in an environment of general inflation, the salaries of British academics fell further and further behind those of groups which had once been academics' equals or inferiors in income terms. Over the 1980s, academics averaged less than a 10 per cent increase in real terms, compared to 35 per cent for NHS doctors and for teachers and 37 per cent for private-sector non-manual workers overall. For the ten years ending in the mid 1990s the average gross increase for all non-manual earners – Classes I, II *and* III – was 101 per cent, but for academic staff it was 68 per cent, or barely ahead of inflation.[54]

Was this inevitable? Or can countries create mass university systems *and* sustain salaries and per-student spending? It is true that few countries have exerted quite such a dramatic downward pressure on per-student spending as the UK. Indeed, if we look at the last quarter-century as a whole, a good many European countries have actually increased expenditure per student faster than the rate of inflation. France, for example, was spending 17 per cent more per university student in real terms in 1997 than in 1975, while Spain increased per-student spending by 27 per cent in the early to mid 1990s.[55] Yet, in all these countries, university academics and administrators alike complain constantly of underfunding. The bigger increases are generally from a lower starting base, so the outcome is very similar. The typical university building, all over Europe, is shabby, ugly and overcrowded. To academics, this is simply the visible tip of an iceberg of inadequate resources.

Academics' complaints are not simply the inevitable self-serving grumbles of a public-sector group jostling for taxpayers' money. What education shares with health is that it does not and cannot register regular large efficiency gains, because it depends on human beings, not machines. The quality of what you receive is directly related to how much time you, as a student or patient, receive from others. The British government's descriptions of cuts in per-student spending as 'efficiency gains' are, in this context, not merely cynical but almost certainly a lie.

As Paul Ryan has pointed out, public services suffer from 'cost disease'.[56] In large parts of the economy we can register 'real' increases in income from the fact that new factories are more productive, turning out more goods with fewer workers, less energy input, less waste. Hence we can now buy a washing machine with an average of, say, a week's wages rather than three weeks'. But education isn't like that (and nor are most other public services). We haven't yet found methods of changing the way that teachers and students interact. We don't have clever strategies for making sure you get the same sort of learning with twice as many students per tutor, or with half as much detailed feedback given on students' essays, or with didactic lectures instead of seminar groups. With washing machines, productivity gains regularly deliver more machines that are cheaper *and* as good as or better than before; but with education the equivalent simply doesn't happen.

Looked at in this way, 'real' spending increases start to look a bit less real. The French may be spending 17 per cent more in 'real' terms per student than twenty years ago, but that doesn't mean that students are necessarily getting 17 per cent more teaching, or better staff, or even better labs and libraries. Average incomes have gone up much more than 17 per cent in 'real' terms during that same period. If lecturers' salaries rose with the rest, then that expenditure increase will account for a smaller portion of a lecturer's time than before. In growing economies where people's earnings are rising steadily, doing no more than maintain 'real' levels of spending per student will mean that, as a percentage of GDP, spending per student falls.

Even in countries which didn't actually cut student spending, the 1990s were a period of spluttering funding for higher education. Leaving aside countries where significant amounts of money already came from student fees (the USA, Australia, Canada), OECD figures indicate that, in most industrialized countries, small increases in nominal spending per head masked a fall in real terms (once inflation is taken into account). Almost all these countries, moreover, were turning in clear falls in expenditure per student compared to GDP per head, as Table 7.6 makes clear.

Table 7.6 *Expenditure per student in higher education as a percentage of GDP per capita*

	1993	1997
Austria	45	43
Finland	n/a (1995: 40)	35
France	32	33
Germany	43	43
Italy	29	n/a (1995: 26)
Netherlands	49	45
Spain	29	32
Switzerland	75	63
UK	49	40

Sources: OECD 1999a, 2000a, 2001a

What price quality? Are we getting less for more?

It is hard to believe – and I certainly don't – that in the longer term this pattern won't affect the quality of countries' higher education. Far and away the bulk of higher-education spending (and indeed of education spending generally) goes on salaries. If spending falls as a percentage of GDP, this effectively means either that a given student is going to be getting a smaller proportion of people's time devoted to him or her or that the quality of the people working in education will fall. In the latter case, students may get as much time, but it will be from people who are less desirable in labour-market terms, and so can be bought for a smaller proportion of GDP than their predecessors. Salary may not be everything, but it certainly isn't irrelevant; and, as academics' relative pay falls, people who might have entered the profession a generation ago turn elsewhere. In some areas this is already evident: in 1998 and 1999, several of the UK's top-ranked and internationally famous economics departments reported that not a single one of their new Ph.D. students was from the UK. Fewer and fewer of their best new graduates showed any interest in an academic career; conversely, companies, especially in the City, were hiring them eagerly at far higher salaries than academe can offer. As the authors of a Research Councils report on Ph.D. recruitment point out, clever students demand clever teachers. What happens when companies hiring well-trained young economists find that 'the country's universities have not got the intellectual firepower to provide them'?[57]

For economics, read any other subject with a thriving alternative market. In the short term, a number of things mask this effect. The most important is that current university staff are trapped. Many chose their careers decades before; now they find their relative earnings shrinking vis-à-vis their contemporaries in other professions, but they have no real alternative but to stay put. They may work harder – see more students, give more lectures, spend their evenings on paperwork for the next inspection or audit. But they also can and do change the product. Increasing the numbers at a given lecture doesn't obviously affect the quality of anybody's learning. But what about when you double the numbers in each seminar group? Abolish small-group tutorials altogether? Reduce the quantity of student work that academics mark and provide feedback on? By the time most of these latter changes have cut in – and they most definitely have – it is very hard to convince oneself that quality has not suffered.[58]

You can, of course, argue that these changes are counterbalanced by students working harder and more independently – though, if active teaching and comments on student work are so unimportant, why do we have university teaching staff at all? You might also convince yourself, as many politicians apparently have, that the whole problem will shortly be solved by the development of wonderful interactive software, which will enable students to learn more effectively and cheaply from computers than ever they were able to with conventional teaching. You will, however, have to depend entirely on faith when you do so, for to date there is not a shred of empirical evidence available in support of such a position. The one demonstrable effect of IT on the way in which students are taught is the spread of computer-delivered and computer-marked 'objective' testing – which in practice means mutiple-choice tests of factual knowledge, illustrated in Figure 7.3.

Figure 7.3 *'Objective' IT-based testing in higher education: exemplar questions*

(a) Indicate whether the reason given is correct:

Assertion Increased government spending increases inflation under all conditions

BECAUSE

Reason Government spending is not offset by any form of production.

(b) Which of the following rhyme schemes could be used for a sonnet?
abba cdde efg efg
abab cdcd efef gg
abba abba caca

(c) The Food Division of the Brickbat Corporation is undertaking a capital budgeting analysis. This division has a different level of systematic risk from that typical for the corporation as a whole. The most appropriate method for estimating the division's beta is to:

(i) calculate the regression coefficient from a time-series regression of corporation stock returns on a market index.

(ii) multiply the company beta by the ratio of the division's total assets to the corporation's total assets.

(iii) calculate the regression coefficient from a time-series regression of the division's net income on the corporation's return on assets.

(iv) calculate the regression coefficient from a time-series regression of the division's return on assets on a market index.

Sources: Adapted from questions appearing in Brown 1997 and Medweb

These certainly make it easier to test students more frequently, but the sort of testing and learning they encourage is hardly what most of us associate with higher education.

Expand a public-sector service enormously, especially when voters are hugely resistant to tax increases, and what happens? Exactly what you might expect – and the cost squeeze in British universities, and the overcrowding and poor facilities typical of many European institutions, bear witness to it. By the time that Laura Spence applied to Oxford, these pressures had convinced large parts of the academic workforce in the 'top' part of the British higher-education hierarchy that their salvation had to lie outside the Treasury, otherwise they could only sink against North American competition. So the Laura Spence affair broke against a background of debate over university funding, and especially over the desirability (and legitimacy) both of fees (introduced by Labour in 1998 with Conservative support, paraded against by students, and attacked out of hand by the Liberal Democrats) and of differential 'top-up fees' (outlawed by the Labour ministers then in office and endorsed by a good many figures from the top Russell Group universities).

The Russell Group universities are increasingly convinced that global stratification is proceeding apace, and that they need to increase funding levels quickly if they are not to find themselves doomed to what will be effectively a mediocre backwater, however pretty its buildings. To do this, they need to break free of government egalitarianism. It is not at all clear that they will do so. He who pays the piper calls the tune, and as David Robertson, a major contributor to current higher-education debates, has observed, the last big review by Dearing 'offers up a model of higher education composed of new hierarchies, greater centralised administrative control and the prospect of vastly more paperwork . . . [T]he driving intelligence of the report is the conviction that the sector must be controlled.'[59] This is certainly the vision most enthusiastically embraced by recent British ministers.

None of this is likely to cheer the academic heart, or make university life the employee's promised land. But does that matter? Thus far in this book I have resolutely ignored education as anything but an economic input, although one of the obvious casualties of universities' financial straits and increased bureaucratization must be time for scholarship and disinterested learning. So, what about the twin economic goals for higher education: imparting skills to its graduates and developing research with direct economic relevance? Taking all the trends in higher education together, are they good or are they bad for skills provision, research and growth?

My own view is that what is happening is very bad: and that it is bad for *growth*, not just for intellectual creativity, education in its broad liberal sense, and the quality of national life. This is the case even though universities are not the only source of scientific breakthroughs, let alone of practical, technological developments.

As we saw above, it *is* possible to have growth without a vibrant university sector. In research terms, in-company research and development (as in Japan) or independent networks of research laboratories, like those of France, offer alternative models. In other cases, institutional structures can encourage small and medium-size firms to thrive by improving and developing products which are well inside the technological envelope.[60] Equally, if other aspects of your economy and society don't encourage effective application of research and efficient, well-managed businesses, then (like the UK in the 1960s and 1970s) you can perfectly well combine world-class scientific research with economic failure.[61]

However, if all your universities are mediocre, then, as a country, you will certainly not have any Silicon Valleys. Governments of large developed countries (such as the UK, France, Germany and Japan) hate the idea of being avowedly and intentionally second class in terms of new ideas, patents and industries. It is also pretty risky knowingly to forswear research-led growth, because the changing international scene suggests that good research universities may become increasingly important to countries' economic futures as well as their cultural ones. It is not just the close association between university research and the technological breakthroughs of the last twenty years that matters, but also the increasing tendency of good people (and not just capital) to move towards the most productive, innovative and exciting areas in their field of expertise. It is hard to be confident, in advance, that you can maintain a successful economy and retain your best people while consciously consigning your university sector to third- or fourth-class status.

And what about the 'skill-training' side of universities? This has been the central theme of political (and business) rhetoric about the need for ever more graduates, conjuring up a vision of 'supply-side' growth developing once ever more university-educated young people pour into the workforce, creating the 'knowledge economy' around them as they come.

But suppose that more does indeed mean worse? Not in the sense that the new graduates are less able or less deserving than previous generations, but in the sense that they are *all* less well educated and well trained. Suppose you move from 100,000 to 400,000 graduates a year. All the latter have *some* of what the former had, but you no longer have 100,000, or anything like it, educated in the way the 'old' graduates were – whether in engineering, law, philosophy, mathematics or archaeology. Is that obviously, in economic terms, a good bargain?

It is always difficult to measure the quality of education, and enormously difficult the minute one goes beyond performance in the basic academic skills which are taught not in universities, but in primary and secondary schools. So I certainly can't measure in any precise way whether and how far the quality and skills of graduates today are any different from, or generally lower than, those of graduates a decade or five decades ago. Which graduates? Compared to whom? Which subjects? Which skills? What we can do, however, is delineate our current situation. It is one where:

- individuals' demand for higher education goes on rising (for totally rational, self-interested reasons);
- the economy probably already has an over-supply of graduates, as we saw in Chapters 2 and 6;
- funding per student is falling, and the most probable prognosis is a continuing decline in real funding levels;
- we have, or are set for, a progressive decline in the real amounts of teaching (and learning) offered on each degree, and in the quality of university staff.

Opening up universities has provided cultural, social and intellectual opportunities on an unprecedented scale, even if many students *are* only there because of the labour market. But for our politicians, who are so overwhelmingly and insistently focused on higher education as simply an input into a growth equation, the result may be net loss, not net gain. One result of the recent university explosion is that many of those entering graduate jobs probably do so with *lower* skill levels than in previous years, since their studies are less well funded and less effective. Should governments really be confident that, overall, they are boosting the growth rate and getting good returns on their inflated expenditures? Is it really a good idea to reduce real funding per student when your graduates are continuing to feed into professional, managerial and research jobs in pharmaceutical companies, software houses, merchant banks, electricity-generating companies and hospitals? Suppose we spent less on expanding the whole higher-education sector and more on schools and teachers, so that fundamental academic skills were better taught between ages five and sixteen. Would that obviously be a 'bad thing' for growth?

For the UK, these choices are particularly acute. It is not only that we have a prestigious and intellectually productive university sector with an uncertain future. It is not only that we have cut per-student funding to levels where the impact on teaching and facilities is visible and obvious. It is also that we have no alternative system. Our higher-education capacity and our research capacity *are* our universities. We have a single and supposedly 'unified' sector, unlike the tripartite French (*Grandes Écoles*, universities, CNRS) or Germans (universities, polytechnics and research centres). If higher education declines, there is no obvious backstop.

Like their counterparts in other countries, at some levels UK politicians and civil servants recognize this. Yet their record, over the last quarter-century, gives little cause for optimism. It is one of an unbalanced quest for growth, to the exclusion of the other, central, concerns of education. It is also one based on a persistent tendency to misunderstand how education and a modern economy actually relate to each other, and an associated and equally extraordinary faith that in this sector, still, central planning should rule. The final chapter summarizes where this has left us, and the lessons we would do well to learn for the future.

8 Conclusion

So, does education matter? The lesson of the last century must be that, for individuals, it matters more than ever before in history. And not just any education: having the right qualifications, in the right subjects, from the right institutions, is of ever growing importance. Fewer and fewer jobs and opportunities are open to those who are denied, or reject, formal education; and, for the young, long periods in school and university increasingly appear not as an option, but as pretty much a necessity.

But does education matter in the ways in which governments the world over believe it does? And are these governments' education policies accordingly well conceived? To those questions the answer must be 'No'. As this book has documented, two naive beliefs have a distorting influence: the belief in a simple, direct relationship between the amount of education in a society and its future growth rate, and the belief that governments can fine-tune education expenditures to maximize that self-same rate of growth. Neither is correct.

If you put either proposition baldly to politicians or civil servants, they might well deny believing anything so simple. But, as the previous chapters have shown, their actions speak otherwise. In the UK at least, for the last quarter-century education policy has been driven consistently by a preoccupation with growth and with workplace skills, and has involved more and more government intervention at everything from national to classroom and shop-floor level. The results have been frequently disastrous.

Let us be clear: education does have major economic importance, and to argue the opposite would be stupid. Our societies depend on more or less universal education, taking people to levels of literacy and mathematics which were rare even a century and a half ago. Modern lifestyles depend on continuing scientific and technological developments, and on large numbers of very highly educated people building on the accumulated wisdom of an ongoing scientific revolution. So governments do have a legitimate economic reason to be concerned for the provision and quality of mainstream school education in all the basic (and traditional) subjects, and to provide the infrastructure for a thriving university and research sector that produces the practitioners and innovators in medicine, engineering, physics, chemistry and genetics. Moreover, people really do acquire 'human capital' during education and work, and this makes them, and so their societies, more productive, even though education alone is far from able to deliver a prosperous society.

The problem arises when, as has happened in recent decades, we move to extrapolating the benefits of education in much the same mood of boundless and groundless optimism as investors caught up in a stock-market bubble. The result has been expansion as an end in itself: more vocational qualifications and diplomas, more training, more university places are treated as self-evidently desirable. Such expansion is neither costless nor, in my view, the top priority, or even a major priority, for a modern government. It is not, first of all, the best policy for delivering rapid growth, but rather threatens to undermine the real, if partial, symbiosis between education and the economy that currently exists. Second, despite the rhetoric, these educational policies are ill-conceived as a way of helping society's least advantaged and least successful members. And last, but not least, this approach progressively narrows and devalues our whole conception of education. Let us take each of these charges in turn.

> **The best things carried to excess are wrong.**
>
> Charles Churchill (1761)
>
> **Any measure used for control is unreliable.**
>
> Goodhart's Law[1]

The last twenty-five years have been the heyday of education policy directed purposefully towards economic ends. One result has been a fixation on quantitative targets which allow governments to monitor progress and pronounce success. These necessarily emphasize what can be easily counted and easily measured; so we have policies intended, above all, to increase numbers, whether these be of qualifications gained or of students enrolled. The most extreme manifestations of this trend – such as outcome-related funding which paid people for NVQs delivered, or franchising schemes which offered backpackers free scuba-diving courses – have foundered because they so visibly undermined quality and invited abuse. But the basic principle of targets has not vanished. How could it? For this is the quintessential approach of any centrally run and directed system which measures success by quantity. If you believe that more education equals more growth, and that government can and should deliver one through the other, then, like a compass needle to the pole, you will be drawn towards quantitative targets, whether they are the NVQs of the early 1990s or the 50 per cent enrolment in higher education that currently enthuses our political classes.

This approach is precisely analogous to the way in which Soviet planners ran their economy, and it has precisely the same drawbacks. Numerical targets have to be concerned with things that can be counted easily (like tractors or examination grades), not with more complex attributes which require judgement and are open to debate (such as whether those tractors work at all well, or the quality of different curricula). In a centrally funded, target-driven, top-down organization, the main and inevitable concern of lower-level functionaries is the satisfaction of their paymasters. If the things they are being asked to produce are genuinely simple to define and inspect, then the system may indeed produce them – albeit not very efficiently. But if they are complex and difficult to measure, like the quality of a university degree, then the effects of such systems tend to be pernicious.

This is especially true when one marries centralized, target-driven controls with financial pressures. That, of course, is exactly the situation that modern education systems find themselves in. As we saw in Chapters 6 and 7, the huge expansion of university education has been accompanied by a constant downward pressure on costs and on real levels of spending. These pressures are not specific to any particular political party or any particular country: they are inherent in any large-scale expansion of state-funded post-compulsory education. They are most obvious in higher education, because that is where change has been so recent and rapid. But the repercussions are not confined to this level.

To support research and innovation, countries need a sizeable, but not vast, number of top-class, superbly trained researchers and developers, not a very large number of imperfectly trained ones. Within a vast university sector, no government can afford to equip all teaching institutions with state-of-the-art scientific facilities. Yet, as we saw, it is extremely hard for any democratic government to treat publicly funded institutions unequally; and, once a sizeable part of the electorate has come to consider itself entitled to a publicly funded education at primary, secondary *and* degree level, the political pressures for equal funding become stronger still. At the same time, teaching young people effectively is a very labour-intensive activity, where we have not found any low-cost, high-technology alternatives to expert human teachers. As universities have expanded, the amount of time and attention that students receive from teachers has declined. Some of the evidence for this is large-scale and quantitative – such as student–teacher ratios, average number of instructional hours, and the like. Other evidence is anecdotal – for example, comparisons of the demands made and feedback given to students following a given course as compared to their predecessors' experience a decade or so ago.[2]

Comparable pressures are visible in further education, where the average number of teaching or 'contact' hours per student declined markedly in the 1980s and 1990s. Elsewhere in the system the strains are rather different. There are simply far more teachers needed at every single level than at any previous period: for new pre-school classes and smaller primary classes, and for more and more students in upper-secondary education. There are also more administrators, more inspectors, more coordinators and advisers, more classroom aides to help disabled or 'statemented' pupils. All this creates upward pressures on costs, and strong incentives for governments of any persuasion to keep teacher salaries down.

What has this done to quality? Until recently, one safeguard has been an ever-growing pool of educated recruits on which to draw. As we saw in Chapter 1, for much of the twentieth century teaching was *the* modal destination for an upwardly mobile child – notably for clever working-class children as they gained the secondary and tertiary education their parents were denied. But this is decreasingly the case. The number of alternative professional and managerial jobs has grown enormously, and the change is especially marked for women. For the first half of the twentieth century, teaching was almost the only professional job open to women, and if you read university and college alumni magazines it is striking just how high a proportion of women graduates, even of the 1950s and 1960s, went into teaching. Their successors are very different. Only a tiny proportion of young male or female graduates from highly regarded universities can be found entering (or indeed thinking of entering) schoolteaching.

The change is not specific to Britain. Read the autobiography of someone like the French novelist and essayist André Maurois, who attended a small provincial *lycée* early in the twentieth century, and you find that many of the *lycée* teachers of that generation were people who without doubt would today be university academics (if they were in education at all). The same is true for the great public and day schools of England, or the (state-funded) *Gymnasien* of pre-1939 Austria. There are still a few schoolteachers like these; but with so many alternative opportunities can there possibly be as many as before? On a broader scale, studies of the academic records of successive generations entering teacher training bear out what one would expect. Over time, as alternative opportunities *and* the number of teachers have expanded, the teaching profession boasts a smaller and smaller proportion of the academically high-achieving.[3]

The vast expansion at tertiary level compounds the problem. It increases the number of teachers needed yet further, while at the same time the downward pressure on academic pay and conditions in most university systems (notably the UK's) is increasingly deterring the most able students, many of whom, even a generation ago, would have sought university positions.

Altogether, it is very likely that in the UK we are now producing 400,000 graduates a year who have, on average, been considerably less well and intensively educated than the 200,000 a year who were produced just a little while before. We know why the students themselves are continuing to flock in; but is this a good bargain for the country? Suppose (and I am pulling numbers out of the air here) that university students are, on average, learning about 75 per cent as much as their predecessors did, and having only about 60 per cent as much attention and money spent on each of them. That might look like a good bargain: you get one and a half times as much 'skill' in total for just 20 per cent more total spending. However, reverse the figures (60 per cent of the skill, 75 per cent of the cost) and it doesn't look so good at all. And it could just as well be that way round as the other. Either way, moreover, the change threatens one key link between education and the economy: the training of a small cadre of first-rate researchers and innovators.

To summarize: low-level, uniform funding of a vast sector precludes first-rate facilities in which to train first-rate students, and deters such students from entering university research or teaching. Meanwhile, recruitment for a huge tertiary sector has a knock-on effect on recruitment for the secondary schools, on secondary-school teaching quality, and so, one must assume, on the average skill levels of secondary-school graduates. At the very least, it makes it harder for governments to find the increased funding for teacher salaries which is needed to maintain recruitment in an increasingly competitive job market. And remember that the one and only part of current education where we found clear evidence of economic benefits was the central 'academic' skills of primary and secondary education, such as mathematics and reading and writing skills.

We can't know whether we are currently getting a great bargain from our huge, cut-price expansion or – as I suspect – are well into declining returns. Moreover, while I have focused here on the wider effects of cheap mass higher education, similar arguments apply to the money spent on the failed vocational initiatives described in earlier chapters. We badly need to stop taking for granted that more spending on education is always a good idea – not least because it precludes spending on other areas for which a far better case can be made.

> **The poorest he that is in England hath a life to live as the greatest he.**
> Thomas Rainborowe (d. 1648)

> **Social exclusion . . . damages lives and wrecks communities . . . It is up to government to do everything it can to help ensure that no individual and no community is left behind.**
> Labour Party manifesto, 2001[4]

Contemporary Britain shares with other modern democracies a number of bedrock values which are rarely enunciated in any formal way. It is simply assumed that everyone subscribes to them. One of these is that children all deserve equal opportunities to use their abilities and succeed in life. (By contrast, in a society which believes in castes, or indeed estates, or in religiously sanctioned differences in men's and women's roles, the assumption is that birth brings with it different deserts and opportunities.) In practice, the children of any society clearly don't enjoy such equality; so the live issue is how much the state can and should do to equalize chances. A second bedrock assumption is that we owe it to our adult fellow citizens not to let them fall below a certain level in terms of income, health, living conditions, safety, and the chance to continue playing a full role in society.

Education is frequently invoked as a, or even the, key instrument for securing equal opportunity for children, and for helping adults improve their life chances. I agree wholeheartedly with the former – though only where primary and secondary education are concerned. A modern society which does not do its utmost to ensure that all children master the basic academic skills, and have the chance to progress, is indeed failing its citizens. On the other hand, as this book demonstrates in detail, governments that see rapid growth in higher education as a major tool for equalizing opportunity delude themselves.

As for education being the best way to help adults, including young adults, I demur. Our current obsession with education does not automatically increase everyone's well-being. On the contrary: it can be a very poor way of promoting some of the core social values summarized above – including helping the least advantaged, or what 2001 policy-speak labels the 'socially excluded'.

It is all too easy to slide from facts about education to education as opportunity. We look at the higher salaries that not only graduates but holders of HNDs or A levels command, and then at the higher unemployment rates, worse pay, and, indeed, poorer health and shorter lives of the uneducated, and see education as the way to deal with the latter. Give the uneducated education, extrapolate those rates of return, and the problem of social exclusion will be solved. In the shorter term, when companies fold and industries disappear, we see this same process at work, as politicians fall back on the mantra of 'training' and 'retraining' as the solution to redundant workers' woes.

Clearly, people without good levels of basic academic skills are at a permanent disadvantage in our world. But if there is one thing which this book will, I hope, have made clear it is that education is a 'positional good' (as the economists call it) – one which gains much of its value from whether you have more than other people – and is not just about acquiring skills in some absolute way. The rewards your education bring are as much to do with being labelled a 'top' or a 'near-the-top' sort of person as they are to do with the curriculum you studied. And *not everyone can be top*. So, as we saw, secondary education becomes segmented as it becomes universal; universities form themselves into ever clearer hierarchies; and fourteen-year-olds who are failing academically quite rationally lose motivation. Pile more and more education on top of what is there already, and you end up with the same segmentation, the same positioning, and even greater problems of cost and quality.

This in itself should make us pause before seeing education as the answer to all our social problems; but there are other considerations too. Vocational training and special training programmes have been used as a panacea for the disadvantaged and the unemployed for many years now. Hopefully, the history and arguments presented in earlier chapters will have given pause for thought about whether such training really is such a wonderful idea, either for the recipients or for the economy. Such programmes, whether for the young (such as Britain's YTS), or for the unemployed (such as the raft of special training and retraining programmes run by almost every Western country), are very expensive and inefficient. This is partly because for any programme – whether its clients are ill-educated youngsters or long-term unemployed adults – you need a huge infrastructure of civil servants, administrators, accountants, trainers, evaluators and the like; and partly because, in substantive terms, the effects of such programmes are rather slight. Jim Heckman,[5] the Nobel Prize-winning economist, has calculated the probable cost of using education and training schemes to raise American high-school dropouts' skills to a level where their earnings also rise significantly – or, to be precise, get back to the same real, average level as they had been a decade earlier.[6] The answer, for males alone, was a staggering $284 *billion*[7] – considerably more than the federal government's spending on health, and orders of magnitude more than it has ever spent on education and training.[8]

But should we care about the cost? Don't we owe those at the bottom of the heap whatever it takes to get a slightly more equal chance at things? And what is the alternative?

Well, there is one. Moreover, the evidence for its effectiveness in promoting 'social inclusion' is far more persuasive than the evidence in favour of remedial training or vocational education, let alone central targets for the social origins of university students. It is simply to subsidize jobs.

The most eminent and eloquent proponent of wage subsidies for the low-paid is the American economist Edmund Phelps.[9] His and related ideas have had some substantial influence on policy-makers on both sides of the Atlantic, but less than they should; and they are far too little known in education circles. Education policy needs to recognize the evidence showing how various types of work operate as a route back into successful longer-term, and indeed permanent, employment – especially when contrasted with the overwhelmingly discouraging picture we get from education and training programmes for the disadvantaged.

Temporary contracts and short-term jobs generally have a bad name. Yet the evidence from large-scale national surveys such as the British Household Panel Survey is that almost everyone who holds them moves on to other employment, very often permanent, and only a small proportion head straight back into unemployment. Among low-income families and single parents, obtaining a 'mini-job' (i.e. a part-time job of less than sixteen hours a week) greatly increases the likelihood that the adult concerned will secure a more substantial or full-time job in the near future, whereas government-funded training programmes seem to have no discernible effect at all on the employment and income prospects of most of their recipients. Moreover, as we noted above when discussing affluent teenagers' greater access to part-time jobs, a smooth transition from education to employment is itself strongly associated with having worked already. Jobs now lead to jobs later, across the developed world.[10]

In recent decades, our obsessive focus on growth through educational engineering has had the side effect of narrowing policy thinking to the detriment of the least advantaged. It is not just that education has come to be seen as the only policy worth thinking about. Worse, the chant in favour of more education is actually a chant in favour of regressive taxation. The fight against university fees isn't a major campaign for equal opportunity – quite the contrary. The poor don't go to university. The children of the middle classes do.

In reviewing Edmund Phelps's proposals, a commentator in the *Economist* noted that politicians were unlikely to implement job subsidies, because their costs were far too clear and simple to calculate. This would make them politically 'impossible'. And yet 'give those same politicians a few hundred small ideas for spending money uselessly . . . and . . . they will have no trouble at all' in equalling the amount.[11] Too much of recent education and training policy bears out this gloomy conclusion. Moreover, middle-class voters are an electorally potent group, and they want more education spending – and easy access to university – not less. But let us at least be clear: many of our governments' education priorities have precious little to do with social justice.

Where there is no vision, the people perish.
Proverbs 29.18

The final reason for worrying about current education policy is very different, but no less serious. Our preoccupation with education as an engine of growth has not only narrowed the way we think about social policy. It has also narrowed – dismally and progressively – our vision of education itself.

This book reflects that narrowing. It has concentrated on contemporary preoccupations and beliefs about education, and shown how overwhelmingly economic they are. It argues that the links between education and the economy are more tenuous and complex than most people suppose, and that our beliefs about 'education for growth' have produced a series of misguided policies. But, if we want better policy-making in the future, we must do more than evaluate 'education for growth' in its own terms. We must also recognize how this obsession has damaged our notion of what education is about. This has not been the main subject of this book, but it is what first led me to worry about its dominant theme.

The contribution of education to economic life is an important subject, and an interesting subject, and it can actually be investigated empirically. But it is only one aspect of education, not the entirety, and it does not deserve the overwhelming emphasis which it now enjoys. Reading modern political speeches and official reports and then setting them alongside those of twenty-five, let alone fifty or a hundred, years ago is a revelation. Contemporary writers *may* pay a sentence or two of lip-service to the other objectives of education before passing on to their real concern with economic growth. Our recent forebears, living in significantly poorer times, were occupied above all with the cultural, moral and intellectual purposes of education. We impoverish ourselves by our indifference to these.

'The wisdom that a democratic community needs is the wisdom of the entire population,' wrote Robert Hutchins, a past chancellor of the University of Chicago. '[O]ne of the most important elements in the strength of a country . . . is its educational system . . . provided that the educational system will be directed to moral, intellectual, aesthetic and spiritual growth.'[12] The history of public education in any modern democratic state concerns issues of identity and citizenship quite as much as the instilling of more or less utilitarian skills. How far this is publicly enunciated, and whether it evokes bitter battles over values and control, can vary. In nineteenth-century France the village school-masters were famously the shock troops of a secular Republic opposed to the power of the Church. The reluctance of the different English churches to cede control of their schools to the state delayed universal and compulsory primary education for decades. Communist states have always used schools as a major organ of indoctrination, so that every post-Communist state has moved rapidly to authorize private schools. The role that schools play in creating citizens, and in passing on to new generations both an understanding of their own history and society and particular moral, intellectual or religious values, should concern any modern state with a public education system – which means each and every one of them.[13]

These issues have not gone away because we in the UK have chosen to ignore them – but ignore them we largely have of late. This has been true at both school and university level: the supposed economic rationale for higher education swamps any other considerations. The 1997 Dearing Report was the last major review of UK university policy, and its effects are only now working through the system. In its first pages it offers a ritual obeisance to the notion that education 'contributes to the whole quality of life', but then proceeds to ignore this for the remaining 466 pages of the main report. The background papers it commissioned are devoted exclusively to issues of economics and access.[14] Do we really believe that economic relevance is the only justification for a university? And that universities' futures should be justified entirely by the rates of return that we have examined sceptically above, or by the 'job-placement rates' for graduates on which UK government inspectors currently place such emphasis?

A century and a half ago, Cardinal Newman examined the 'idea' of a university, and in so doing argued passionately that 'knowledge is not merely a means to something beyond it, or the preliminary of certain arts into which it naturally resolves, but an end sufficient to rest in and to pursue for its own sake'. Of course, it had other functions too; for

Newman its relation to religion was fundamental, while he and today's politicians would agree on its importance for 'professional skill'. But in Newman's analysis the foremost concern was 'knowledge [as] the indispensable condition of expansion of mind, and the instrument of attaining to it'.[15] His rallying call should surely resonate today, when so much of what is good about our world is owed not to vocational degree programmes, or 'useful' research projects commissioned by business, but to the traditions of independent thought and critical enquiry.

This book offers no detailed policy alternatives for governments to follow. In fact, given the dismal effects of detailed, centralized education planning, alternative encompassing blueprints are surely the last thing we need. However, what governments could and should do, ideally, is to concentrate on their core educational responsibility, which is to provide their citizens with a good basic education at primary and secondary levels. An end to myriad initiatives and micro-management would give both politicians and bureaucrats more time, energy and money to do this properly, and would also allow people to develop the variety of educational approaches, curricula and purposes that a large and complex society demands.

Let me end with the University of Chicago's Robert Hutchins again. It was his gloomy conclusion, in a book whose object was to promote independent thought and liberal education, that 'Industrialization seems to charm people into thinking that the prime aim of life and hence of education is the development of industrial power.'[16] This certainly describes the dominant and increasingly triumphant philosophy of recent UK education policy. Ironically, this has become more apparent the more the economy itself recovers from its mid-century travails and the less plausible it becomes that we need to remake education to avoid economic perdition. It is hard to be optimistic that this attitude will change, for governments everywhere love simple, all-embracing principles.[17] But perhaps by calling into doubt some of today's received truths and clichés we can also start to think again, in broader perspective, about the sort of education we want for ourselves and for our children.

References

Introduction

1. Blair 1999; Labour Party 2001.
2. For example Callaghan 1976 or Blair 1999.
3. Blunkett 2000a, para. 10.
4. Leadbetter 1999: vii.
5. Finegold & Soskice 1988.
6. Blair 1999.
7. See Clanchy 1981. In pre-industrial societies many more people could read than write, and exact estimates of literacy rates are impossible. However, the number of people in the eleventh century who had seals (a proxy for literacy, and far less common than in the thirteenth century) suggests very low levels of literacy in England at that time.

Chapter 1: A truly world-beating industry: the growth of formal education

1. In the West, the Roman Empire attained 'high' literacy levels estimated at around 10 per cent for *males*; many tribal societies had no developed script, while large sections of society and large geographical areas would rely on oral bargaining and mental arithmetic in commerce even in societies where literacy was well established in connection with religion (for example Islam, Buddhism, Christianity), and would operate local government and politics without any written records. See Morgan 2001 and Goody 1968.

2. Figures for 1997 are the most recent available. Student numbers by level and by continent are as in Table A.

Table A *Worldwide student numbers: 1997*

	Primary	*Secondary*	*Tertiary*
Africa	100,226,000	33,708,000	4,780,000
America	112,083,000	53,899,000	25,486,000
Asia	406,661,000	237,861,000	34,844,000
Europe	46,304,000	69,547,000	21,794,000
Oceania	3,176,000	3,101,000	1,251,000
World total	668,450,000	398,116,000	88,155,000

Source: UNESCO 1999

3. UNESCO 1999. UNESCO calculates enrolment ratios by taking total enrolments at a given level as the proportion of the age cohort which, according to national regulations, should be enrolled at this level. The absolute increase is a function of population growth plus higher participation rates.

4. Figures for 1997 are the most recent available. Teacher numbers by level and by continent are as in Table B.

Table B *Worldwide teacher numbers: 1997*

	Primary	*Secondary*	*Tertiary*	*Total*
Africa	2,927,000	1,585,000	242,000	4,754,000
America	5,148,000	3,451,000	1,881,000	10,480,000
Asia	13,763,000	12,185,000	2,339,000	28,287,000
Europe	2,814,000	5,568,000	1,759,000	10,141,000
Oceania	165,000	228,000	62,000	455,000
World total	24,817,000	23,017,000	6,283,000	54,117,000

Source: UNESCO 1999

5. That is, 30 out of 39 did (Jackson & Marsden 1966: 178–9).

Chapter 2: Elixir or snake oil? Can education really deliver growth?

1. Labour Party 1996.

2. Recent major statements on education by the DfEE, Downing Street and the DTI respectively are Blunkett 2000a and 2000b, Blair 1999 and DTI 1998. All embody these views. (See for example quotations in the Introduction and later in this chapter.)

3. DES 1991: Aims.

4. DfEE 1998: 1.

5. Blunkett 2000b: 3.

6. Quotes from Blunkett 2000a and Leadbetter 1999.

7. A and O levels (Advanced and Ordinary levels, General Certificate of Education) were established in the 1950s as single-subject, publicly examined and graded qualifications. A levels – typically taken at age eighteen, at the end of upper-secondary education – still exist and are the main English university-entrance qualification. O levels were typically taken at age sixteen, and were supplemented in the 1960s by the less academically demanding CSEs (Certificates of Secondary Education). In the late 1980s O levels and CSEs were abolished and replaced by GCSEs – General Certificates of Secondary Education – taken by almost all sixteen-year-olds. They are graded from A to E.

8. In 1988, GCSEs replaced O levels and CSEs, providing a single public academic examination for all sixteen-year-olds in England, Wales and Northern Ireland which can be taken in a range of different subjects (usually between six and ten). Before that, a top-grade (grade-1) pass in a CSE was treated as equivalent to an O-level pass. In the GCSEs, grades A–C are designed to cover the same range of achievement as O levels (and grade-1 CSE); these grades are now (2001) commonly referred to as a 'pass' by young people and employers, and the cut-off has now been institutionalized in the government's new National Qualifications Framework, where passes at A–C and D–F are assigned to different levels.

9. Robinson's figures are taken from Labour Force Survey data. A recent detailed re-analysis of these figures, alongside data from the National Child Development Study and the International Adult Literacy Survey, confirms the general pattern (Dearden et al. 2000a), as do data from the General Household Survey. One significant difference of emphasis in the work of Dearden et al. is that they underline that *returns* to qualifications (how much you get back on your 'investment' of so many years of studying, during which you forgo earnings)

are very sensitive to the length of time it takes to get a qualification – which is commonly less for vocational than for academic qualifications.

10. Most strikingly in the 1980s and early 1990s, since when they appear to have levelled off (Atkinson 1999).

11. US Department of Education 1997.

12. It would be unwise to extrapolate these figures too enthusiastically, let alone treat them as a very precise reflection of the productivity of graduates: returns to university degrees fell in the USA in the early 1970s, and were higher in the UK in 1975 than in 1979. However, the increase in the earnings gap between the unqualified and graduates is a piece of evidence frequently cited by enthusiasts for the idea that the economy is changing fundamentally.

13. See later in this chapter (pp. 32–6) and Chapters 6 and 7 for a more detailed discussion.

14. The difference is not huge, but holds even allowing for family background and qualifications. See for example Scholarios & Lockyer 1999 and Naylor et al. 1998.

15. The basic assumption here is a very simplified one: namely that the sixth-form student has two years' less working life and a fixed 5 per cent income advantage. As we saw earlier, higher levels of education are also associated with a lower risk of unemployment, so this may not be a reasonable assumption to make. (More sophisticated calculations look at lifetime earnings, taking account of lower unemployment rates.) On the other hand, the situation is not far off the truth for many adult workers. If you look back at Figure 2.1 you will see that men with just one A level to show for their sixth-form studies are, on average, barely making more than those with five or more GCSEs/O levels.

16. This is a rather lower figure than in some previous studies: for example, the Department of Education and Science estimated the average 'private rate of return' for young people graduating between 1980 and 1984 at 25 per cent. The source for these DES figures was a report, *Top-up Loans for Students* (DES 1988), which made the case for student loans; the more recent figures are discussed in detail in National Committee of Inquiry into Higher Education 1997.

17. These estimates (from Dearden et al. 2000a) are before controlling for family background, ability measures and other factors. The effect, and importance, of such factors is discussed in the next section.

18. Harmon & Walker 2000.

19. M. Campbell 2000:3.

20. For a clear statement of the underlying assumptions in such analysis, see Dutta et al. 1999. The difficulty with rate-of-return calculations has been

recognized for many years – certainly since Edward Denison's important and influential work on the 'residual factor' in economic growth. Denison's attempts to produce quantitative estimates of the effects of knowledge and education on economic growth were carefully qualified; but they did, nonetheless, offer an attractive set of numbers and hypotheses – such as that 'almost one-fourth of a 59 point gap' between Italian and US national income per person is due to 'differences in the education of the labour force alone' (Denison in OECD 1964: 51). Governments were duly seduced.

21. Becker 1993: 15. Becker's work popularized the term 'human capital', and is discussed in more detail in Chapter 5.

22. In calculating returns to UK degrees in the mid 1990s, the Dearing committee calculated that four-fifths of undergraduate teaching costs were being borne from the public purse, as were more than half of full-time students' living costs. Recent changes have increased the cost to students somewhat, but not (yet) by a substantial margin. Spending totals in the chapter text are from the 2001 Spending Review (HM Treasury).

23. National Committee of Inquiry into Higher Education 1997: para. 630.

24. Depending on how you classify the tax attorneys, Japan has a maximum of 68,000 lawyers, the USA over a million – or seven times as many per head of population.

25. Across the whole OECD, only Iceland and Switzerland have higher proportions of the working-age population employed (OECD 2000b and 2001b), and only Norway and Switzerland have higher average GDP per head. Denmark also has more engineers and research scientists per head than any OECD country except Norway, Sweden and the USA. One possible explanation of the differences in returns to education is that they are higher the worse a country's basic education (and so the less skilled the less educated are). But not only is there no simple and obvious relationship between relative returns to education levels within a country and that country's performance in international surveys of student achievement: countries' rankings in terms of returns to education vary over time far more markedly than can plausibly be explained by changes in the quality of their basic education.

26. See World Bank 1995, especially pp. 10–14. Comparing wages in different countries is fraught with difficulty: exchange rates can give a very misleading picture of what incomes will actually buy. It is therefore important to use 'purchasing-power parity' (PPP) figures for comparison; but these are also difficult to calculate. Moreover, many poor people are farmers, or depend on other non-cash sources of income. The World Bank has carried out extensive work to define and measure poverty: for example, its 1990 World Development

Report focused on poverty, and selected two global poverty lines of $275 and $370 per person per year at 1985 PPP prices (approximately $440 and $590 in 2000 prices, or well under $2 (or £1.50) per day). Compare this with the current UK minimum wage of over £4 per hour.

27. The whole notion of 'productivity' is a minefield in itself. How do you judge the productivity of, for example, a teacher in a (publicly funded) primary school?

28. I am indebted to my colleague Gareth Williams for this excellent summing up of the situation.

29. For a clear typology of all of them, see Dore 1976b.

30. See for example FEDA et al. 1997 and Payne 2001.

31. In the USA, people who complete associate (two-year) degrees, taken in a local community (FE) college, do not, on average, have significantly higher 'ability' scores (or, rather, scores on high-school performance tests) than do those who obtain just a high-school diploma before entering the labour market – although those who complete a four-year degree do, on average, have higher high-school test scores (Arkes 1999). The associate degree nonetheless has labour-market value: its holders earn significantly more on average than those with just the high-school diploma. How much is this because of what the associate degree teaches, and how much because it shows perseverance and motivation?

32. See Hunter & Hunter 1984 and Schmidt & Hunter 1998. Even if education were used *purely* as a way of screening for ability, this could help increase the efficiency of employers' hiring decisions. However, it is hard to believe that the gains, in that situation, would outweigh the huge costs of public education.

33. A common approach looks at employed versus self-employed workers, on the assumption that the self-employed don't need to signal their ability to employers: instead, their incomes (and returns to their education) reflect their 'human capital'. But the employed and the self-employed are very different groups (notably in their taste for self-employment), so this is not comparing like with like; nor is it clear that formal qualifications are as irrelevant as 'signals' in the self-employed sector as this approach assumes. Comparisons of identical twins (to see how education differences affect the pay of genetically identical people) are also problematic, because of the small and non-random nature of the samples who can be studied. (See for example Bound & Solon 1998, Harmon & Walker 1999 and 2000, and Bonjour et al. 2000.) One recent paper concluded that 'the real problem is that ability and schooling appear to be inseparable – all interaction and no main effects' (Heckman & Vytlacil 2000: 10). However, some researchers (including Blundell and Dearden, whose work on individual rates of return (Blundell et al., 1999 and 2000) includes extensive adjustment for background variables such as social class and early 'ability', or rather

achievement, measures) believe that new techniques should allow researchers to arrive at some better estimates.

34. See for example Ashworth 1998: *passim* for how some quite plausible assumptions of this kind reduce the social rate of return for higher education below what is normally considered a sound level for public investment.

35. In the United States, employers appear not to distinguish between one high-school diploma and another, whereas where you went to college, and your subject, matter a great deal (see for example Halperin 1998, Frank & Cook 1995 and Monks 2000). High-school diplomas are awarded by students' own schools, and employers probably feel unable to tell if standards are high or low at a given school. At college level, however, there is a great deal of information on quality, which – accurate or not – may be feeding into their decisions.

36. See also Naylor et al. 1998 and 2001 for related and similar findings.

37. The differences are particularly marked for those in the lowest group: these fare much worse than the average, while the differences between groups with 'average' and 'good' basic skills is less marked. See Bynner & Parsons 1997a, 1997b and 2000.

38. Among younger people, good GCSEs almost invariably lead on to A-level entry, and nearly all A-level students go on to university. This was less true twenty or twenty-five years ago, and so it is easier to distinguish the effects of different qualifications from each other.

39. Dolton & Vignoles 1999b and 2000.

40. In the US context, scores on tests such as the SATs (Scholastic Assessment Tests) are important in determining life changes, in the absence of any equivalent to A levels, the *baccalauréat* and the like.

41. See Pryor & Schaffer 1999.

42. Of course it may be that it is some sort of 'general' ability that is increasingly valued in the labour market; but, while we know this to be highly correlated with academic test results, disentangling the two is effectively impossible.

43. Finegold & Soskice 1988: 23. See for example Blair 1999 (quoted in the Introduction, p. xii) for an example of how this typology has taken hold.

44. It recurs in studies using quite different methods of analysis. See for example Patrinos 1994, Pritchett 1996, Mingat & Tan 1996 and 1998, and Lopez et al. 1998. These studies focus on developing countries. Others, which examine developed economies, also find a complex mixture of effects, varying by stage of education, gender of students, etc. See Krueger & Lindahl 1999 and Kim & Kim 1999. As with most such large comparative studies, the quality of the data is open to question; but there is certainly no evidence of a simple, strong relationship between education and growth worldwide.

45. These insurrections of Sinhala youth were quite distinct from the civil war with Tamil groups, or anti-Tamil violence.

46. Rate-of-return analyses of this type were actually used in this way during the 1950s, 1960s and 1970s. See Psacharopoulos 1985 and 1994.

47. It may seem obvious that the wages of government bureaucrats are not a precise reflection of productivity – but is it so obvious that other wages are? Rate-of-return analyses cannot have it both ways: either analysing wages is a good general method of estimating economic returns to education or it is not.

48. UNESCO 1972: para. 1012.

49. A recent review of the literature by Sianesi & Van Reenen (2000) emphasizes the importance of education type, quality and investment efficiency, and the difficulty of identifying the direction of causality – i.e. whether education causes growth or vice versa. The authors also conclude that 'human capital increases productivity' and that education is not being used as just a signalling device.

50. The literature is inconsistent in its findings, and underlines the complexity of the relationship and the absence of any simple link between education and growth. See for example Krueger & Lindahl 1999.

51. A. Maddison, *Phases of Capitalist Development* (Oxford: Oxford University Press, 1982), p. 111, quoted in Lal 1989. See also the work of Carpentier (2000), Michel (1999) and others of the Montpellier group of economic historians for comparable conclusions regarding nineteenth-century European growth.

52. 'Purchasing-power parity' comparisons bring Swiss incomes down – but only a bit. Very small oil states such as Brunei are omitted from this comparison (based on World Bank Development Reports).

53. Swiss enrolment rates have now risen to about half the OECD average: for example, in 1996 they were 16 per cent compared to a 34 per cent average – and a figure of over 50 per cent for the USA (OECD 1998).

54. See for example Harris et al. 1997 and Jaworski & Phillips 1999.

55. Robinson 1999b.

56. National Commission on Excellence in Education 1983; Steinberg 1996.

57. Ashton & Green 1996; Finegold & Soskice 1988.

58. The USA imports a great deal of scientific and technological talent, notably through recruitment of graduate students who stay in the country; in particular, a very high proportion of maths and engineering Ph.D. students are from overseas. However, the bulk of the current wave of innovations – in Silicon Valley and elsewhere – remains home-grown; and the vast majority of (productive) US workers are, of course, US-educated.

59. North 1990: 77.

60. Bils & Klenow 1998.

61. All quotes from Blair 1999.

62. Kevin Roberts, chief executive of Saatchi & Saatchi Advertising Worldwide, cited in Keep 1999: 326.

63. Central Statistical Office, *Annual Abstract of Statistics*; Ministry of Labour, *Annual Abstract of Statistics*.

64. Institute for Employment Research 2000.

65. Institute for Employment Research 2000.

66. The major source of data on employment is the Labour Force Survey. The categories are based on the Standard Occupational Classification (SOC). This has been changed recently, making very detailed comparisons over time quite complicated; but at this level of aggregation the changes make very little difference.

67. See for example Wood 1994, Lawrence 1996, and Slaughter 1998 and 1999. The argument centres around the question of how far trade with low-wage countries explains/creates greater wage inequality in developed countries.

68. See for example Alpin et al. 1998, F. Green et al. 1999, Chevalier 2000 and Dolton & Vignoles 1999a. Researchers judge whether 'over-education' exists by looking at the education that people who did the same job used to have, or by actually asking people whether they need and use all their skills.

69. Ashworth 1988; Keep 2000; Murphy 1993 and 1994.

70. If you look at people with the same formal qualifications, those with the better jobs are also somewhat more likely to have higher levels of skill (as measured on independent tests such as those administered for the International Adult Literacy Survey). In other words, employers seem to discriminate – as you would expect – on substantive skill levels as well as on paper qualifications. See F. Green et al. 1999 and Pryor & Schaffer 1999.

71. Detailed studies of jobs where the qualification requirements have changed indicate that, in most cases, the intrinsic requirements of the job have not, and observers conclude that most of this shift is simply a result of a greater supply of people with higher qualifications. In Ashworth's view (1998: 28) 'the only rationale for (further) expansion is a fervent and widely-held belief' that this will generate greater economic growth than would the use of that money for other purposes – a view for which he finds not a shred of evidence.

72. Robinson 1997a.

73. For a summary of the evidence, see Gemmell 1997. The specific argument here is not over whether education makes the educated more productive, but whether the effects of education are or are not entirely captured by (any) increases in the educated workers' own productivity.

74. In its 2001 overview of member states' education systems (OECD 2001a)

the OECD puts forward figures for the contribution of education (human capital) to economic growth in the 1980s and 1990s which suggest that in this period a major part of countries' growth (including that of the UK) was attributable to increases in human-capital stock. The general basis for this argument is endogenous growth theory. The specific figures are drawn from one particular set of econometric analyses, available in an OECD Economics Department working paper (Bassanini & Scarpetta 2001) which uses as its definition of human capital the number of years of education completed by a country's inhabitants. The paper itself is interesting not least because it shows, once again, how very varied the results of such analyses tend to be; but in itself it does nothing to undermine the key point that econometric results are highly sensitive to the assumptions made about the distribution of unobserved attributes and selection processes.

Chapter 3: A great idea for other people's children: the decline and fall of vocational education

1. DES 1991; Blunkett 2001; Unwin 1994; personal conversation with the author.

2. See Sanderson 1999 for a discussion of apprenticeship before the Second World War and shifting views of its importance and effectiveness; also Owen 1999.

3. Chartered occupations (i.e. occupations with a royal charter) are largely self-regulating rather than regulated by government, and their governing bodies exert control over training and over the qualification required for practitioners to term themselves 'Chartered' (for example 'Chartered Accountant' or 'Chartered Surveyor').

4. Numbers taken from Cotgrove 1958.

5. Sanderson 1999.

6. See for example Barnett 1986 and Sanderson 1994 and 1999.

7. A. Neil, 'Class action means Labour MPs live near better schools', *Sunday Business*, 25 July 1999. Press Holdings owns, among others, *The Scotsman* and *Sunday Business*.

8. Nick Davies, 'Schools in crisis: pupils profit', *The Guardian*, 12 July 2000. Davies is atypical in only one way: his promised land is the Netherlands rather than the usual Germany.

9. *Report of the Balfour Committee on Industry and Trade* 1927.

10. Abbott 1933: 214.

11. Ministry of Labour 1962.

12. MSC 1981: 1, 5, 9, 14.

13. Ibid.: 4, 6.

14. It was 20.9 per cent for males aged fifteen to twenty-four in 1983.

15. See for example the exchange between Michael Colvin MP and David Young: House of Commons Employment Committee 1983: 20 April.

16. The official government position on any relationship between YTS and apprenticeships was neutrality (House of Commons Employment Committee 1983: para. 15).

17. See Evans 1992: 56–72.

18. Raggatt & Williams 1999: 46–7 – the words are those of an MSC official.

19. Jessup 1991: 135.

20. Ibid.: 8.

21. Ibid.: 10–11.

22. Thatcher 1993: 421. Thatcher notes here – approvingly – that Young 'revolutionised the working of the Manpower Services Commission'.

23. Barnett 1986: 301.

24. NEDC & MSC 1984: iv.

25. Ibid.: 5, 7, 8.

26. Prais 1995: 72. For the full discussion of the hotel study, see Prais et al. 1989.

27. Prais 1995: 69.

28. Ibid.: 68. See also, inter alia, Prais & Wagner 1983, Daly et al. 1985, Prais & Steedman 1986, Steedman 1987 and 1988, and Prais 1989.

29. Prais himself gave the Keynes Lecture in Economics at the British Academy, on this topic, in 1993.

30. DES figures as cited in Spours 1995. From 1987, young school leavers were no longer entitled to go straight on to benefits.

31. This is clearly an ill-omened building: its previous occupant was the National Union of Mineworkers.

32. Training Agency 1988: 1.

33. 'The overall model stands or falls on how effectively we can state competence and attainment . . . If you cannot say what you require, how can you develop it and how do you know when you have achieved it?' (Jessup 1991: 134). For a discussion of the problems associated with this policy, see Wolf 1995.

34. Anthony Trollope, *The Three Clerks* (1858), Chapter 11.

35. See Appendix 4 in Robinson 1996. It is possible for several NVQs to be based on one set of standards.

36. House of Lords Official Report: Parliamentary Debates (Hansard), Vol. 515, No. 30, 31 January 1990.

37. Personal communication.

38. Dore 1993.

39. Unwin 1994.

40. See for example Andrews et al. 1999 and Ryan 2001 for a general discussion of the evidence.

41. See for example A. Green et al. 1999. The GCSE, by providing a unified certificate which gave more students clear evidence of A-level 'potential', definitely played a role in the sudden increase in sixth-form numbers in England and Wales. (See for example Gray et al. 1994.) However, the underlying trend is one common to all developed countries.

42. See for example Gregg & Wadsworth 1999 and Hakim 1998.

43. See especially Gregg & Wadsworth 1999: Chapter 7. Average job tenure for the workforce as a whole seems to have changed very little over the period 1975–2000, but has risen for women with children, and fallen significantly for the young, and for men over fifty.

44. See for example Hakim 1998.

45. See for example OECD 1997b.

46. Paul Ryan (2001) notes that, in all OECD countries, the young change jobs more often than older workers, but that absolute rates vary considerably. Job movement by the young is especially high in the USA, and especially low in Japan and Germany. See also OECD 1999d.

47. Crowley-Bainton & Wolf 1994.

48. Hutchins 1953: 15.

49. See Wolf 1997.

50. The income gap between adult males in skilled 'craft' jobs and those who are university graduates is essentially identical in Germany and the United States. See Heckman 1994 and Harhoff & Kane 1994, and see Chapter 5 below for a discussion of the continuing importance of the respected German apprenticeship system, which recruits after the end of upper-secondary schooling.

51. A. Green et al. 1999: Figure 4.2.

52. A. Green et al. 1999.

53. Dr L. Lassnig, quoted in A. Green et al. 1999: 159.

54. Dronkers 1993: 18.

55. Parkes 1993; Kehm 1999; Dore 2000.

56. DES 1991.

57. For details on these statistics, and other material covered here, see FEU et al. 1994 and FEDA et al. 1995 and 1997.

58. FEDA et al. 1997. One would not know, from government statistics of the late 1990s, that BTEC diplomas were still thriving. As part of the drive to create

a tidy framework of levels, education qualifications were categorized far more neatly on the page than in reality, with diplomas and the like folded into the 'GNVQ and related' category for reporting purposes.

59. FEU et al. 1994; FEDA et al. 1995 and 1997.

60. Centre for Curriculum and Assessment Studies & International Centre for Research and Assessment 1995; FEU et al. 1994; Wolf 1998b and 1998c.

61. Blunkett 2001.

62. Institute for Employment Research 2000.

63. That is, five or more at grades A–C.

64. Blunkett 2001.

65. Ibid.

66. 'Plumbing to be taught in schools', *The Times*, 6 July 2000.

Chapter 4: Does business know best?

1. Employment Department 1988; DTI 2001a.

2. In 2000 Rover became independent again, after BMW disposed of it for (effectively) nothing; but it survives only as a small niche manufacturer in twenty-first-century car-industry terms.

3. See pp. 131–3.

4. Speech to the Nottingham branch of the Institute of Marketing, 11 January 1971, quoted in P. J. C. Perry 1976: 276. Powell is now remembered mostly for his controversial speeches warning against the dangers of immigration; but before these he was one his generation's more influential advocates of market economics.

5. The precise status of the ITBs changed during the 1970s. The boards were first subordinated to the Manpower Services Commission, then saw levies replaced largely by grants, then had levies reimposed on all but small firms.

6. Elliott & Mendham 1981, quoted in Senker 1995: 17.

7. As noted in Chapter 3, British apprenticeships were, until very recently, not regulated by government. Generally an apprentice qualified by 'serving his time', without any formal examination process. In most cases, apprentices would also, as part of the formal, college-based part of their training, take a vocational qualification – typically City & Guilds – but this was not a compulsory part of apprenticeship. Equally, non-apprentices could and did take the qualifications.

8. This close connection between the Post Office and the education world was to continue. Other Post Office chief executives would include Michael Heron – another future NCVQ chairman – and Ron Dearing, a former civil servant

who, as Sir Ron, conducted three influential reviews for the Tories (of the National Curriculum, of sixteeen-to-nineteen education and of higher education) and then, as Lord Dearing, ran UfI (the University for Industry), the Labour government's flagship project to encourage 'lifelong learning'.

9. CBI 1989: 9.

10. Ibid.: 19.

11. Headed by a senior businessman, the Council's members included the director-general of the CBI, the general secretary of the Trades Union Congress, and two former Post Office chairmen now involved in running quangos and government inquiries (Dearing and Heron), along with representatives of various government departments and quangos (though not the IoD or the Chambers of Commerce).

12. CBI 1991: 7–8 (italics mine).

13. Total numbers of exam passes for the country, compiled from individual schools' results, are, of course, one of the things fed into the National Targets.

14. CBI 1993b: 5.

15. DfEE & DENI 1997: 3, 5.

16. NACETT 1999: Foreword.

17. In Scotland there were LECs (Local Enterprise Councils) rather than TECs.

18. Although in principle other qualifications at the same level could be substituted, this required active renegotiation and agreement, and was rarely done.

19. See Stanton 1996.

20. Sources: minutes and papers of the Publishing Qualifications Board and NCVQ annual NVQ statistics.

21. See for example Prais 1991 and Steedman & Hawkins 1994; see also Callender 1992.

22. The most detailed account of NVQ assessment in practice is in Eraut et al. 1996.

23. CBI 1991: 10.

24. CBI 1993b: 6.

25. CBI 1994a: 5, 9, 13, 14, 69.

26. SVQs: Scottish Vocational Qualifications, based on the same principles and standards as the NVQs, but run by SCOTVEC – the Scottish Vocational Education Council – rather than NCVQ. SCOTVEC is now part of the Scottish Qualifications Authority, which merged SCOTVEC with the Scottish Examinations Board.

27. CBI 1995: 29.

28. CBI 1994a: 14.

29. Ibid.: 56.

30. CBI 1995: 22.

31. The 'Beaumont Report' (Beaumont 1996), named after Gordon Beaumont, chair of the CBI Training Committee and the chair and author of the review, is, overall, a rather extraordinary document. It is innocent of any information on numbers surveyed, numbers responding, or methodology, though it does scatter a large number of percentages around the text as evidence of employer support for the 'NVQ concept'. A large body of evidence already existed on the way in which NVQs were operating: some largely polemical (on both sides of the debate), but much of it the result of well-funded research studies sponsored both by the Department of Employment itself and by a variety of research councils and foundations. However, all of this was pretty much ignored. Instead, the inquiry set out to measure business opinion by using a properly representative (stratified) sample and a postal survey. Unfortunately, business enthusiasm for NVQs did not extend to completing questionnaires about them. Only around 100 responses (roughly 15 per cent) were received. There followed extensive follow-up calls and contacts, plus more add-on mailings. All this was largely ad hoc, and, though the numbers of responses crept up, the process destroyed any possibility that figures could be treated as representative of national employer opinion and practice. They nonetheless remained the main, and often the only, source of evidence for what followed.

32. Labour Force Survey data.

33. Institute of Directors 1994: 6, 8.

34. Callaghan 1976: the widely reported speech is commonly known as 'the Ruskin College speech'.

35. See opinion polls in 1997; also Wolf 2000.

36. Baker 1993: 203.

37. The Quality Assurance Agency, the quango established by government to oversee university teaching quality, demands that courses be presented in the form of a Programme Specification giving intended outcomes of programmes of study, including what were called core and are currently called key skills. It is also promoting a uniform 'Progress File' for all students, documenting what they are achieving, again including core or key skills. For further information see http://www.qaa.ac.uk/public/hq/hq4/specs.htm. See also http://www.dfee.-gov.uk/heqe/publication.htm for related projects on key skills in higher education.

38. Speech by the Secretary of State for Education, 28 September 1992, quoted as Exhibit 5 in CBI 1993a: 15.

39. CBI 1995: 8.

40. A preoccupation with skills such as these, and with highly general ones such

as problem-solving, has hardly been unique to the UK. The familiar-looking list below is from a US government report which purports to reflect American businesses' priorities, and correspondingly urges the 'SCANS' workplace 'competencies' upon US schools and colleges. (The competencies are so called after their drafters: the Secretary's Commission on Achieving Necessary Skills – i.e. SCANS. See SCANS 1991.)

WORKPLACE COMPETENCIES: Effective workers can productively use:

- **Resources** – They know how to allocate time, money, materials, space, and staff.

- **Interpersonal skills** – They can work on teams, teach others, serve customers, lead, negotiate, and work well with people from culturally diverse backgrounds.

- **Information** – They can acquire and evaluate data, organize and maintain files, interpret and communicate, and use computers to process information.

- **Systems** – They understand social, organizational, and technological systems; they can monitor and correct performance; and they can design or improve systems.

- **Technology** – They can select equipment and tools, apply technology to specific tasks, and maintain and troubleshoot equipment.

FOUNDATION SKILLS: Competent workers in the high-performance workplace need:

- **Basic skills** – reading, writing, arithmetic and mathematics, speaking and listening.

- **Thinking skills** – the ability to learn, to reason, to think creatively, to make decisions, and to solve problems.

- **Personal qualities** – individual responsibility, self-esteem and self-management, sociability, and integrity.

41. CBI 1993a: 17.
42. Beaumont 1996: 15.
43. 'Modern Apprenticeships' with government subsidies were launched in 1995. See Chapter 5 for a discussion of apprenticeship policy.
44. Key Skills Position Paper: DfES web site (http://www.dfes.gov.uk/) ref. ks315.
45. Problems with core skills were the major subject of criticism in a series of

critical reports on GNVQs. Until recently, core-skills units were a compulsory part of GNVQs, and the largely negative overall judgements on the awards found in schools inspectorate (HMI) and Further Education Funding Council reports reflect, to a large degree, problems in delivering core skills (see Wolf 1998b and 1998c). The recent HMI report on the pilot of the Key Skills Qualification (Ofsted et al. 2000) is even more openly critical. Woodhead attacked the whole 'pedagogic nonsense' of key skills in a feature for *The Times* ('Gradgrind knew a fact or two': 16 April 1999).

46. Jenkins 2001; CIPD 2001; Schmidt & Hunter 1998.

47. See Ofsted et al. 2000 and the evaluations of Modern Apprenticeship, especially those of Steedman et al. 1998 and Winterbotham et al. 2000.

48. Earlier MSC publications about learning on youth training programmes were similarly committed. See for example MSC 1975 and 1984.

49. Adam Smith, *Wealth of Nations* (1783), Book 1, Chapter 2.

50. Preface to Tullock 1965/1987: 2.

51. By contrast, this suspicion – shared by both main political parties – *is* also found in the USA, where the political and policy-making classes are similarly convinced that educational standards have been destroyed by self-regarding, organized teachers' unions and an 'educational establishment' wedded to misconceived progressive theories.

52. Surveys carried out for the Skills Task Force in 1999 (discussed for example in Skills Task Force 2000) found that just 14 per cent of businesses (almost all large ones) had any employees working for NVQs.

Chapter 5: Why worry about training?

1. Labour Party 2001; House of Lords debate on the Learning and Skills Bill, 17 January 2000 (Hansard col. 889).

2. Playfair's book, *Industrial Instruction on the Continent*, had been published in 1852; he saw the 1867 exhibition as amply supporting his earlier prediction that, without reform, Britain was bound to fall behind mainland Europe.

3. Quoted in Sanderson 1999: 20.

4. *Report of the Balfour Committee on Industry and Trade* 1927: 200, 207.

5. Ministry of Labour 1962: para. 3.

6. The title of his seminal book is *Human Capital: A Theoretical and Empirical Analysis with Special Reference to Education* (emphasis mine).

7. Even though the skills may be valued only in that particular workplace, employers need to feel some confidence that trained workers will not leave for

other jobs the minute the training is over. Shared costs promote that confidence, and give employees an incentive to stay after training, to recoup/enjoy the higher wages.

8. Becker 1993: 33.

9. It is actually very difficult to pin down whether and when on-the-job training boosts individual wages or firms' profits, let alone to calculate by exactly how much. Any large-scale analysis has to depend on questionnaire-based surveys which ask about formal training sessions (especially those which are in fact 'off the job'), whereas learning takes place at least as much in the course of working as it does through formal encounters. In addition, there are huge problems in knowing how far the people who receive training are actually different, in terms of existing abilities/propensity to learn, etc., from those who don't. If there are real differences between the trained and the untrained, then greater gains in wages by the trained may not be because of the training at all. Similarly, the fact that more training is being carried out by (some of) the fastest-growing firms in (some of) the most profitable sectors may be quite as much a result as a cause of the firms' success. An innovative and expanding firm is likely to do a fair amount of training; but you won't turn its failing neighbour into a success with a training programme. Researchers have tried to control for these problems, but (as they acknowledge) with only some success. The number of studies which put a value on the outcomes of training is actually quite small: one quickly finds the same references turning up again and again. Moreover, they tend to be concerned with only a part of the economy (typically manufacturing – which, as we have seen, employs a declining share of the workforce), and some of the most cited deal with very short periods of time, or even a single company. The main relevance of these studies to the argument being made here is that they underscore the difficulty of creating any direct causal link between providing training and an x per cent or y per cent increase in firms' (or national) productivity; but anyone interested in the detailed findings and methodology is referred to Acemoglu & Pischke 1998 and 1999, Bartel 1995, Black & Lynch 1996, Blundell et al. 1999, Booth & Snower 1996, Dearden et al. 2000b, Goux & Maurin 1997, L. A. Lillard & Tan 1992, Lynch 1994, Lynch & Black 1995 and OECD 1999d.

10. If the employee had really borne all the costs of the 'general' part of his training, and if replacing him were more or less cost-free, the employer should be indifferent to his leaving. But, as we discuss later, in practice it is unlikely that the employee did pay. Becker argues that, if your skills mean you are going to get more money later, you should be willing to invest in the training process; but people are often not at all confident of higher wages tomorrow in return for

skills today. In spite of their current employers' worries over poaching, their future employers may fail to recognize the skills or to offer the higher wage, so accepting lower wages in the meantime can look pretty risky.

11. 'Electronics companies oppose inward investment', *Financial Times*, 17 February 2000.

12. The general point is that, the less confident people are of reaping the benefits, the less willing they will be to make financial sacrifices in pursuit of training.

13. See Walter Greenwood's novel *Love on the Dole* (1933) for a vivid picture of the changing dynamic of apprenticeship at a time of economic slump: from being an essential source of skilled workers, to a source of cheap indentured labour, to a cost of which employers wanted rid altogether.

14. Blunkett 2001: paras. 62–4. The key arguments for sub-optimality are presented as (1) the issue of 'general' skills, which we have just discussed; (2) lack of information about skill requirements (which is an argument for providing information, and fairly uncontroversial – although there is little evidence that people actually need information from government services); and (3) 'spillover' of skills into general growth. This last argument was discussed in Chapter 2 (pp. 52–3), where we noted that, while the argument sounds quite plausible, there is actually no concrete evidence for such a phenomenon.

15. National Commission on Excellence in Education 1983: 5.

16. Public Law 103–227, 31 March 1994: the Goals 2000: Educate America Act, sections 2 and 102.

17. Growth (average annual percentage change) of real GDP per worker per year.

18. Including the UK. Source: DTI: 2001b.

19. Per worker: 25 per cent per hour worked.

20. America has had its share of special training programmes (CETA, JTPA, Job Corps, for example), but these have been more or less uniformly aimed at, and indeed reserved for, special disadvantaged groups – particularly young unemployed from low-income backgrounds. They are conceived as measures to combat unemployment, not as a method of raising general productivity. See for example Friedlander et al. 1997 and Ryan 2001.

21. See for example Ashton & Green 1996, especially pp. 126–35.

22. This is true for a period longer than the last decade (as, indeed, one might expect from the summary data on occupational growth presented in Chapter 2). Nor is this just a right-wing economist's viewpoint. Erik Olin Wright, the USA's leading Marxist sociologist, predicted in the 1970s a general tendency for jobs to be 'deskilled' under capitalism; but since then his own empirical analyses have led him to the opposite conclusion (Wright 1979 and 1997).

23. NEDC & MSC 1984: iv, 1.

24. See Wolf 1998a.

25. See for example Marshall & Tucker 1993, Pennington 1995 and Jeong 1995. The great French enthusiast was Edith Cresson, one of the French prime ministers of the Mitterrand presidency.

26. Büchtemann & Soloff 1998: 12.

27. The closest equivalents are in its German-speaking neighbours, Austria and (parts of) Switzerland, and in Denmark.

28. The very low wages paid to German apprentices, and the length of the apprenticeship, are what make apprenticeships profitable for small companies. See for example Euwals & Winkelmann 2001.

29. They also, very rationally, train a disproportionate number of apprentices – considerably more than their share of total employment. See for example Soskice 1994 and Ryan 2001.

30. Less in wages than in the major overheads associated with large training workshops, permanent training staff, extra payments to the qualified shop-floor trainers, and lost production. See for example Soskice 1994, Berg 1994 and Arnold & Münch 1996.

31. Works councils are appointed by the workforce as a whole, not by the trade unions as such, but the unions are the dominant influence.

32. Accepting a low wage during training and skill acquisition is the obvious way for employees to make their (partial or full) contribution to the costs; but it is not obvious why they should unless they are confident of a pay-off.

33. Bischof & Smith 1999: 19.

34. Heckman 1994; Blundell et al. 1996; Freeman & Schettkat 2000. While there is greater dispersion overall in American than in German wages, this manifests itself at the two extremes. What the German system is doing, contrary to most people's perceptions, is shifting more of the cost on to employers (since the vast bulk of US college costs are borne by the state).

35. One of the great merits of the apprenticeship system is the way in which it provides all but a small proportion of young people with a structured route into adult working life, and a clear occupational identity. However, the arguments for more workplace training which this chapter is examining (rather critically) are being made on straight productivity grounds, in terms of 'optimal' human-capital formation and 'market failure'. In that context, it is the straight economic benefits of other countries' approaches which are relevant.

36. See for example Büchtemann & Soloff 1998: 12: 'The risk of under-investment in human capital is particularly acute in the case of *workforce training* . . . Britain has been frequently cited as a typical case in which insti-

tutional factors have reinforced instead of compensated for market failures in providing a sufficient amount of workplace training ("*low-skill equilibrium*").' (Italics in the original.)

37. Wolf 1998a; Sanderson 1994 and 1999.

38. Finegold & Soskice 1988: 22.

39. Finegold & Soskice 1988. See also Ashton & Green 1996, Crouch et al. 1999 and M. Campbell 2000.

40. Blunkett 2001: 24.

41. Figures from the International Adult Literacy Survey, as summarized in OECD 1995 and 1997c and O'Connell 1999, are also consistent with those collected since 1985 for European economies through the Labour Force Survey. A number of other surveys, summarized in Machin & Wilkinson 1995, also show the UK at above the European average but below Scandinavian countries and the USA on measures of formal training, very broadly defined to include not only employer-funded courses but also adult education.

42. Labour Force Survey 1998 and 1999.

43. The percentage of large firms providing some sort of formal training is much higher than for small firms – which is not surprising, given that the former will generally have more new employees in any given year, more types of job, and more formal and regulated procedures. Thus, for example, 91 per cent of large firms (500-plus employees) do some formal training, compared to 72 per cent of those with 25–99 employees. However, the percentage of employees *in* such firms receiving off-the-job training shows a rather different pattern – 20 per cent in the biggest firms, and 28 per cent in those with 25–99 employees report some formal training in the previous year. (Learning and Training at Work Survey 1999, carried out for the Skills Task Force. Results from DfEE: Statistical First Release 7/2000.)

44. Learning and Training at Work Survey, November/December 1999 (DfEE: Statistical First Release 7/2000). The average is fairly similar across employers except for the very smallest (where the average is lower); among sectors, it is higher for manufacturing, and lower for finance and business services.

45. F. Green 1999.

46. The 1998 Labour Force Survey showed 39 per cent of employer-funded training to be qualification-related; the International Adult Literacy Survey (OECD 1997c; O'Connell 1999) produced the near-identical figure of 41 per cent.

47. One reason for this may be that, even if you are acquiring skills in one workplace which would be useful in others, it is often not easy to cash them in. There is some interesting American evidence that suggests that employers

frequently don't find out much about new employees' specific past jobs and acquired skills when they hire them. If they did, they would hire more effectively, because that same study shows that relevant previous work experience affects new workers' productivity substantially (as does previous formal training, though to a far smaller extent). See Bishop 1994.

48. For many years, UK (and other countries') data showed women to be less likely to receive training than men; but this is no longer the case. For example, in the early 1990s, Labour Force Survey data in the UK showed a slightly higher incidence of training among women overall, but a lower proportion of employer-funded training (Dearden et al. 1997 and 2000b). Other data sets (see for example O'Connell 1999) show a similar picture for Europe and North America. All round the world, training is also much more likely to go to younger than to older workers – which is exactly what you would predict, given that the former have more working years ahead of them in which they and their employers can recoup their investment. See for example L. A. Lillard & Tan 1992.

49. The difference is less marked for those in jobs grouped as 'managerial and administrative', although they still receive training much more often than those in manual occupations.

50. British Household Panel Study 1991–5; figures quoted in F. Green 1999.

51. Blundell et al. 1996: 2. Their average time in their current job is also much higher.

52. The general point here is that education and training may often be complementary, not substitutes for each other; so training the educated is the most efficient (or productive) thing an employer can do. The extent to which this is the case – and, within that, the degree to which it is a very general complementarity or a case of tight links involving content and prior skills – is something of which we have no clear idea.

53. Wolf & Jenkins 2001.

54. There is generally remarkably little evidence of 'poaching' as a genuine issue and practice. Not only are individuals who are getting training less likely to move than those who receive none, the tendency of individuals to stay put is also stronger the longer and more intensive the training they receive, and the effect holds regardless of whether there is a qualification involved. See Dearden et al. 1997.

55. Lynch 1994; Hocquet 1996. These findings apply to adult workers receiving in-company training, not to the returns to completed apprenticeships.

56. Groot 1995; Booth 1993; Blundell et al. 1999.

57. M. Campbell 2000: 2.

58. Blunkett 2001: 23. The reference is to work by Institute for Fiscal Studies

researchers, some of which relates only to the manufacturing sector. The researchers themselves are careful not to make any general extrapolations to the effects of more training.

59. See for example Blundell et al. 1999.

60. Groot et al. 1994; Groot 1995; OECD 1999d.

61. It should be noted that not all studies come up with positive returns to in-company training. The OECD (1999d) cites a study by Goux and Maurin of French matched firm–worker data which finds no such effects, and another by Pischke showing insignificant returns for men.

62. Groot 1995. 'Other' training has the highest returns of all. The data are from a large Dutch cohort study.

63. Groot 1995: 330.

64. A. Green et al. 1999.

65. As described in Chapter 4, the ITBs foundered on the twin reefs of financial crisis and attacks on their bureaucracy and form-filling requirements.

66. Wolf 1995.

67. An additional problem is that NVQs are organized into units which are designed not as free-standing sub-parts of a qualification, or as something which it is easy to deliver as a chunk, but around some general function. Take Vehicle Mechanics as an example. A small business may well specialize in bodywork, or brakes, or heating and cooling systems; but no NVQ units align with these (unlike in older qualifications such as City & Guilds). Instead they are about 'routine servicing' of all aspects of a vehicle, or 'identifying faults' that affect performance across the whole range of a vehicle's parts. This compounds the difficulty of delivering/acquiring an NVQ. See Stanton 2000: 50–52.

68. Learning and Training at Work Survey (DfEE: Statistical First Release 7/ 2000).

69. Robinson 1996.

70. Retail NVQs have an informative history. There were no formal certificates for basic retail jobs for many years, and some of the large companies (for example Tesco and Safeway) have been happy to use NVQs so long as they fit their own training plans, seeing this as a way to reward workers and respond to government and CBI encouragement. But NVQs are used only when, and in so far as, they fit company needs – which means that some big companies have used them for a while and then dropped them, others have used them for years, and others have never used them. And their market value is very doubtful. A recent unpublished study of Saturday work in Glasgow, reported on at a meeting at the DfEE in December 2000, showed a middle-class accent winning over an NVQ any time.

71. In that year, five colleges – less than 2 per cent of the total – received 16 per

cent of the total extra funding allocated by FEFC: all were heavy franchisers (Gravatt 1997).

72. For more details on franchising, see Gravatt 1997 and Lucas et al. 1999.

73. Mager et al. 2000: Chapter 5.

74. The FTSE 100 is the *Financial Times* list of the 100 most highly valued companies listed on the UK Stock Exchange.

75. Gravatt 1997: 19.

76. Pennington 1995. See also the report of the Commission on the Skills of the American Workforce 1990.

77. Eagle Forum web site: http://www.eagleforum.org/educate/.

78. See OECD 1999e. For a fuller discussion of these, and comparable programmes in other countries, see Ryan 2001.

79. Owen 1999: 414–15. Owen adds that, of course, 'None of this shows that British industry would not have performed better' with reformed apprenticeships, technical schools, more workplace training, etc. But the issue in this chapter (as in his) is whether such things were really important. Other historians are also questioning both how bad training actually was in the Victorian and Edwardian periods and how important it was in explaining the relative decline of UK industry (Sanderson 1999: 32; McClelland 1990; Floud 1982 and 1984).

80. Aristotle, *Politics*, quoted in Dixon 1993.

81. See A. Green et al. 1999.

82. Ryan 2000b and 2001; see also Steedman et al. 1998.

83. Sutherland & Wolf 1995.

84. Modern Apprenticeships were the first to be introduced; they were confined to more advanced training, leading to qualifications at NVQ level 3.

85. In other words, subsidies would be justified on 'equity' grounds, not as a way of boosting efficiency and company productivity.

86. For discussions of different aspects of the system, see for example Soskice 1994, Oulton & Steedman 1994, Berg 1994, Arnold & Munch 1996, Crouch et al. 1999 and Ryan 2000b.

87. BIBB 1993.

88. See for example Dore 2000.

89. See especially Euwals & Winkelmann 2001 and Soskice 1994.

90. See for example Harhoff & Kane 1994 and Heckman 1994.

91. See for example Dore 2000: 208. Factory production, using unskilled workers, was replacing family-based artisan production. In the period since Bismarck's legislation, other modern associations, such as that of the engineers, have developed spontaneously, with no state sponsorship.

92. Owen 1999.

Chapter 6: The tyranny of numbers and the growth of the modern university

1. National Committee of Inquiry into Higher Education 1997; Blunkett 2000a.
2. Gillian Shephard, launching the Dearing Review of Higher Education, 10 May 1996.
3. Blunkett 2000a: 14.
4. CBI 1994b: 6.
5. The 1862 Land Grant Act steered income from federal land sales towards new educational institutions which included vocational courses.
6. See Chapter 2, and later in this chapter, for a further discussion of the extent to which graduates are over-qualified for their jobs; also the work of Murphy (1993), Robinson (1997a) and Chevalier (2000).
7. W. D. Furneaux, *The Chosen Few* (Oxford: Oxford University Press, 1961), quoted in Appendix 1 ('Demand for places in higher education') of Robbins 1963.
8. Robbins 1963: 71 (para. 183).
9. The American Freshman Survey, which surveys a large sample of first-year university students on an annual basis, collects students' opinions on (among many other things) the likelihood that they will not complete a bachelor's degree or will get an average grade (degree-class equivalent) below a certain level. On both counts, replies indicate that many students are more optimistic about what is likely to happen than national statistics indicate should be the case.
10. Williams 1996 gives recent figures indicating that current annual IUT expenditure per student is half as much again as for university students as a whole, but less than for university engineering faculties.
11. Boudon 1982.
12. And those who do take courses which will enable them to (re-)enter university after two years, with the relevant credit, and continue to a full degree (*licence* or *maîtrise*): see Cam 2001.
13. Foundation Degrees: Q and A Briefing, DfEE Website 2000 (www.dfee. gov.uk/heqe/foundqanda.htm).
14. These two-year programmes can lead on to a full degree, completed at a university, apparently with the addition of just one extra session at summer school compared to conventional degree students. See Foundation Degrees: Q and A Briefing, DfEE Website 2000 (www.dfee.gov.uk/heqe/foundqanda.htm).
15. Pratt 2000: 16.
16. Parker 1983: 154–5.

17. The 'upper classes' are so tiny in number as not to figure in any national statistics. In any case, the old landed elite no longer dominates government, finance or industry in any Western country, though it increasingly mirrors the upper middle classes in its attitude to education. The girls schools which once turned out wealthy girls without a formal certificate to their name now mostly compete for custom on their academic records.

18. These figures are derived from a number of different sources, not all of which use exactly the same occupational definitions and divisions. The earliest figures come from a large survey of 10,000 men living in England and Wales in 1972: figures are for that cohort which would have entered university (aged eighteen to nineteen) in the late 1940s and early 1950s (Halsey et al. 1980). The occupational classification used for the analysis is different from the more familiar Standard Occupational Classification which yields the I to V division shown in the table, but can be roughly aligned with it. The 1960 figures are from a survey carried out for the Robbins inquiry into higher education (Robbins 1963). All other figures comes from information on parental occupation collected from university applicants by the centralized system set up first for the universities before 1992 (UCCA) and then for the unified system of 'old' and 'new' (ex-polytechnic) universities (UCAS) and analysed variously by (among others) Edwards & Roberts (1980), Egerton & Halsey (1993), HEFCE Advisory Group (1996) and Robertson & Hillman (1997). The period between 1977 and 1990 (when the polytechnics grew fast but were outside the UCCA system) is omitted, and all figures are for full-time young undergraduate entries. It is important to note, however, that the allocation of individuals to classes is at best a very approximate affair. The UCCA/UCAS system does it on the basis of self-reported occupation of the head of household, but many responses/occupations are not easily allocated to a particular class, and for a significant minority of students UCAS reports that they cannot be classified. A study of the accuracy of classification (HEFCE Advisory Group 1996) concluded that it was about 75 per cent accurate. On top of this, many people feel that the whole classification system is increasingly ill-suited to modern society, in which many of the least advantaged families are effectively outside the occupational structure altogether and in which family breakdown and the decline of marriage make it unclear who is the 'head of household' for many young applicants. Finally, some observers feel that the system is particularly misleading for some immigrant groups, and that apparent increases in access for lower occupational classes (for example IV and V) may to a significant degree reflect the progress of young people from immigrant families where the occupational classification of the father does not fully reflect the educational or cultural background and milieu

of the family. Nonetheless, provided the figures are taken as representing general trends, rather than too much weight being assigned to a particular number, they do provide a good general picture of access to higher education over the last half-century.

19. There have been changes in the nature and definition of higher education (including the merging of the universities and polytechnics in 1991) and also in the class structure of the country. Obviously you can't work out exactly what are the chances of children from a particular group entering university if you don't know the size of the group concerned – and, while one can make some reasonable estimates from regular surveys such as the Labour Force Survey and the General Household Survey, censuses happen only every ten years. In between, the overall structure of jobs changes – and many individual families are socially mobile.

20. These figures apply only to those for whom family origins are known, and do not allow for changes in the occupational structure in 1960-99. These may be summarized as in Table C.

Table C *Percentage of eighteen-year-olds by social class of birth family*

	1981	2000
I (professional, higher management)	6.0	9.3
II (middle managers, teachers)	22.5	25.0
III (non-manual)	10.0	10.6
III (skilled manual)	38.0	36.2
IV and V (semi-skilled and unskilled)	23.5	18.9

Source: DES/DfEE annual statistics

21. A study by Muller, cited in Halsey 1993, looked at nine European countries over the period 1930–70. On average, Class-I-type families made up about 10 per cent of the primary-school and 45 per cent of the university student body, with France above average at 55 per cent from Class I and the UK below average at 35 per cent for this period as a whole. The International Adult Literacy Survey, carried out among the 16-to-65-year-old population in a sample of OECD countries by the OECD, collected data which indicate the relative odds of going to university in relation to your parents' education. The relative odds for those whose parents had tertiary education compared to those whose parents

did not complete upper-secondary education range from 5.6 (Switzerland) to 1.9 times higher (Australia) for older respondents, and from 6.6 (Poland) to 2.4 (Australia) for younger ones. UK values are 3.1 and 3.3 respectively (OECD 1997c: Table A2.1). For the USA, see also Davies & Guppy 1997 and D. Lillard & Gerner 1999.

22. See Windolf 1997 and Anderson 1990. The percentage fall in German students from blue-collar homes was more than half as large again as the drop in the civilian-employment share of blue-collar jobs (Robinson 1997c).

23. US Census Bureau 2001.

24. Dolton & Vignoles 1997; Dolton & Stilles 2001; Elias & Rigg 1990; Chevalier 2000; Robinson 1995. See also Brennan et al. 2001, Lindley 1981 and Murphy 1993.

25. Atkins et al. 1993.

26. All the information in this section is drawn from Richard L. Kagan's fascinating account: 'Universities in Castile' (Kagan 1975).

Chapter 7: Pyramids and payments: the higher-education market

1. CBI 1994b: 4; personal conversation with the author; Dow-Jones advertisements.

2. Even after controlling for a multitude of other factors: see Naylor et al. 1998 and 2001.

3. See Monks 2000. Students at the top institutions (classified in terms of academic selectivity, cost, and the institution's own resource base) were also by far the most likely to enjoy very high earnings within just ten years of leaving high school, but only if they went on to do a postgraduate qualification as well – which in the US context would typically mean law, medicine (both strictly postgraduate) or an MBA. The scenario here is that, through a selective (and expensive) education, you also get a higher chance than your peers of getting into one of the most prestigious graduate schools, and then of converting the overall educational package into a very high salary very fast (Zemsky et al. 1997).

4. Recent papers by the Vice-Chancellor of Aberdeen (Rice 1999a and 1999b) and the head of Pembroke College, Oxford, (Stevens 1998) encapsulate current preoccupations.

5. Frank & Cook 1995.

6. Atkinson 1999.

7. Law Society Omnibus Salary Data: average for salaried partners. See also Adonis & Pollard 1997.

8. Frank & Cook 1995: 69.

9. The FTSE 100 is the *Financial Times*'s list of the 100 most highly valued companies listed on the UK Stock Exchange. The Argentinian is Carlos Criado-Perez of Safeway, the Irishman Matt Barrett of Barclays, and the Belgian Luc Vandevelde of Marks & Spencer.

10. This is a finding from ongoing research being conducted at the Institute of Education on recruitment practices.

11. See Isaacs 2001.

12. Dore 1976a and 1997: 48–9.

13. Cam 2001. Students are distributed between higher-technician and second-cycle university courses respectively in the proportion 5:1 among children of manual workers – and 1:5 among upper-middle-class students (who are also far more likely, in absolute terms, to enter higher education).

14. The University of California is a very atypical public institution. Of the fifteen top-rated state universities in 1999/2000, five were University of California campuses.

15. The United States has unusually good data on student access to different university programmes, notably from two major longitudinal studies of high-school graduates and a yearly survey of freshmen across US higher education. All figures cited here derive from these surveys. The 'American Freshman National Norms' are published annually by the Cooperative Institutional Research Program, currently administered by the Higher Education Research Institute at the University of California, Los Angeles. Among the factors affecting access to top colleges is family composition: those living with both biological parents are significantly more likely to attend 'selective schools', even after controlling for family income (D. Lillard & Gerner 1999). Rich kids are not only more likely to attend selective colleges (at any academic attainment level) but also more likely to pick the areas of study which offer more lucrative career opportunities and higher post-graduation incomes (Davies & Guppy 1997).

16. Mortensen 1998.

17. This is least true of some of the small private undergraduate-only colleges; but the whole of American higher education rests on a huge structure of federal grants and loans to students which are not tied to public institutions.

18. Data for the 1990s, from the federally funded National Center for Postsecondary Improvement, show that US higher education can be best understood in terms of different institutions catering for seven different market segments.

19. 1999 figure.

20. Soares (1999) notes that undergraduates with family ties ('legacies') averaged around 20 per cent of the student body even after a (high) minimum academic level was introduced in the 1960s.

21. In 1990, for example, the average SAT score of undergraduates entering Harvard was 1,370; for those with family ties it was 1,335 (Soares 1999: 274). (To put this into context, the Albany campus of the State University of New York (SUNY) – a 'top' state university – has an average SAT score for freshmen of 1,205; while at the big, unselective campuses of SUNY scores hover round 1,050, and in the colleges of technology at about 950.)

22. The UK (less than 1 per cent of world population) still did very well in the publication stakes in the 1980s, with 9 per cent of scientific publications – compared to 7 per cent for Japan with over 2 per cent of world population.

23. Ben-David & Zloczower 1962; Ben-David 1977. The Americans were particularly influenced by German models – see B. R. Clark 1995.

24. Centre National de la Recherche Scientifique: the CNRS is a public-sector organization devoted to basic research, with eighteen regional offices and 25,000 employees, including more than 11,000 researchers. Many units operate in association with higher-education institutions, but CNRS has its own separate directorate and national committees.

25. See especially Porter et al. 2000.

26. The Max Planck Society (largely funded by the central, federal, government) runs its own institutes, and there is also a large network of state-supported, industry-linked 'independent' research institutes and myriad smaller institutes with national or state ministry support.

27. This pattern is most visible to the outsider in France, where constituent universities were once part of a single national university, and where the vast majority of academic researchers work for the single state organization of research laboratories, the CNRS. But it is just as important in understanding the way that, for example, Italian public universities work, with everything set by national laws – or, indeed, the German system, where, although education is formally a state rather than a federal function, most of the major decisions that affect higher education are reached consensually by the collaborative Bund-Länder Kommission für Bildungsplanung und Forschungsföderung (the Federal Government and States Joint Commission for Educational Planning and Research Promotion) and by the Standing Conference of the States' Ministers of Culture and Education.

28. Capano 1999: 206.

29. Ibid.

30. In 2001, the top-ranking non-US business schools (on a composite measure)

were INSEAD (no. 7: average post-graduation salary $129,000) and London Business School (no. 8: average post-graduation salary $116,000); first and second overall were Pennsylvania's Wharton and Harvard ($163,000 and $173,000 respectively) (*Financial Times*, 22 January 2001).

31. This information is reported in Cannadine 1999, although it is not original to this.

32. In 1992/3, international students funnelled at least £716 million into the UK economy – or twice the value of coal, gas and electricity exports combined. By 2000 the UK's vice-chancellors estimated that this had risen to £1.5 billion (Greenaway & Tuck 1995; CVCP 2000).

33. The phrase is originally that of A. H. Halsey, one of the leading analysts of British universities and academics, who refers to 'A pyramid of prestige' and to the development of 'a graded system of schools and colleges which reflects the power and prestige pyramid of the wider society' (1961: 341).

34. Author's analysis of college records and data supplied by Oxford University Registry and by a sample of twenty colleges.

35. In the mid nineteenth century the small provincial university of Giessen became internationally famous for its hugely successful institute of chemistry – the first of the great German university research laboratories.

36. The British universities are not technically nationalized; but, while in theory they may be independent, in practice they operate as fully public-sector, government-directed institutions.

37. So called because the vice-chancellors of this informal, self-selected group had their early meetings in London's Russell Hotel. Members are Birmingham, Bristol, Cambridge, Cardiff, Edinburgh, Glasgow, Imperial, King's College London, Leeds, Liverpool, LSE, Manchester, Newcastle, Nottingham, Oxford, Sheffield, Southampton, University College London, and Warwick.

38. Considerably more at Cambridge than at Oxford. In the latter, the colleges retain more autonomy and power, although change in the level of and the allocation mechanism for college fees is now shifting power within Oxford.

39. Halsey & Trow 1971; Halsey 1992. These voting patterns are consistent with a more general tendency for public-sector workers at all levels to be more left-wing politically than their private-sector counterparts.

40. Stevens 1998: 16–17.

41. QAA 2001.

42. The twenty-two-subject framework was set up in 1999 and was intended to be all-encompassing. The NHS, however, insisted on the separate development of eleven sets of benchmark standards for 'vocational' medically related degrees, and another ten specialist sets of standards are also under discussion.

43. See Newstead 1996 for a discussion of the evidence on degree standards.

44. The Robbins Report of 1963 bemoaned the dominance of Oxford and Cambridge, and the fact that this was likely to increase, the more effectively colleges sought out the most academically able pupils from all schools. '. . . so great a concentration tends to set up new distinctions and exclusions,' it warned. 'It is not a good thing that Oxford and Cambridge should attract too high a proportion of the country's best brains' (Robbins 1963: 81). But, short of calling for 'at least some other institutions' to be made highly attractive, it offered no obvious counterweight to this process.

45. There are also moral and religious constraints. I am not suggesting that people are inspired only by financial motives, as caricatures of the 'rational' human being sometimes imply.

46. Glennerster 1998: 14.

47. Halsey 1992: 7.

48. Ibid.: 50.

49. Free tuition for all students (regardless of family income) was actually introduced by Harold Wilson's first (Labour) government of 1964–6; the affluent British middle classes of the 1950s paid fees, though not full-cost ones.

50. See for example Williams 1996.

51. Direct spending by government from tax revenues is continuing to fall: the overall level is maintained through (compulsory) student fees.

52. Excluding doctors and other medical professionals with medical-school appointments.

53. University salary figures from the Association of University Teachers; salary quintiles drawn from the annual National Statistics publication *Social Trends* (London: The Stationery Office).

54. The Retail Price Index rose 57 per cent in this period. Information taken from reports to the Board of Education by individual universities (pre-1914); University Grants Commission reports; Robbins 1963: Appendix 3; Association of University Teachers reports; CVCP 2000; COSHEP 1999; Bett 1999; National Committee of Inquiry into Higher Education 1997.

55. OECD 2000a. Figures are all adjusted using overall GDP consumer price deflators. Italy has gone even further than the UK in reducing per-student spending in the last twenty-five years: see Table 7.6 for its low absolute levels.

56. Ryan 1992.

57. Machin & Oswald 1999: 19.

58. There is also evidence that the proportion of staff in administrative (rather than teaching and research) jobs increases, further reducing student access to academic staff: see Gumport & Pusser 1995.

59. Robertson 1998a: 13.

60. Italy is the obvious and most successful example.

61. See for example Owen 1999 on how the institutional context – not education or investment – has been the key to UK economic revival in the last ten to twenty years.

Chapter 8: Conclusion

1. 'Goodhart's Law' is a shorthand version of the economist Charles Goodhart's observation that any observed statistical regularity will tend to collapse once pressure is placed upon it for control purposes. See A. Perry 2000: 63 for this and other discussions of how using performance indicators to control people creates bias and corruption of the measure.

2. You can, if you wish, choose to believe that students make up the shortfall by doing far more independent learning than their forebears, but you will find very few people in further and higher education who believe a word of it. How much work do *you* do without either an immediate incentive or a deadline?

3. See for example Lakdawalla 2001.

4. Labour Party 2001.

5. See Heckman 1993; also Heckman 1994, Heckman & Smith 1998 and US Department of Labor 1995.

6. As noted before, the 1980s and 1990s were a period of growing income inequality, and in the USA the real earnings of high-school dropouts fell 13 per cent during the 1980s.

7. David Willetts (2001: 14) calculates that, to achieve a comparable effect in the UK to the ones Heckman analyses, one would have to spend £240 billion.

8. Heckman's estimates are for 1979–89, expressed in 1989 dollars. A comparable calculation for 1989–99 would imply even higher spending levels. The calculations for high-school dropouts focused on males, as they were the big losers at this education level during the 1980s; but Heckman also provides comparable estimates for women. For comparisons between these estimates and actual federal spending levels on different programmes, see the web site of the US Office of Management and Budget (http://www.whitehouse.gov/omb/), or the White House web site (http://www.whitehouse.gov/).

9. Phelps 1997.

10. See especially Iacovou & Berthoud 2000 and Booth et al. 2000. Of course there are no miracles on offer: people who were unemployed before entering a job are four times more likely to be laid off than those who entered their current

job from a previous one, suggesting that the ex-unemployed have fewer good jobs on offer (Böheim & Taylor 2000). And in the early to mid 1990s around a fifth of those who had been unemployed and found a job were back in unemployment for at least a while during the following year. But, compared to the high costs and limited benefits of training courses for the unemployed, this still looks pretty encouraging.

11. 'The World Economy Survey', *The Economist*, 20 September 1997, p. 55.

12. Hutchins 1953: 14.

13. See for example A. Green 1990 and 1997 and Schuller 2001.

14. National Committee of Inquiry into Higher Education 1997: 7. The background reports discuss student and staff 'experiences and expectations'; approaches to widening participation; rates of return; externalities and the new growth literature; developing a qualifications framework; and (three reports) funding options.

15. Newman 1852/1873, Part 1.

16. Hutchins 1953: 1.

17. A previous mantra was 'investment'. More was good – and even more was better – regardless of what it was for.

Bibliography

Abbott, A. (1933). *Education for Industry and Commerce in England* (Oxford: Oxford University Press)

Acemoglu, D., & Pischke, J.-S. (1998). *The Structure of Wages and Investment in General Training*, NBER Working Paper 6357 (Cambridge, Mass.: National Bureau of Economic Research, Inc.)

—— (1999). 'Beyond Becker: training in imperfect labor markets', *Economic Journal*, 109, February, 112–42

Adelman, C. (n.d.). *The Way We Are: The Community College as American Thermometer* (Washington, DC: Department of Education)

Adonis, A., & Pollard, S. (1997). *A Class Act: The Myth of Britain's Classless Society* (London: Hamish Hamilton)

Alpin, C., Shackleton, J. R., & Walsh, S. (1998). 'Over- and undereducation in the UK graduate labour market', *Studies in Higher Education*, 23.1, 17–34

Altonji, J. G. (1994). 'The effects of high school curriculum on education and labour market outcomes', *Journal of Human Resources*, 30.3, 409–38

Anderson, D. (1990). *Access to University Education in Australia 1852–1990: Changes in the Undergraduate Social Mix*, History of Australian Universities Series (Canberra: Research School of Social Sciences, Australian National University)

Andrews, M., Bradley, S., & Upward, R. (1999). 'Estimating youth training wage differentials during and after training', *Oxford Economic Papers*, 51.3, 517–44

Arkes, J. (1999). 'What do educational credentials signal and why do employers value credentials?' *Economics of Education Review*, 18, 133–41

Arnold, R., & Münch, J. (1996). *Questions and Answers on the Dual System of*

Vocational Training in Germany (Bonn: Federal Ministry of Education, Science, Research and Technology)

Ashenfelter, O., & Rouse, C. (1999). *Schooling, Intelligence and Income in America: Cracks in the Bell Curve*, NBER Working Paper 6902 (Cambridge, Mass.: National Bureau of Economic Research, Inc.)

Ashton, D., & Green, F. (1996). *Education, Training and the Global Economy* (Cheltenham: Edward Elgar)

Ashworth, J. (1998). 'A waste of resources? Social rates of return to higher education in the 1990s', *Education Economics*, 6.1, 27–44

Astin, A. W., Korn, W. S., Sax, L. J., & Mahoney, K. M. (1994). *The American Freshman: National Norms for Fall 1994* (Los Angeles: University of California)

Atkins, M. J., Beattie, J., & Dockrell, W. B. (1993). *Assessment Issues in Higher Education* (Sheffield: Employment Department Group)

Atkinson, A. B. (1999). 'The distribution of income in the UK and OECD countries in the twentieth century', *Oxford Review of Economic Policy*, 15.4, 56–75

AUT [Association of University Teachers] (n.d.). *Professional Pay in Universities* (London: AUT)

—— (1995). *Higher Education: Preparing for the 21st Century* (London: AUT)

—— (1996). *Efficiency Gains or Quality Losses? How Falling Investment Affects Higher Education's Capacity to Contribute to the UK's Economic Success* (London: AUT)

AUT, NATFHE [Association of University Teachers, National Association of Teachers in Further and Higher Education] Confederation (1993). *UK Universities: Bursting at the Seams. Why Universities Need Additional Resources to Fund the Recent Rapid Expansion of Students Numbers* (London: AUT)

Baker, K. (1993). *The Turbulent Years: My Life in Politics* (London: Faber and Faber)

Baker, T. L., & Vélez, W. (1996). 'Access to and opportunity in postsecondary education in the United States: a review', *Sociology of Education*, extra issue, 82–101

Barnett, C. (1986). *The Audit of War: The Illusion and Reality of Britain as a Great Nation* (London: Macmillan)

Barron, J. M., Black, D. A., & Loewenstein, M. A. (1989). 'Job matching and on-the-job training', *Journal of Labour Economics*, 7.1, 1–19

Bartel, A. P. (1994). 'Productivity gains from the implementation of employee-training programmes', *Industrial Relations*, 33, 411–25

—— (1995). 'Training, wage growth, and job performance: evidence from a company database', *Journal of Labour Economics*, 13.3, 401–25

Bassanini, A., & Scarpetta, S. (2001). *Does Human Capital Matter for Growth in OECD Countries? Evidence from Pooled Mean-Group Estimates*. Economics Department Working Paper 282 (Paris: OECD)

Beaumont, G. (1996). *Review of 100 NVQs and SVQs. A Report Submitted to the Department for Education and Employment* (London: National Council for Vocational Qualifications)

Becker, G. S. (1993). *Human Capital: A Theoretical and Empirical Analysis with Special Reference to Education*, 3rd edn (Chicago: University of Chicago Press)

Ben-David, J. (1968a). *Fundamental Research and the Universities: Some Comments on International Differences* (London: HMSO for OECD)

—— (1968b). 'The universities and the growth of science in Germany and the United States', *Minerva*, 7, 1–35

—— (1977). *Centers of Learning: Britain, France, Germany, United States: An Essay Prepared for the Carnegie Commission on Higher Education* (New York and London: McGraw-Hill)

Ben-David, J., & Zloczower, A. (1962). 'Universities and academic systems in modern societies', *European Journal of Sociology*, 3, 45–84

Bennett, R., Glennerster, H., & Nevison, D. (1995). 'Investing in skill: expected returns to vocational studies', *Education Economics*, 3.2, 99–117

Berg, P. B. (1994). 'The German training system', in R. Layard, K. Mayhew & G. Owen (eds.), *Britain's Training Deficit* (Aldershot: Avebury Press)

Bett, M. (1999). *Independent Review of Higher Education Pay and Conditions* (London: The Stationery Office)

Betts, R. (1991). 'The issue of technical education 1867–1868', *History of Education Society Bulletin*, 48

—— (1998). 'Persistent but misguided? The technical educationalists 1867–1889', *History of Education*, 27.3, 267–78

BIBB [Bundesinstitut für Berufsbildung] (1993). *Training Ordinances and the Procedure for Producing Them* (Berlin and Bonn: BIBB)

Bierhoff, H., & Prais, S. J. (1993). *Britain's Industrial Skills and the School-Teaching of Practical Subjects*, NIESR Discussion Paper 33 (London: National Institute of Economic and Social Research)

Bils, M., & Klenow, P. J. (1998). *Does Schooling Cause Growth or the Other Way Around?*, NBER Working Paper 6963 (Cambridge, Mass.: National Bureau of Economic Research, Inc.)

Bischof, B., & Smith, D. (1999). 'Is Germany now the sick man of Europe?' *Prospect*, July, 18–21

Bishop, J. H. (1994). 'The impact of previous training on productivity and wages', in L. M. Lynch (ed.), *Training and the Private Sector* (Chicago: University of Chicago Press)

Black, S., & Lynch, L. M. (1996). 'Human capital investments and productivity', *American Economic Review*, 86, 263–7

Blair, T. (1999). *The Learning Habit*, Romanes Lecture delivered by the Prime Minister at Oxford University, 2 December: available on the 10 Downing Street web site: http://www.number-10.gov.uk/news.asp?NewsId=416&SectionId=32

Blundell, R., Dearden, L., & Meghir, C. (1996). *The Determinants and Effects of Work-Related Training in Britain* (London: Institute for Fiscal Studies)

Blundell, R., Dearden, L., Goodman, A., & Reed, H. (2000). 'The returns to higher education in Britain: evidence from a British cohort', *Economic Journal*, 110, F82–F99

Blundell, R., Dearden, L., Meghir, C., & Sianesi, B. (1999). *Human Capital Investment: The Returns from Education and Training to the Individual, the Firm and the Economy* (London: Institute for Fiscal Studies)

Blunkett, Rt Hon. D., MP (2000a). *Modernising Higher Education – Facing the Global Challenge*, speech delivered at the University of Greenwich, 15 February (London: Department for Education and Employment)

—— (2000b). *Opportunity for All: Skills for the New Economy. Initial Response to the National Skills Task Force Final Report from the Secretary of State for Education and Employment* (London: Department for Education and Employment)

—— (2001). *Education into Employability: The Role of the DfEE in the Economy*, speech delivered at the Institute of Economic Affairs, London, 24 January (London: Department for Education and Employment)

Board of Education (1900). *Report of the Board of Education* (London: HMSO)

Böheim, R., & Taylor, M. P. (2000). *The Search for Success: Do the Unemployed Find Stable Employment?* (Colchester: Institute for Social and Economic Research, University of Essex)

Bonjour, D., Cherkas, L., Haskel, J., Hawkes, D., & Spector, T. (2000). 'Estimating returns to education using a new sample of UK twins', unpublished paper from Queen Mary & Westfield College, London, available at http://www.qmw.ac.uk/~ugte153

Booth, A. L. (1991). 'Job-related formal training: who receives it and what is it worth?', *Oxford Bulletin of Economics and Statistics*, 53, 281–94

—— (1993). 'Private sector training and graduate earnings', *Review of Economics and Statistics*, 75, 164–70

Booth, A. L., & Snower, D. J. (eds.) (1996). *Acquiring Skills* (Cambridge: Cambridge University Press/Centre for Economic Policy Research)

Booth, A. L., Francesconi, M., & Frank, J. (2000). *Temporary Jobs: Who Gets Them, What are They Worth and Do They Lead Anywhere?* ISER Working Paper 2000–13 (Colchester: Institute for Social and Economic Research, University of Essex)

Boudon, R. (1982). *The Unintended Consequences of Social Action* (London: Macmillan)

Bound, J., & Solon, G. (1998). *Double Trouble: On the Value of Twins-Based Estimation of the Return to Schooling*, NBER Working Paper 6721 (Cambridge, Mass.: National Bureau of Economic Research, Inc.)

Bound, J., & Turner, S. (1999). *Going to War and Going to College: Did World War II and the G.I. Bill Increase Education Attainment for Returning Veterans?*, NBER Working Paper 7452 (Cambridge, Mass.: National Bureau of Economic Research, Inc.)

Bourdieu, P. (1989). *La Noblesse d'état: Grandes Écoles et esprit de corps* (Paris: Editions de Minuit)

Braun, D., & Merrien, F.-X. (eds.) (1999). *Towards a New Model of Governance for Universities? A Comparative View* (London: Jessica Kingsley)

Brennan, J., Higher Education Funding Council for England, & Open University Centre for Higher Education Research and Information (2001). *The Employment of UK Graduates: Comparisons with Europe and Japan* (Bristol: Higher Education Funding Council for England)

Bridges, P. H. (1996). *The Fluttering Standard: How Should Higher Education Approach Academic Standards in the 21st Century?* (Derby: University of Derby)

Brown, G., with J. Bull & M. Pendlebury (1997). *Assessing Student Learning in Higher Education* (London: Routledge)

Brown, S., & Sessions, J. G. (1999). 'Education and employment status: a test of the strong screening hypothesis in Italy', *Economics of Education Review*, 18, 397–404

Büchtemann, C. F., & Soloff, D. J. (1998). 'Education, training and the economy', *European Journal for Vocational Training*, 13, 9–21

Bynner, J., & Parsons, S. (1997a). *Does Numeracy Matter?* (London: Basic Skills Agency)

—— (1997b). *It Doesn't Get Any Better: The Impact of Poor Basic Skills on the Lives of 37-year-olds* (London: Basic Skills Agency)

—— (2000). 'The impact of poor numeracy on employment and career progression', in C. Tikly & A. Wolf (eds.), *The Maths We Need Now: Demands, Deficits and Remedies* (London: Institute of Education)

Callaghan, Rt Hon. J., MP (1976). *Speech by the Prime Minister ... at a Foundation Stone-Laying Ceremony at Ruskin College Oxford*, 18 October, first printed as 'Towards a national debate: the Prime Minister's Ruskin speech', *Education*, 148.17 (22 October 1976), 332–3

Callender, C. (1992). *Will NVQs Work? Evidence from the Construction Industry*, IMS Report 228 (Brighton: Institute of Manpower Studies, University of Sussex)

Cam, P. (2001). 'The French baccalaureate since 1985: level of qualification or type of diploma?' *Assessment in Education*, 8.3, 291–314

Campbell, A. (1991). 'Issues of training strategy in British manufacturing', in J. Stevens & R. Mackay (eds.), *Training and Competitiveness* (London: National Economic Development Office)

Campbell, M. (2000). *Learning Pays and Learning Works: A Review of the Economic Benefits of Learning* (London: National Advisory Council for Education and Training Targets)

Cannadine, D. (1999). *Making History Now: An Inaugural Lecture* (London: Institute of Historical Research, University of London)

Capano, G. (1999). 'Italy: the endless transition', in D. Braun & F.-X. Merrien (eds.), *Towards a New Model of Governance for Universities? A Comparative View* (London: Jessica Kingsley)

Carnevale, A. P. (1998). *Education and Training for America's Future* (Washington, DC: The Manufacturing Institute)

Carpenter, P. G., Hayden, M., & Long, M. (1998). 'Social and economic influences on graduation rates from higher education in Australia', *Higher Education*, 35, 399–422

Carpentier, V. (1999). 'Dépenses publiques d'éducation et croissance économique de long terme au Royaume-Uni', *Colloque International: Laboratoire Montpelliérain d'Economie Théorique et Appliquée* (Montpellier: LAMETA)

—— (2000). 'Développement educatif et performances économiques au Royaume-Uni: XIXe et XXe siècles', unpublished doctoral thesis, University of Montpellier

Carr, R. V., Wright, J. D., & Brody, C. J. (1996). 'Effects of high school work experience a decade later: evidence from the National Longitudinal Survey', *Sociology of Education*, 69, 66–81

Carswell, J. (1985). *Government and the Universities in Britain: Programme and Performance 1960–1980* (Cambridge: Cambridge University Press)

Cassells, J. (1990). *Britain's Real Skill Shortage and What to Do about It* (London: Policy Studies Institute)

CBI [Confederation of British Industry] (1989). *Towards a Skills Revolution –*

a Youth Charter, interim report of the Vocational Education and Training Task Force (London: CBI)

—— (1991). *World Class Targets* (London: CBI)

—— (1993a). *Routes for Success. Careership: A Strategy for All 16–19 Year Olds Learning* (London: CBI)

—— (1993b). *Training: The Business Case* (London: CBI)

—— (1994a). *Quality Assessed: The CBI Review of NVQs and SVQs* (London: CBI)

—— (1994b). *Thinking Ahead: Ensuring the Expansion of Higher Education into the 21st Century* (London: CBI)

—— (1995). *Realising the Vision: A Skills Passport* (London: CBI)

Central Statistical Office (1999). *Annual Abstract of Statistics* (London: HMSO)

Centre for Curriculum and Assessment Studies & International Centre for Research and Assessment (1995). *Evaluation of the Use of Set Assignments in GNVQ. Final Report* (Bristol and London: University of Bristol and University of London Institute of Education)

Chambers, R. (1995). *'Lewisham – not Lewes!' Profligate Colleges or Penalised Students*, Lewisham College Praxis Paper 1 (London: Lewisham College)

Chapman, K. (1997). 'Degrees of difference: variability of degree results in UK universities', *Higher Education*, 33, 137–53

Chevalier, A. (2000). *Graduate Over-Education in the UK*, Discussion Paper 7 (London: Centre for the Economics of Education)

Chevalier, A., & Walker, I. (1999). *Further Results on the Returns to Education in the UK* (Keele: University of Keele Department of Economics)

CIPD [Chartered Institute of Personnel and Development] (2001). *Recruitment* (London: CIPD)

City & Guilds (1993). *City & Guilds of London Institute: A Short History 1878–1992* (London: City & Guilds)

Clanchy, M. (1981). 'Literate and illiterate; hearing and seeing: England 1066–1307', in J. Graff Harvey (ed.), *Literacy and Social Development in the West: A Reader* (Cambridge: Cambridge University Press)

Clark, B. R. (1995). *Places of Inquiry: Research and Advanced Education in Modern Universities* (Berkeley: University of California Press)

—— (1998). *Creating Entrepreneurial Universities* (Oxford: Elsevier)

Clark, T., & Taylor, J. (1999). 'Income inequality: a tale of two cycles?', *Fiscal Studies*, 20.4, 387–408

Clotfelter, C. T. (1999). 'The familiar but curious economics of higher education: "Introduction to a Symposium"', *Journal of Economic Perspectives*, 13.1, 3–12

Coffield, F. (1999). 'Breaking the consensus: lifelong learning as social control', *British Educational Research Journal*, 25.4, 479–500

Cohn, E., Hughes, J. R., & Woodrow, W. (1994). 'A benefit-cost analysis of investment in college education in the United States: 1969–1985', *Economics of Education Review*, 13.2, 109–23

Commission on the Skills of the American Workforce (1990). *America's Choice: High Skills or Low Wages* (Rochester, NY: National Center on Education and the Economy)

COSHEP [Committee of Scottish Higher Education Principals] (1999). *Submission to Committee of Inquiry into Student Finance* (Edinburgh: COSHEP)

Cotgrove, S. F. (1958). *Technical Education and Social Change*. (London: Allen & Unwin)

Crouch, C., Finegold, D., & Sako, M. (1999). *Are Skills the Answer? The Political Economy of Skill Creation in Advanced Industrial Countries* (Oxford: Oxford University Press)

Crowley-Bainton, T., & Wolf, A. (1994). *Access to Assessment Initiative* (Sheffield: Employment Department Research Strategy Branch)

CVCP [Committee of Vice-Chancellors and Principals] (2000). *Investing in Universities and Colleges for Global Success. The CVCP Submission to the 2000 Spending Review* (London: CVCP)

Daly, A., Hitchens, D. M. W. N., & Wagner, K. (1985). 'Productivity, machinery and skills in a sample of British and German manufacturing plants: results of a pilot enquiry', *National Institute Economic Review*, February

Davies, S., & Guppy, N. (1997). 'Fields of study, college selectivity, and student inequalities in higher education', *Social Forces*, 75.4, 1417–38

Dearden, L., Machin, S., Reed, H., & Wilkinson, D. (1997). *Labour Turnover and Work Related Training* (London: Institute for Fiscal Studies)

Dearden, L., McIntosh, S., Myck, M., & Vignoles, A. (2000a). *The Returns to Academic, Vocational and Basic Skills in Britain*, DfEE Research Report 192 (London: Department for Education and Employment)

Dearden, L., Reed, H., & Van Reenan, J. (2000b). *Who Gains When Workers Train? Training and Corporate Productivity in a Panel of British Industries*, IFS Working Paper WOO/04 (London: Institute for Fiscal Studies)

Dearing Report (1997). *See* National Committee of Inquiry into Higher Education (1997)

Dench, S., Perryman, S., & Giles, L. (1998). *Employers' Perceptions of Key Skills*, IES Report 349 (Brighton: Institute for Employment Studies)

DES [Department of Education and Science] (1972). *Education: A Framework for Expansion* (London: HMSO)

—— (1988). *Top-up Loans for Students* (London: HMSO)

—— (1991). *Education and Training for the 21st Century* (London: HMSO)

DES/DfEE [Department of Education and Science/Department for Education and Employment] (1981–). *Annual Statistics on Participation in Education and Training by Young People* (London: HMSO/The Stationery Office)

Desai, T., Gregg, P., Julian S., & Wadsworth, J. (1999). 'Gender and the labour market', in P. Gregg & J. Wadsworth (eds.), *The State of Working Britain* (Manchester: Manchester University Press)

DfEE [Department for Education and Employment] (1996). *1995–1996 Quinquennial Review of the National Council for Vocational Qualifications, Stage Two Report* (London: DfEE)

—— (1998). *The Learning Age: A Renaissance for a New Britain* (London: DfEE)

—— (2000). *Foundation Degrees: A Consultation Document* (London: DfEE)

—— (2001). *National Learning Targets* DfEE Website 2001: http://www.dfee. gov.uk/nlt/targets.htm

DfEE & DENI [Department for Education and Employment & Department of Education for Northern Ireland] (1997). *Targets for Our Future: A Consultation Document* (London and Belfast: DfEE and DENI)

Dickens, R., & Ellwood, D. (2001). *Whither Poverty in Great Britain and the United States? The Determinants of Changing Poverty and Whether Work will Work*, J. H. Kennedy School of Government Faculty Research Working Papers Series (Cambridge, Mass.: Harvard University Press)

Dixon, M. (1993). 'Self-imposed stranglehold on recovery', *Financial Times*, 23 June, 14

Dolton, P. J. (1993). 'The economics of youth training in Britain', *Economic Journal*, 103, 1261–78

Dolton, P. J., & Stilles, M. (2001). *Overeducation in the Graduate Labour Market: Some Evidence from Alumni Data*, Discussion Paper 9 (London: Centre for the Economics of Education)

Dolton, P. J., & Vignoles, A. (1997). 'Graduate overeducation: a European perspective', *Higher Education Europe*, 22.4, 475–84

—— (1999a). 'Overeducation: problem or not?', in M. Henkel & B. Little (eds.), *Changing Relationships between Higher Education and the State*, Higher Education Policy Series, 45 (London and Philadelphia: Jessica Kingsley)

—— (1999b). *Reforming A Levels: Is a Broader Curriculum Better?* (Newcastle and London: University of Newcastle upon Tyne and the Centre for Economic Performance, London School of Economics)

—— (2000). 'The pay-off to mathematics A-level', in C. Tikly & A. Wolf (eds.), *The Maths We Need Now: Demands, Deficits and Remedies* (London: Institute of Education)

Dolton, P. J., Greenaway, D., & Vignoles, A. (1997). ' "Whither higher education?": an economic perspective for the Dearing Committee Inquiry', *Economic Journal*, 107, 710–26

Dore, R. (1976a). *The Diploma Disease: Education, Qualification and Development* (London: Allen & Unwin)

—— (1976b). 'Human capital theory, the diversity of societies and the problem of quality in education', *Higher Education*, 5, 79–102

—— (1993). 'The Siamese twins of the training debate: a case for surgery?', unpublished paper

—— (1997). *The Diploma Disease. Education, Qualification and Development*, 2nd edn (London: Institute of Education)

—— (2000). *Stock Market Capitalism, Welfare Capitalism: Japan and Germany versus the Anglo-Saxons* (Oxford: Oxford University Press)

Dougherty, C. (1996). *Putting Training in Perspective: A Longitudinal Case-Study Approach*, CEP Discussion Paper 283 (London: Centre for Economic Performance, London School of Economics)

Dronkers, J. (1993). 'The precarious balance between general and vocational education in the Netherlands", in A. Wolf (ed.), *Parity of Esteem: Can Vocational Awards Ever Achieve High Status?* (London: Institute of Education)

DTI [Department of Trade and Industry] (1998). *Our Competitive Future: Building the Knowledge Driven Economy* (London: DTI)

—— (2001a). *Opportunity for All in a World of Change* (London: HMSO)

—— (2001b). *UK Competitiveness Indicators*, 2nd edn (London: DTI)

Dutta, J., Sefton, J., & Weale, M. (1999). 'Education and public policy', *Fiscal Studies*, 20, 351–86

Edwards, E. G., & Roberts, I. J. (1980). 'British higher education: long-term trends in student enrolment', *Higher Education Review*, 12.2, 7–43

Egerton, M., & Halsey, A. H. (1993). 'Trends by social class and gender in access to higher education in Britain', *Oxford Review of Education*, 19.2, 183–96

Elias, P., & Bynner, J. (1997). 'Intermediate skills and occupational mobility', *Policy Studies*, 18.2, 101–24

Elias, P., & Rigg, M. (eds.) (1990). *The Demand for Graduates* (London: Policy Studies Institute)

Elliott, C., & Mendham, S. (1981). *Industrial Training Boards: Why They Should be Dismantled* (London: Centre for Policy Studies)

Employment Department (1988). *Employment for the 1990s* (London: HMSO)

Eraut, M., Steadman, S., Trill, J., & Porkes, J. (1996). *The Assessment of NVQs*, Research Report 4 (Brighton: University of Sussex Institute of Education)

Euwals, R., & Winkelmann, R. (2001). *Why Do Firms Train? Empirical Evidence on the First Labour Market Outcomes of Graduated Apprentices*, CEPR Discussion Paper 2880 (London: Centre for Economic Policy Research)

Evans, B. (1992). *The Politics of the Training Market: From Manpower Services Commission to Training and Enterprise Councils* (London: Routledge)

FEDA [Further Education Development Agency], Institute of Education and the Nuffield Foundation (1995). *GNVQs 1994–5: A National Survey Report. The Second Interim Report of a Joint Project: The Evolution of GNVQs: Enrolment and Delivery Patterns and their Policy Implications* (London: FEDA)

—— (1997). *GNVQS 1993–7: A National Survey Report. The Final Report of a Joint Project: The Evolution of GNVQs: Enrolment and Delivery Patterns and their Policy Implications* (Bristol: FEDA)

Feinstein, C. H. (1999). 'Structural changes in the developed countries during the twentieth century', *Oxford Review of Economic Policy*, 15.4, 35–55

Fernández, R., & Rogerson, R. (1999). *Equity and Resources: An Analysis of Education Finance Systems*, NBER Working Paper 7111 (Cambridge, Mass.: National Bureau of Economic Research, Inc.)

FEU [Further Education Unit], Institute of Education and the Nuffield Foundation (1994). *GNVQs 1993–4: A National Survey Report. The Interim Report of a Joint Project: The Evolution of GNVQs: Enrolment and Delivery Patterns and their Policy Implications* (London: FEU)

Finegold, D. (1999). 'Creating self-sustaining high-skill ecosystems', *Oxford Review of Economic Policy*, 15.1, 60–81

Finegold, D., & Soskice, D. (1988). 'The failure of training in Britain: analysis and prescription', *Oxford Review of Economic Policy*, 4.3, 21–53

Floud, R. (1982). 'Technical education and economic performance in Britain 1850–1914', *Albion*, 14

—— (1984). *Technical Education 1850–1914: Speculations on Human Capital Formation*, CEPR Discussion Paper 12 (London: Centre for Economic Policy Research)

Fossey, R., & Bateman, M. (eds.) (1998). *Condemning Students to Debt: College Loans and Public Policy* (New York: Teachers College Press)

Frampton, D. (1995). *Towards a Nation of Shopkeepers: The Devocationalising of the FE Curriculum*, Lewisham College Praxis Paper 2 (London: Lewisham College)

Frank, R., & Cook, P. (1995). *The Winner-Take-All Society* (New York: Free Press)

Freeman, R., & Schettkat, R. (2000). 'Skill compression, wage differentials and employment: Germany *vs* the US', paper presented to an International Conference on Skill Measurement and Economic Analysis, University of Kent at Canterbury

Friedlander, D., Greenberg, D., & Robins, P. (1997). 'Evaluating government training programs for the economically disadvantaged', *Journal of Economic Literature*, 35.4, 1809–55

Führ, C. (1995). 'The German university: basically healthy or rotten? Reflections on an overdue reorientation of German higher education policy', in D. Phillips (ed.), *Education in Germany: Tradition and Reform in Historical Context* (London and New York: Routledge)

Gellert, C. (1993). 'The German model of research and advanced education', in R. C. Burton (ed.), *The Research Foundations of Graduate Education: Germany, France, Britain, United States, Japan* (Berkeley, Los Angeles and London: University of California Press)

Gemmell, N. (1997). *Externalities to Higher Education: A Review of the New Growth Literature*, Report 8 of *Higher Education in the Learning Society* (The Dearing Report) (London: HMSO)

Glennerster, H. (1998). 'Education: reaping the harvest', in H. Glennerster & J. Hills (eds.), *The State of Welfare: The Economics of Social Spending* (Oxford: Oxford University Press)

Golding, C., & Katz, L. F. (1999). 'The shaping of higher education: the formative years in the United States, 1890–1940', *Journal of Economic Perspectives*, 13.1, 37–62

Goody, J. (ed.) (1968). *Literacy in Traditional Societies* (London: Cambridge University Press)

Gosden, P. H. J. H. (1972). *The Evolution of a Profession: A Study of the Contribution of Teachers' Associations to the Development of School Teaching as a Professional Occupation* (Oxford: Blackwell)

Gosling, A., Machin, S., & Meghir, C. (1994). *What has Happened to Wages?* (London: Institute for Fiscal Studies)

Goux, D., & Maurin, E. (1997). *Returns to Continuous Training: Evidence from French Worker–Firm Matched Data* (Paris: CREST)

Grabher, G. (1993). *The Embedded Firm: On the Socioeconomics of Industrial Networks* (London: Routledge)

Granovetter, M. (1995). *Getting a Job: A Study of Contacts and Careers* (Chicago: University of Chicago Press)

Gravatt, J. (1996). *Funding Learning or Funding Awarding Bodies? Colleges and the Qualifications Cartel*, Lewisham College Praxis Paper 3 (London: Lewisham College)

—— (1997). *Deepening the Divide: Further Education Franchising and the Diversion of Public Funds*, Lewisham College Praxis Paper 6 (London: Lewisham College)

—— (1999). *Following the Money: FE Funding in 1999/2000* (London: Further Education Development Agency)

Gravatt, J., & Pert, I. (1996). *ISR: Institutional Surveillance and 'So Called Data'*, Lewisham College Praxis Paper 4 (London: Lewisham College)

Gravatt, J., & Sorrell, G. (1996). *Equity vs. Equality: The Impact of Convergence on Colleges and Students*, Lewisham College Praxis Paper 5 (London: Lewisham College)

Gray, J., Jesson, D., & Tranmer, M. (1994). *England and Wales Youth Cohort Study. Local Labour Market Variations in Post-16 Participation: Evidence from the End of the Eighties* (Sheffield: Employment Department Research Strategy Branch)

Green, A. (1990). *Education and State Formation: The Rise of Education Systems in England, France and the USA* (London: Macmillan)

—— (1997). *Education, Globalization and the Nation State* (Basingstoke: Macmillan)

Green, A., Wolf, A., & Leney, T. (1999). *Convergence and Divergence in European Education and Training Systems* (London: Institute of Education)

Green, F. (1999). 'Training the workers', in P. Gregg & J. Wadsworth (eds.), *The State of Working Britain* (Manchester: Manchester University Press)

Green, F., McIntosh, S., & Vignoles, A. (1999). *'Overeducation' and Skills – Clarifying the Concepts* (London: Centre for Economic Performance, London School of Economics)

Greenaway, D., & Haynes, M. (2000). *Funding Universities to Meet National and International Challenges*, a report commissioned by the Russell Group of Universities (Nottingham: University of Nottingham School of Economics)

Greenaway, D., & Tuck, J. (1995). *Economic Impact of International Students in UK Higher Education* (London: Committee of Vice-Chancellors and Principals)

Gregg, P., & Wadsworth, J. (eds.) (1999). *The State of Working Britain* (Manchester: Manchester University Press)

Groot, W. (1995). 'Type specific returns to enterprise-related training', *Economics of Education Review*, 14.4, 323–33

Groot, W., Hartog, J., & Oosterbeek, H. (1994). 'Returns to within-company schooling of employees', in L. M. Lynch (ed.), *Training and the Private Sector* (Chicago: University of Chicago Press)

Grubb, N. W., & Gardner, D. (1999). *Learning and Earning in the Middle: The Economic Benefits of Sub-Baccalaureate Education* (New York: Columbia University Community College Research Center)

Gumport, P. J., & Pusser, B. (1995). 'A case of bureaucratic accretion: context and consequences', *Journal of Higher Education*, 66.5, 493–520

Hakim, C. (1998). *Social Change and Innovation in the Labour Market: Evidence from the Census SARs on Occupation Segregation and Labour Mobility, Part-Time Work and Student Jobs, Homework and Self-Employment* (Oxford: Oxford University Press)

Halperin, S. (ed.) (1998). *The Forgotten Half Revisited: American Youth and Young Families 1988–2008* (Washington, DC: American Youth Policy Forum, Inc.)

Halsey, A. H. (1961). 'A pyramid of prestige', *Universities Quarterly*, September, 341–5

—— (1992). *Decline of Donnish Dominion: The British Academic Professions in the Twentieth Century* (Oxford: Clarendon Press)

—— (1993). 'Trends in access and equity in higher education: Britain in international perspective', *Oxford Review of Education*, 19.2, 129–40

Halsey, A. H., & Trow, M. A., with the assistance of O. Fulton (1971). *The British Academics* (London: Faber and Faber)

Halsey, A. H., Heath, A. F., & Ridge, J. M. (1980). *Origins and Destinations: Family, Class and Education in Modern Britain* (Oxford: Clarendon Press)

Hanushek, E. A., & Rivkin, S. G. (1996). *Understanding the 20th Century Growth in US School Spending*, NBER Working Paper 5547 (Cambridge, Mass.: National Bureau of Economic Research, Inc.)

Hanushek, E. A., & Somers, J. A. (1999). *Schooling, Inequality, and the Impact of Government*, NBER Working Paper 7450 (Cambridge, Mass.: National Bureau of Economic Research, Inc.)

Harhoff, D., & Kane, J. T. (1994). 'Financing apprenticeship training: evidence from Germany', unpublished paper from the University of Mannheim and Zentrum für Europäische Wirtschaftsforschung

Harkness, S., & Machin, S. (1999). *Graduate Earnings in Britain, 1974–95*, DfEE Research Report 95 (London: Department for Education and Employment)

Harmon, C., & Walker, I. (1995). 'Estimates of the economic return to schooling for the United Kingdom', *American Economic Review*, 85, 1278–85

—— (1999). 'The marginal and average return to schooling in the UK', *Economic Review*, 43.4–6, 879–87

—— (2000). 'The returns to the quantity and quality of education: evidence for men in England and Wales', *Economica*, 67, 19–35

Harris, S., Keys, W., & Fernandes, C. (1997). *Third International Mathematics and Science Study: Second National Report, Part 1* (Slough: National Foundation for Educational Research)

Haskel, J., & Holt, R. (1999). *Anticipating Future Skill Needs: Can It be Done? Does It Need to be Done?*, Skills Task Force Research Paper 1 (London: Department for Education and Employment)

Heckman, J. J. (1993). *Assessing Clinton's Program on Job Training, Workfare and Education in the Workplace*, NBER Working Paper 4428 (Cambridge, Mass.: National Bureau of Economic Research, Inc.)

—— (1994). 'Is job training oversold?', *The Public Interest*, spring, 91–115

Heckman, J. J., & Smith, J. A. (1998). *Evaluating the Welfare State*, NBER Working Paper 6542 (Cambridge, Mass.: National Bureau of Economic Research, Inc.)

—— (1999). 'The pre-programme earnings dip and the determinants of participation in a social programme: implications for simple programme evaluations strategies', *Economic Journal*, 457, 313–48

Heckman, J. J., & Vytlacil, E. (2000). *Identifying the Role of Cognitive Ability in Explaining the Level of and Change in the Return to Schooling*, NBER Working Paper 7820 (Cambridge, Mass.: National Bureau of Economic Research, Inc.)

HEFCE [Higher Education Funding Council for England] (1997). *The Influence of Neighbourhood Type on Participation in Higher Education* (London: HEFCE)

HEFCE [Higher Education Funding Council for England] Advisory Group on Access and Participation (1996). *Widening Access to Higher Education* (Bristol: HEFCE)

Heller, D. E. (1997). 'Student price response in higher education', *Journal of Higher Education*, 68.6, 624–59

Henkel, M., & Little, B. (eds.). *Changing Relationships between Higher Education and the State*, Higher Education Policy Series, 45 (London and Philadelphia: Jessica Kingsley)

Higher Education (1992). *Oxford Review of Economic Policy*, 8.2 (special issue) (Oxford: Oxford University Press)

Hocquet, L. (1996). *Vocational Training and the Poaching Externality: Evidence for France*, Working Paper (Oxford and Paris: University of Oxford, Institute of Economics and Statistics/LAMIA, University of Paris 1, Panthéon-Sorbonne)

Hodgson, A., & Spours, K. (2000). *Expanding Higher Education: From 'System Slowdown' to 'System Acceleration'* (London: Institute of Education, Lifelong Learning Group)

House of Commons Employment Committee (1983). *Minutes of Evidence: The Youth Training Scheme* (London: HMSO)

Hunter, J. E., & Hunter, R. F. (1984). 'Validity and utility of alternative predictors of job performance', *Psychological Bulletin*, 96, 72–98

Hutchins, R. M. (1953; 2nd edn 1964). *The University of Utopia: Charles R. Walgreen Foundation Lectures* (Chicago: University of Chicago Press)

Iacovou, M., & Berthoud, R. (2000). *Parents and Employment*, DSS Research Report 107 (Leeds: Corporate Document Services for the Department of Social Security)

IMS [Institute of Manpower Studies] (1989a). *Access to Higher Education in the 1990s and Beyond*, IMS Working Paper 155 (Brighton: IMS, University of Sussex)

—— (1989b). *How Many Graduates in the 21st Century?*, IMS Working Paper 177 (Brighton: IMS, University of Sussex)

Institute of Directors (1994). *Performance and Potential: Education and Training for a Market Economy* (London: Institute of Directors)

Institute for Employment Research (2000). *Projections of Occupations and Qualifications 1999/2000* (Coventry and London: University of Warwick and Department for Education and Employment)

Isaacs, T. (2001). 'Entry to university in the United States: the role of SATs and advanced placement in a competitive sector', *Assessment in Education*, 8.3, 391–406

Jackson, B., & Marsden, D. (1966). *Education and the Working Class* (Harmondsworth: Penguin)

Jarausch, K. H. (ed.) (1983). *The Transformation of Higher Learning 1860–1930: Expansion, Diversification, Social Opening and Professionalization in England, Germany, Russia and the United States* (Chicago: University of Chicago Press)

Jaworski, B., & Phillips, D. (eds) (1999). *Comparing Standards Internationally: Research and Practice in Mathematics and Beyond*, Oxford Studies in Comparative Education 9.1 (Oxford: Symposium Books)

Jenkins, A. (2001). *Companies' Use of Psychometric Testing and the Changing Demand for Skills: A Review of the Literature*, Discussion Paper 12 (London: Centre for the Economics of Education)

Jeong, J. (1995). 'The failure of recent state vocational training policies in Korea from a comparative perspective', *British Journal of Industrial Relations*, 33.2, 237–52

Jessup, G. (1991). *Outcomes: NVQs and the Emerging Model of Education and Training* (London: Falmer)

Johnes, G. (1993). 'A degree of waste: a dissenting view', *Oxford Review of Education*, 19, 459–64

Johnson, J. A. (1990). *The Kaiser's Chemists: Science and Modernization in Imperial Germany* (Chapel Hill: University of North Carolina Press)

Kagan, R. L. (1975). 'Universities in Castile', in L. Stone (ed.), *The University in Society*, Vol. 2: *Europe, Scotland and the United States from the 16th to the 20th Century* (Princeton: Princeton University Press)

Keep, E. (1999). 'UK's VET policy and the "Third Way": following a high skills trajectory or running up a dead end street?', *Journal of Education and Work*, 12.3, 323–46

—— (2000). 'The future of work may not be highly-skilled', *The Edge*, 5, 16–17

Kehm, B. M. (1999). *Higher Education in Germany: Developments, Problems and Perspectives* (Wittenberg and Bucharest: Institute for Higher Education Research and UNESCO European Centre for Higher Education)

Kim, S.-J., & Kim, Y. J. (1999). *Growth Gains from Trade and Education*, IMF Working Paper 99/23 (Washington, DC: International Monetary Fund)

Koelman, J. B. J. (1998). 'The funding of universities in the Netherlands: developments and trends', *Higher Education*, 35, 127–41

Krueger, A. B., & Lindahl, M. (1999). *Education for Growth in Sweden and the World*, NBER Working Paper 7190 (Cambridge, Mass.: National Bureau of Economic Research, Inc.)

Labour Party (1996). *The Skills Revolution* (London: The Labour Party)

—— (2001). *Ambitions for Britain – Labour's General Election Manifesto* (London: The Labour Party); the manifesto can also can be found at http://www.labour.org.uk/lp/new/labour/labour.wwv main.main?p full=1&p language=us&p cornerid=364783

Lakdawalla, D. (2001). *The Declining Quality of Teachers*, NBER Working Paper 8263 (Cambridge, Mass.: National Bureau of Economic Research, Inc.)

Lal, D. (1989). *Nationalised Universities: Paradox of the Privatisation Age* (London: Centre for Policy Studies)

Lascelles, D. (1998). *Quant and Mammon: Meeting the City's Requirements for Post-Graduate Research and Skills in Financial Engineering* (London: Engineering and Physical Sciences Research Council and Centre for the Study of Financial Innovation)

Laslett, P. (1967). 'The university in high industrial society', in B. Crick (ed.), *Essays on Reform: A Centenary Tribute* (Oxford: Oxford University Press)

Lawrence, R. Z. (1996). *Single World, Divided Nations? International Trade and OECD Labor Markets* (Paris: Brookings Institution Press and OECD Development Centre)

Layard, R., Mayhew, K., & Owen G. (eds.) (1994). *Britain's Training Deficit* (Aldershot: Avebury Press)

Leadbetter, C. (1999). *Living on Thin Air: The New Economy* (London: Penguin)

Lee, V. E., & Frank, K. A. (1990). 'Students' characteristics that facilitate the transfer from two-year to four-year colleges', *Sociology of Education*, 63, 178–93

Lee, V. E., Mackie-Lewis, C., & Marks, H. M. (1993). 'Persistence to the baccalaureate degree for students who transfer from community college', *American Journal of Education*, 102, 80–114

Leslie, L. L. (1990). 'Rates of return as informer of public policy with special reference to the World Bank and Third World countries', *Higher Education*, 20, 271–86

Lillard, D., & Gerner, J. (1999). 'Getting to the Ivy League: how family composition affects college choice', *Journal of Higher Education*, 70.6, 706–30

Lillard, L. A., & Tan, H. W. (1992). 'Private sector training: who gets it and what are its effects', *Research in Labor Economics*, 13, 1–62

Lin, Y., & Vogt, P. W. (1996). 'Occupational outcomes for students earning two-year college degrees', *Journal of Higher Education*, 67.4, 446–75

Lindley, R. (ed.) (1981). *Higher Education and the Labour Market* (Guildford: Society for Research into Higher Education, University of Surrey)

Lopez, R., Vinod, T., & Wang, Y. (1998). *Addressing the Education Puzzle: The Distribution of Education and Economic Reform*, Policy Research Working Paper 2031 (Washington, DC: World Bank)

Lucas, N., McDonald, J., & Taubman, D. (1999). *Learning to Live with It. The Impact of FEFC Funding, Further Evidence from Fourteen Colleges* (London: National Association of Teachers in Further Education)

Lynch, L. M. (ed.) (1994). *Training and the Private Sector* (Chicago: University of Chicago Press)

Lynch, L. M., & Black, S. (1995). *Beyond the Incidence of Training: Evidence from a National Employers' Survey*, NBER Working Paper 5231 (Cambridge, Mass.: National Bureau of Economic Research, Inc.)

McClelland, K. (1990). 'The transmission of collective knowledge: apprenticeship in engineering and shipbuilding 1850–1914', in P. Summerfield & E. Evans (eds.), *Technical Education and the State since 1850* (Manchester: Manchester University Press)

McCormick, K. (1986). 'The search for corporatist structures in British higher technological education: the creation of the National Advisory Council on Education in Industry and Commerce (NACEIC) in 1948', *British Journal of Sociology of Education*, 7.3, 293–317

Machin, S. (1999). 'Wage inequality in the 1970s, 1980s and 1990s', in P. Gregg & J. Wadsworth (eds.), *The State of Working Britain* (Manchester: Manchester University Press)

Machin, S., & Oswald, A. (1999). *Signs of Disintegration: A Report on UK Economics PhDs and ESRC Studentship Demand*, report to the Economic and Social Research Council (London and Coventry: University College London and University of Warwick)

Machin, S., & Wilkinson, D. (1995). *Employee Training: Unequal Access and Economic Performance* (London: Institute for Public Policy Research)

McPherson, M. S., & Schapiro, M. O. (1998a). *An Overview of Trends and Patterns in Participation and Financing in US Higher Education* (Paris: OECD)

—— (1998b). *The Student Aid Game: Meeting Need and Rewarding Talent in American Higher Education* (Princeton: Princeton University Press)

Mager, C., Robinson, P., Fletcher, M., Stanton, G., Perry, A., & Westwood, A. (2000). *The New Learning Market* (London: Institute for Public Policy Research and Further Education Development Agency)

Marquand, J. (1989). *Autonomy and Change: The Sources of Economic Growth* (New York: Harvester Wheatsheaf)

Marshall, R., & Tucker, M. (1993). *Thinking for a Living. Education and the Wealth of Nations* (Washington, DC: National Center on Education and the Economy)

Mason, G. (1999). *The Labour Market for Engineering, Science and IT Graduates: Are There Mismatches between Supply and Demand?*, DfEE Research Report 112 (Sheffield: Department for Education and Employment)

Mason, G., Beltrano, J.-P., & Paul, J. J. (2000). *Knowledge Infrastructure, Technical Problem-Solving and Industrial Performance: Electronics in Britain and France* (London and Dijon: National Institute of Economic and Social Research and Université de Bourgogne, Institut de Recherche sur l'Économie de l'Education)

Medweb site at the University of Birmingham: medweb.bham.ac.uk

Meen, G. (1988). 'International comparisons of the UK's long-run economic performance', *Oxford Review of Economic Policy*, 4.1, xxii–xli

Michel, S. (1999). *Éducation et croissance économique en longue période* (Paris and Montreal: L'Harmattan)

Mingat, A., & Tan, J.-P. (1996). *The Full Social Returns to Education: Estimates Based on Countries' Economic Growth Performance*, Human Capital Development Working Paper 73 (Washington, DC: World Bank)

—— (1998). *The Mechanics of Progress in Education: Evidence from Cross-Country Data*, Policy Research Working Paper 2015 (Washington, DC: World Bank)

Ministry of Labour (1962). *Industrial Training: Government Proposals* (London: HMSO)

Mommsen, W. J. (1987). 'The academic profession in the Federal Republic of Germany', in R. C. Burton (ed.), *The Academic Profession: National, Disciplinary, and Institutional Settings* (Berkeley, Los Angeles and London: University of California Press)

Monks, J. (2000). 'The returns to individual and college characteristics: evidence from the National Longitudinal Survey of Youth', *Economics of Education Review*, 19, 279–89

Morgan, T. (2001). 'Oral examinations at German universities', *Assessment in Education*, 8.1, 25–34

Mortensen, T. G. (1998). 'How will we do more with less? The public policy dilemma of financing postsecondary educational opportunity', in R. Fossey & M. Bateman (eds.), *Condemning Students to Debt: College Loans and Public Policy* (New York: Teachers College Press)

MSC [Manpower Services Commission] (1975). *Vocational Preparation for Young People: A Discussion Paper* (Sheffield: MSC)

—— (1981). *A New Training Initiative: A Consultation Document* (Sheffield: MSC)

—— (1984). *Youth Training Scheme: Guide to Scheme Design and Content* (Sheffield: MSC)

MSC & DES [Manpower Services Commission & Department of Education and Science] (1986). *Review of Vocational Qualifications in England and Wales* (London: HMSO)

Murnane, R. J., Willett, J. B., & Levy, F. (1995). 'The growing importance of cognitive skills in wage determination', *Review of Economics and Statistics*, 77, 251–66

Murnane, R. J., Willett, J. B., & Tyler, J. H. (1999). *Who Benefits from Obtaining a GED? Evidence from High School and Beyond*, NBER Working Paper 7172 (Cambridge, Mass.: National Bureau of Economic Research, Inc.)

Murphy, J. (1993). 'A degree of waste', *Oxford Review of Education*, 19, 9–31

—— (1994). 'A degree of waste: reply to Johnes', *Oxford Review of Education*, 20, 81–92

NACETT [National Advisory Council for Education and Training Targets] (1999). *National Targets Action Plan* (London: NACETT)

National Center for Education Statistics (1997). *Postsecondary Persistence and Attainment* (Washington, DC: US Department of Education)

National Commission on Excellence in Education (1983). *A Nation at Risk* (Washington, DC: US Department of Education)

National Committee of Inquiry into Higher Education (1997). *Higher Education in the Learning Society. Summary Report* (The Dearing Report) (London: HMSO)

Naylor, R., Smith, J., & McKnight, A. (1998). *Determinants of Occupational Earnings: Evidence for the 1993 UK University Graduate Population from the USR* (Coventry: University of Warwick Department of Economics)

—— (2001). *Sheer Class? The Extent and Sources of Variation in the UK Graduate Earnings Premium* (mimeograph) (Coventry: University of Warwick)

NCVQ [National Council for Vocational Qualifications] (1992). *Developing and Piloting the NCVQ Core Skill Units* (London: NCVQ)

—— (1993). *Specifications for the Core Skill Units in GNVQs* (London: NCVQ)

Neave, G. (1973). 'Breaking the working class barrier', *Comprehensive Education*, 24, 16–17

NEDC & MSC [National Economic Development Council & Manpower Services Commission] (1984). *Competence and Competition: Training and Education in the Federal Republic of Germany, the United States and Japan* (London: NEDC)

Newman, J. H. (1852/73). *The Idea of a University* (London: Longmans Green & Co.)

Newstead, S. E. (1996). 'The psychology of student assessment', *The Psychologist*, 9, 543–7

Nickell, S. (1999). 'Unemployment in Britain', in P. Gregg & J. Wadsworth (eds.), *The State of Working Britain* (Manchester: Manchester University Press)

Nolan, M. A., Felix, R. F., & Burke, A. E. (1998). *Lower Qualifications and Earnings in Britain* (St Andrews: University of St Andrews Department of Economics)

North, D. (1990). *Institutions, Institutional Change and Economic Performance* (Cambridge: Cambridge University Press)

O'Connell, P. J. (1999). *Adults in Training: An International Comparison of Continuing Education and Training* (Paris: OECD)

OECD (1964). *The Residual Factor and Economic Growth* (Paris: OECD)

—— (1991). *Further Education and Training of the Labour Force in OECD Countries: Evidence and Issues* (Paris: OECD)

—— (1995). *Literacy, Economy and Society. Results of the First International Adult Literacy Survey* (Paris and Ontario: OECD and Statistics Canada)

—— (1997a). *Education at a Glance: OECD Indicators* (Paris: OECD)

—— (1997b). *Employment Outlook* (Paris: OECD)

—— (1997c). *Literacy Skills for the Knowledge Society. Further Results from the International Adult Literacy Survey* (Paris and Ontario: OECD and Statistics Canada)

—— (1998). *Education at a Glance: OECD Indicators* (Paris: OECD)

—— (1999a). *Education at a Glance: OECD Indicators* (Paris: OECD)

—— (1999b). *Overcoming Exclusion through Adult Learning* (Paris: OECD)

—— (1999c). *Thematic Review of the Transition From Initial Education to Working Life. Country Note: United Kingdom* (Paris: OECD)

—— (1999d). *Employment Outlook* (Paris: OECD)

—— (1999e). *Thematic Review of the Transition from Initial Education to Working Life. Country Note: United States of America* (Paris: OECD)

—— (2000a). *Education at a Glance: OECD Indicators* (Paris: OECD)

—— (2000b). *Employment Outlook* (Paris: OECD)

—— (2001a). *Education at a Glance: OECD Indicators* (Paris: OECD)

—— (2001b), *Employment Outlook* (Paris: OECD)

Ofsted [Office for Standards in Education], the Further Education Funding Council and the Training Standards Council (2000). *Pilot of New Key Skills Qualification 1997–99* (London: Ofsted)

Ong, L. L., & Mitchell, J. D. (1998). *Professors and Hamburgers: An International Comparison of Real Academic Salaries* (Nedlands: Department of Accounting and Finance, University of Western Australia)

O'Rourke, K. H., & Williamson, J. G. (1995). *Around the European Periphery 1870–1913: Globalization, Schooling and Growth*, NBER Working Paper 5392 (Cambridge, Mass.: National Bureau of Economic Research, Inc.)

Osborne, M., Leopold, J., & Ferrie, A. (1997). 'Does access work? The relative performance of access students at a Scottish university', *Higher Education*, 33, 155–76

Oulton, N., & Steedman, H. (1994). 'The British system of youth training: a comparison with Germany', in L. M. Lynch (ed.), *Training and the Private Sector* (Chicago: University of Chicago Press)

Owen, G. (1999). *From Empire to Europe: The Decline and Revival of British Industry since the Second World War* (London: HarperCollins)

Parker, T. (1983). *The People of Providence: A Housing Estate and Some of Its Inhabitants* (London: Hutchinson)

Parkes, D. (1993). 'Can parity between academic and vocational awards ever be achieved? Germany in European context', in A. Wolf (ed.), *Parity of Esteem: Can Vocational Awards Ever Achieve High Status?* (London: Institute of Education)

Patrinos, H. A. (1994). *Notes on Education and Economic Growth: Theory and Evidence*, Human Resources Development and Operations Policy Working Paper 39 (Washington, DC: World Bank)

Payne, J. (2001). *Student Success Rates in Post-16 Qualifications: Data from the England and Wales Youth Cohort Study*, DfEE Research Report 272 (London: Department for Education and Employment)

Payne, J., Cheng, Y., & Witherspoon, S. (1996). *Education and Training for 16–18 Year Olds: Individual Paths and National Trends* (London: Policy Studies Institute)

Pennington, H. (1995). 'The evolution of the School-to-Work Opportunities Act', in J. F. Jennings (ed.), *National Issues in Education: Goals 2000 and School-to-Work* (Bloomington: Phi Delta Kappa International)

Perry, A. (2000). 'Performance indicators: "Measure for Measure" or "A Comedy of Errors"?', in C. Mager, P. Robinson, M. Fletcher, G. Stanton, A. Perry & A. Westwood, *The New Learning Market* (London: Institute for Public Policy Research and Further Education Development Agency)

Perry, P. J. C. (1976). *The Evolution of British Manpower Policy from the Statute of Artificers 1563 to the Industrial Training Act 1964* (London: British Association for Commercial and Industrial Education)

Phelps, Edmund (1997). *Rewarding Work* (Cambridge, Mass.: Harvard University Press)

Phillips, D. (ed.) (1995). *Education in Germany: Tradition and Reform in Historical Context* (London and New York: Routledge)

Porter, M. J., Hirotaka T., & Mariko, S. (2000). *Can Japan Compete?* (Basingstoke: Macmillan)

Prais, S. J. (1989). 'Qualified manpower in engineering: Britain and other industrially advanced countries', *National Institute Economic Review*, February

—— (1991). 'Vocational qualifications in Britain and Europe: theory and practice', *National Institute Economic Review*, May

—— (1995). *Productivity, Education and Training. An International Perspective* (Cambridge: Cambridge University Press)

Prais, S. J., & Steedman, H. (1986). 'Vocational training in France and Britain: the building trades', *National Institute Economic Review*, May

Prais, S. J., & Wagner, K. (1983). 'Some practical aspects of human capital investment in training standards in five occupations in Britain and Germany', *National Institute Economic Review*, August

Prais, S. J., Jarvis, V., & Wagner, K. (1989). 'Productivity and vocational skills in services in Britain and Germany: hotels', *National Institute Economic Review*, November

Pratt, J. (2000). 'The uncertain future of foundation degrees', *Times Higher Education Supplement*, 3 March

Pritchett, L. (1996). *Where has All the Education Gone?*, Policy Research Working Paper 1581 (Washington, DC: World Bank)

Pryor, F. L., & Schaffer, D. L. (1999). *Who's Not Working and Why: Employment, Cognitive Skills, Wages and the Changing US Labor Market* (Cambridge: Cambridge University Press)

Psacharopoulos, G. (1985). 'Returns to education: a further international update and implications', *Journal of Human Resources*, 20.4, 583–97

—— (1994). 'Returns to investment in education: a global update', *World Development*, 22.9, 1325–43

Psacharopoulos, G., & Sanyal, B. (1982). 'Student expectations and graduate market performance in Egypt', *Higher Education*, 11, 27–49

QAA [Quality Assurance Agency] (2001). QAA web site: http://www.qaa.ac.uk

Raggatt, P., & Wilhams, S. (1999). *Government, Markets and Vocational Qualifications: An Anatomy of Policy* (London: Falmer Press)

Reid, I. (1989). *Social Class Differences in Britain: Life-Chances and Life-Styles* (Glasgow: Fontana)

Report of the Balfour Committee on Industry and Trade (1927). (London: HMSO)

Rice, D. C. (1999a). *An Open Letter to All Members of the Scottish Parliament, on Scotland and its Universities, at the Outset of Devolution* (Aberdeen: University of Aberdeen)

—— (1999b). *The Role of the Vice Chancellor*, speech delivered at the CASE Conference, University of Aberdeen (Aberdeen: University of Aberdeen)

Richardson, J. T. E., & King, E. (1998). 'Adult students in higher education: burden or boon?', *Journal of Higher Education*, 69.1, 65–88

Robbins, L. R. (1963). *Higher Education: Report of the Committee Appointed by the Prime Minister under the Chairmanship of Lord Robbins, 1961–63* (London: HMSO)

Robertson, D. (1994). 'Proposals for an associate degree – the search for the "missing link" of British higher education', *Higher Education Quarterly*, 48.4, 294–322

—— (1998a). 'The emerging political economy of higher education', *Studies in Higher Education*, 23.2, 221–8

—— (1998b). 'Who won the War of Dearing's Ear?', *Higher Education Review*, 30.2, 7–22

Robertson, D., & Hillman, J. (1997). *Widening Participation in Higher Education for Students from Lower Socio-Economic Groups and Students with Disabilities*, Report 6 of *Higher Education in the Learning Society* (The Dearing Report) (London: HMSO)

Robinson, P. (1995). *Qualification and the Labour Market: Do the National Education and Training Targets Make Sense?*, Working Paper 736 (London: Centre for Economic Performance, London School of Economics)

—— (1996). *Rhetoric and Reality: Britain's New Vocational Qualifications.* (London: Centre for Economic Performance, London School of Economics)

—— (1997a). *Measure for Measure: A Critical Note on the National Targets for Education and Training and International Comparisons of Educational Attainment*, Working Paper 871 (London: Centre for Economic Performance, London School of Economics)

—— (1997b). *The Myth of Parity of Esteem: Earnings and Qualifications*, Discussion Paper 354 (London: Centre for Economic Performance, London School of Economics)

—— (1997c). *Water under the Bridge: Changes in Employment in Britain and the OECD*, Discussion Paper 325 (London: Centre for Economic Performance, London School of Economics)

—— (1999a). 'Education, training and the youth labour market', in P. Gregg & J. Wadsworth (eds.), *The State of Working Britain* (Manchester: Manchester University Press)

—— (1999b). 'Learning from comparing: new directions in comparative educational research', in R. Alexander, P. Broadfoot & D. Phillips (eds.), *Learning from Comparing: New Directions in Comparative Educational Research*, Vol. 1: *Contexts, Classrooms and Outcomes* (Oxford: Symposium Books)

Robst, J. (1995). 'College quality and overeducation', *Economics and Education Review*, 14.3, 221–8

Ryan, P. (ed.) (1991). *International Comparisons of Vocational Education and Training for Intermediate Skills* (London: Falmer)

—— (1992). 'Unbalanced growth and fiscal restriction: public spending on higher education in advanced economies since 1970', *Structural Change and Economic Dynamics*, 3.2, 261–88

—— (2000a). *Apprenticeship in Britain: Tradition and Innovation*. (Cambridge: King's College)

—— (2000b). 'The institutional requirements of apprenticeship: evidence from smaller EU countries', *International Journal of Training and Development*, 4.1, 42–65

—— (2001). 'The school-to-work transition: a cross-national perspective', *Journal of Economic Literature*, 39.1, 34–92

Sanderson, M. (1994). *The Missing Stratum: Technical School Education in England 1900–1990s* (London and Atlantic Highlands: Athlone Press)

—— (1999). *Education and Economic Decline in Britain 1870 to the 1990s* (Cambridge: Cambridge University Press)

Sanyal, B. C., Noonan, R., Balbaa, S., El-Koussy, A. A., Harby, M. K., & Yaici, L. (1982). *University Education and the Labour Market in the Arab Republic of Egypt* (Oxford: Pergamon)

Sax, L. J., Astin, A. W., Korn, W. S., & Mahoney, K. M. (1999). *The American Freshman: National Norms for Fall 1999* (Los Angeles: University of California)

Saxenian, A. (1994). *Regional Advantage. Culture and Competition in Silicon Valley and Route 128* (Cambridge, Mass.: Harvard University Press)

SCANS [Secretary's Commission on Achieving Necessary Skills] (1991). *What Work Requires of Schools* (Washington, DC: US Department of Labor)

Schmidt, F. L., & Hunter, J. E. (1998). 'The validity and utility of selection methods in personnel psychology: practical and theoretical implications of 85 years of research findings', *Psychological Bulletin*, 124.2, 262–74

Scholarios, D., & Lockyer, C. (1999). 'Recruiting and selecting professionals: context, quality and methods', *International Journal of Selection and Assessment*, 7.3, 142–56

Schuller, T. (2001). 'What kind of more means better? Continuous scholarization or lifelong learning?', *Critical Quarterly*, 43.1, 66–72

Schultz, T. W. (1993). 'The economic importance of human capital in modernisation', *Education Economics*, 1.1, 13–19

Senker, P. (1992). *Industrial Training in a Cold Climate* (Aldershot: Avebury)

—— (1995). *Training Levies in Four Countries: Implications for British Industrial Training Policy* (Watford: EnTra Publications)

Shackleton, J., R. (1992). *Training Too Much? A Sceptical Look at the Economics of Skill Provision in the UK*, Hobart Paper 118 (London: Institute of Economic Analysis)

Shackleton, J. R., & Walsh, S. (1997). 'What determines who obtains national vocational qualifications?', *Education Economics*, 5.1, 41–5

Sharp, P. (1998). 'The beginnings of GNVQs: an analysis of key determining events and factors', *Journal of Education and Work*, 11.3, 293–311

Sheldrake, J., & Vickerstaff, S. A. (1987). *The History of Industrial Training in Britain* (Aldershot: Avebury Press)

Sianesi, B., & Van Reenan, J. (2000). *The Returns to Education: A Review of the Macro-Economic Literature*, Discussion Paper 6 (London: Centre for the Economics of Education)

Singer, B. (1983). *Village Notables in Nineteenth-Century France: Priests, Mayors, Schoolmasters* (Albany: State University of New York Press)

Skills Task Force (2000). *Skills for All: Research Report from the National Skills Task Force* (London: Department for Education and Employment)

Slaughter, M. (1998). 'International trade and labor-market outcomes: results, questions, and policy options', *Economic Journal*, 108.450, 1452–62

—— (1999). 'Globalization and wages: a tale of two perspectives', *World Economy*, 22.5, 609–30

Smith, D., Scott, P., Bocock, J., & Bargh, C. (1999). 'Vice-chancellors and executive leadership in UK universities: new roles and relationships?', in M. Henkel & B. Little (eds.), *Changing Relationships between Higher Education and the State*, Higher Education Policy Series, 45 (London and Philadelphia: Jessica Kingsley)

Smith, J., McKnight, A., & Naylor, R. (2000). 'Graduate employability: policy and performance in higher education in the UK', *Economic Journal*, 110, 382–411

Smithers, A. (1993). *All Our Futures: A Dispatches Report on Education.* (London: Channel 4 Television)

Snower, D. J. (1999). *Inequality of Earnings*, CEPR Discussion Paper 2321 (London: Centre for Economic Policy Research)

Soares, J. A. (1999). *The Decline of Privilege: The Modernization of Oxford University* (Stanford: Stanford University Press)

Sommer, J. W. (1995). *The Academy in Crisis* (London: Transaction Publishers)

Soskice, D. (1994). 'Reconciling markets and institutions: the German apprenticeship system', in L. M. Lynch (ed.), *Training and the Private Sector* (Chicago: University of Chicago Press)

Spours, K. (1995). *Post-Compulsory Education and Training: Statistical Trends*, Learning for the Future Working Paper 7 (London and Coventry: Institute of Education and University of Warwick, Centre for Education and Industry)

Stanton, G. (1996). *Output-Related Funding and the Quality of Education and Training* (London: International Centre for Research on Assessment, Institute of Education)

—— (2000). 'The new learning market: who pays and for what?', in C. Mager, P. Robinson, M. Fletcher, G. Stanton, A. Perry & A. Westwood, *The New Learning Market* (London: Institute for Public Policy Research and Further Education Development Agency)

Stanton, G., & Richardson, W. (eds.) (1997). *Qualifications for the Future: A Study of Tripartite and Other Divisions in Post-16 Education and Training* (London: Further Education Development Agency)

Steedman, H. (1987). 'Vocational training in France and Britain: office work', *National Institute Economic Review*, May

—— (1988). 'Vocational training in France and Britain: mechanical and electrical craftsmen', *National Institute Economic Review*, November

Steedman, H., & Hawkins, J. (1994). 'Shifting foundations: the impact of NVQs on youth training in the building trades', *National Institute Economic Review*, August

Steedman, H., Gospel, H., & Ryan, P. (1998). *Apprenticeship: A Strategy for Growth* (London: Centre for Economic Performance, London School of Economics)

Steel, J., & Sausman, C. (1997). *The Contribution of Graduates to the Economy: Rates of Return*, Report 7 of *Higher Education in the Learning Society* (The Dearing Report) (London: HMSO)

Steinberg, L. (1996). *Beyond the Classroom: Why School Reform has Failed and What Parents Need to Do* (Boston: Simon & Schuster)

Stevens, R. (1998). *Barbarians at the Gates: A View from Oxford's City Wall* (Washington, DC: George Washington University)

Sutherland, R., & Wolf, A. (1995). *A Spreadsheet Approach to Mathematical Modelling for Engineering Students*, final project report to the Nuffield Foundation (London: Institute of Education)

Sutton Trust (2000). *Entry to Leading Universities* (London: The Sutton Trust)

Swann, G. M. P., Prevezer M., & Stout, D. (eds.) (1998). *The Dynamics of Industrial Clustering* (Oxford: Oxford University Press)

Tanzi, V., & Schuknecht, L. (2000). *Public Spending in the 20th Century: A Global Perspective* (Cambridge: Cambridge University Press)

Teichler, U. (1999). 'Higher education and changing job requirements: a comparative view', in M. Henkel & B. Little (eds.), *Changing Relationships between Higher Education and the State*, Higher Education Policy Series, 45 (London and Philadelphia: Jessica Kingsley)

Thatcher, M. (1993). *The Downing Street Years* (London: HarperCollins)

Training Agency (1988). *Development of Assessable Standards for National Certification*, Guidance Note 1 (Sheffield: Training Agency)

—— (1989). *Training in Britain: A Study of Funding, Activity and Attitudes: The Main Report* (London: HMSO)

Tribe, K. (1990a). 'The accumulation of cultural capital: the funding of UK higher education in the twentieth century', *Higher Education Quarterly*, 44.1, 21–34

—— (1990b). 'The "US model" for higher education: structure and finance', in P. G. Wright (ed.), *Industry and Higher Education* (Buckingham: The Society for Research in Higher Education and Open University Press)

Tullock, G. (1965/1987). *The Politics of Bureaucracy* (Washington, DC: Public Affairs Press/University Press of America)

Turner, D. (1996). 'Changing patterns of funding higher education in Europe', *Higher Education Management*, 8.1, 101–11

Tyler, J. H., Murnane, R. J., & Willett, J. B. (1999). *Do the Cognitive Skills of School Dropouts Matter in the Labor Market?*, NBER Working Paper 7101 (Cambridge, Mass.: National Bureau of Economic Research, Inc.)

UNESCO (1972). *Draft Medium-Term Outline Plan for 1973–1978* (Paris: UNESCO)

—— (1999). *Statistical Yearbook* (Paris: UNESCO Publishing and Bernan Press)

Universities UK (2001). *New Directions for Higher Education Funding: Funding Options Review Group Final Report* (London: Universities UK)

Unwin, L. (1994). 'The role of employers in vocational education and training: partners or passive recipients?', unpublished doctoral thesis, University of Warwick, Coventry

Unwin, L., & Wellington, J. (2001). *Young People's Perspectives on Education, Training and Employment: Realising their Potential* (London: Kogan Page)

US Census Bureau (2001). American Fact Finder web site on www.census.gov

US Department of Education (1997), *Condition of Education* (Washington, DC: US Department of Education)

US Department of Labor (1995). *What's Working (and What's Not): A Summary of Research on the Economic Impacts of Employment and Training Programs* (Washington, DC: US Government Printing Office)

Vossensteyn, J. J. (1999). 'Where in Europe would people like to study? The affordability of higher education in nine Western European countries', *Higher Education*, 37, 159–76

Welch, A. R. (1997). 'The peripatetic professor: the internationalisation of the academic profession', *Higher Education*, 34, 323–45

Willetts, D. (2001). 'Human capital', *Prospect*, February, 14

Williams, G. (1996). *Resources for Higher Education in OECD Countries* (London: Centre for Higher Education Studies, Institute of Education)

Windolf, P. (1997). *Expansion and Structural Change: Higher Education in Germany, the United States and Japan 1870–1990* (Boulder: Westview Press)

Winston, G. C. (1999). 'Subsidies, hierarchy and peers: the awkward economics of higher education', *Journal of Economic Perspectives*, 13.1, 13–36

Winterbotham, M., Adams, L., & Lorentzen-White, D. (2000). *Modern Apprenticeships: Exploring the Reasons for Non-Completion in Five Sectors*, DfEE Research Report 217 (London: Department for Education and Employment)

Wolf, A. (1995). *Competence-Based Assessment* (Buckingham: Open University Press)

—— (1997). 'Growth stocks and lemons: diplomas in the English market-place 1976–1996', *Assessment in Education*, 4.1, 33–49

—— (1998a). 'Politicians and economic panic', *History of Education*, 27.3, 219–34

—— (1998b). 'Portfolio assessment as national policy: the National Council for Vocational Qualifications and its quest for a pedagogical revolution', *Assessment in Education*, 5.3, 413–45

—— (1998c). 'Rotten core could kill', *Times Educational Supplement*, 14 August

—— (1998d). 'The training illusion', *Prospect*, August/September, 12–13

—— (2000). 'A comparative perspective on educational standards', in H. Goldstein & A. Heath (eds.), *Educational Standards*, Proceedings of the British Academy 102 (Oxford: Oxford University Press for the British Academy)

Wolf, A., & Jenkins, A. (2001). 'The growth of psychometric testing. Why do organisations test, and are there lessons for our education systems?', paper presented at the European Educational Research Annual Conference, Lille

Wolf, A., Burgess, R., Stott, H., & Veasey, J. (1994). *GNVQ Assessment Review Project: Final Report*, Technical Report 23, R & D Series (London: Department of Employment Learning Methods Branch)

Wood, A. (1994). *North–South Trade, Employment and Inequality* (Oxford: Clarendon Press)

Wood, A., & Rido-Cano, C. (1996). *Skill, Trade and International Inequality* (Brighton: Institute of Development Studies)

World Bank (1995). *1995 World Development Report: Workers in an Integrating World* (Oxford: Oxford University Press for the World Bank)

Wright, E. O. (1979). *Class Structure and Income Determination* (New York: Academic Press)

—— (1997). *Class Counts: Comparative Studies in Class Analysis* (Cambridge: Cambridge University Press and Maison des Sciences de l'Homme)

Yorke, M. (1998). 'Non-completion of full-time and sandwich students in

English higher education: costs to the public purse, and some implications',
Higher Education, 36, 81–194

Zemsky, R., Shaman, S., & Iannozzi, M. (1997). 'The landscape: in search of
a strategic perspective. A tool for mapping the market in postsecondary
education', *Choice*, November/December

Index

Note: References to figures and tables are indicated by *italics*; references to annotated text as '25 (n21)'; references to the References section as '261 n21'.